Toby Be␣␣
Jan. 199␣
(Benjamin's —OTTAWA)

D1033128

SELECTED WRITINGS

Remy
de
Gourmont

Selected
Writings

Translated and Edited, with an Introduction,
by
Glenn S. Burne

Ann Arbor
The University of Michigan Press

Contents

Introduction

Coming to Paris from his native Normandy in 1883, Remy de Gourmont took a position as assistant librarian at the Bibliothèque Nationale. Shortly afterward he was dismissed for having written an "unpatriotic" article. About the same time—he was in his mid-twenties—he was afflicted by lupus, a disease which left him almost unrecognizably disfigured. These misfortunes, combined with a naturally contemplative nature, drew a circle of solitude around Gourmont, and he secluded himself in his book-cluttered rooms in the rue des Saints-Pères. Except for an occasional trip to the book-stalls along the Seine or, later, after he had helped found a new journal, to his editorial office at the *Mercure de France,* he devoted the next thirty-odd years to solitary study and the writing of more than forty volumes. These writings in all genres, touching as they do on nearly every current of thought in France between 1885 and 1915, offer a fascinating picture of the intellectual life of the period. He was at the vortex of all the major movements and intellectual controversies of the 1890's and the early twentieth century. Symbolism, "la Décadence," art for art's sake, German idealism, scientific method, Imagism, anthropology and experimental psychology, free verse, the latest developments in philology and linguistics—all came under the erudite and ironical eye of Gourmont, who was, as T. S. Eliot put it, "the critical conscience of his generation" and who possessed "all the general intelligence of Aristotle."

Ironical and detached as he may have seemed, Gourmont was committed to a literary faith. Early in his career he came under the spell of the Symbolists—Baudelaire, Mallarmé, Villiers de l'Isle-Adam, the early Huysmans—and most of his studies and writings were defenses or explanations—direct or oblique—of the principles of Symbolism. And both defenses and explanations were needed. The movement was under fire from many of France's leading critics and scholars, who considered it an excessively obscure, perverse, neurotic debasement of French literature—it was, in a word, "decadent." Gourmont came to the defense of the movement by helping turn the prestigious *Mercure de France* into the "official" Symbolist journal and by bringing to bear on Symbolism's enemies all his considerable knowledge, wit, and courage. One of his first works was a scholarly study entitled *Le Latin mystique* (1892), which drew analogies between late medieval Latin poetry and contemporary verse. It had considerable vogue among the Symbolist writers and later was much admired by Ezra Pound. But many of his works of the early 1890's were of a different order, being primarily novels, poems, and stories in the Symbolist mode. His poems (*Litanies de la Rose, Fleurs de jadis*) were rich in bizarre imagery of rare jewels, exotic flowers, archaic and heavily sonorous words expressive of strange colors and perfumes, all cast in rich rhyme patterns and incantatory rhythms. This heady stuff found its way into some of his tales (*Histoires magiques, Proses moroses, Couleurs*), but his novels were written in a more subtle, lower-keyed style, with a precision and irony more reminiscent of Flaubert than of contemporary decadence. His fiction sought to explore the nature of consciousness and various kinds of sensory and imaginative experience and often involved strange blendings of religion and sex—of "the altar and the alcove," as one critic put it. These works, elegantly written, beautifully printed and bound, were admired and even imitated by a number of prominent writers, English, American, and French, but in some quarters they merely earned him the label of "frivolous erotomane." His cerebral sensuality was the outgrowth not only of his current reading and literary preferences, but also of the company he was keeping. He was involved at that time with a strange and colorful lady named Berthe de Courrières, a dabbler in the occult and a practicing adept of the Black Mass. She was also the mistress, for a time, of Alfred Jarry and reputed to be the protagonist of Huysmans' fictional study of the Black Mass, *Là-Bas*. Other acquaintances included Huysmans and Villiers de l'Isle-Adam, author of the bizarre *Contes cruels* and the influential drama *Axël;* and he was an interested reader of Barbey d'Aurevilly's *Diaboliques*. It was some years before Gourmont could shake off the influence of these "decadents"—whose effect was to impede his intellectual growth—and apply himself to the scholarly pursuits for which he had showed such aptitude in his *Le Latin mystique*.

During this early period Gourmont also produced studies and defenses of "Idealism" and "Symbolism," in which he propounded the subjectivist views that he dramatized in his fiction—in novels which he continued to write well into the twentieth century: *Sixtine, roman de la vie cérébrale* (1890), *Les Chevaux de Diomède* (1897), *Le Songe d'une femme* (1899), *Une Nuit au Luxembourg* (1906), and *Un Coeur virginal* (1907). These novels, while written to demonstrate philosophic and aesthetic principles, have considerable merit as works of art. They are interesting forerunners, in their precise registering of the nuances of feeling and sensation and in their subjectivist view of reality, of the work of Virginia Woolf and Proust.

But during the later 1890's and into the new century Gourmont turned his attention increasingly to serious, scholarly study of language and psychology—to the service of the one obsessive role he had assigned himself: establishing the Symbolist aesthetic on a sound philosophical, even "scientific," basis. As Symbolism meant for him the absolute freedom of the artist to follow and express the impulses of his individual sensibility, he set about to demonstrate scientifically that individual sensibility is the sole source, and concrete sensation the sole material, of the writer—whether he be a poet or a critic. In effecting, with considerable success, a synthesis of current scientific and philosophic thought—that is, Darwinian and Lamarckian discoveries regarding the relation of the individual organism to its environment, and German subjective idealism which placed the individual consciousness at the center of every created universe—Gourmont provided a rationale for both the extreme individualism of the Symbolist poet and the extreme subjectivity of the Impressionist critic. He was at pains to demonstrate, as the following essays indicate, that the best of the Symbolist and Impressionist writers were not as impossibly obscure and irresponsible as they were usually made out to be, but that to the contrary their works took the inevitable form honest creation and criticism must take. They were, moreover, directly in the mainstream of good literary tradition, for Gourmont insisted that the superior sensibility of the good literary critic is itself the product of tradition. The critic is the repository and guardian of that tradition, and the more he consults his own sensibility—the more he "rationalizes his impressions"—the more he will be faithful to that role; concrete sensations and sense impressions are ultimately the only valid and sincere sources of feelings, ideas, and judgments.

Gourmont's critical works consist of dozens of short pieces on diverse subjects gathered together and reprinted in single volumes. His best are the three series of essays, the individual volumes of which appeared at intervals over the years: the *Promenades littéraires* (seven volumes), *Promenades philosophiques* (three volumes), and *Epilogues* (five volumes). He also produced the two-volume *Livres des masques* (1896, 1898), two influential studies of language and style, *Esthétique de la Langue française* (1899) and *Le Problème du Style* (1902), two one-volume collections of essays, *La Culture des Idées* (1900) and *Le Chemin de Velours* (1902). His remarkable study of sexuality in the animal world, *Physique de l'amour, essai sur l'instinct sexual* (1903) was translated by Ezra Pound. The informal essays gathered together in *Lettres à l'Amazone* (1914) and *Lettres intimes à l'Amazone* (1926) are provocative, gracefully written "letters" on a variety of subjects addressed to Natalie Clifford Barney, one of Gourmont's few intimates, an American expatriate lady who conducted a literary salon in Paris during the years preceding World War I.

From this plenitude (and it is only a partial listing) it is difficult to choose those pieces most deserving of translation. There are, however, distinct areas of thought into which his writings naturally fall, and these have provided the basis for the present selections and their arrangement. Gourmont's critical theories—in large part a justification of Impressionism—were not set forth directly but were included in his appraisal of the works of other critics. These essays enjoyed considerable popularity among English and American writers, especially those associated with the Imagist movement. T. S. Eliot, Ezra Pound, T. E. Hulme, John Middleton Murry, Richard Aldington, Amy Lowell, Kenneth Burke, and others quoted and borrowed freely from Gourmont in their own efforts to establish a "new" literature. Eliot called him "the perfect critic" and used his principles (in *The Sacred Wood*) to chastize other Impressionist critics (notably Arthur Symons) who did not measure up. Eliot recognized that Gourmont's theories represented a fine synthesis of artistic sensitivity and scientific learning and, as such, provided highly useful principles with which to support his own critical and poetic predilections. Interestingly enough, Eliot managed to derive from Gourmont's extremely personal Impressionism principles applicable to his own impersonal theory of art. He made extensive use of *Le Problème du style,* especially in his essays on Massinger, Middleton, Ben Jonson, and "The Metaphysical Poets" (in *Selected Essays*), in which he quotes "the great French critic" on the relationship of feelings, ideas, and language in poetry. In the latter essay Eliot also made an interesting application of the concept of "dissociation of sensibility" which Gourmont discusses in "La Sensibilité de Jules Laforgue." This concept—which sees the rational intellect as being dissociated from the sensibility by the intervention of skepticism—Eliot modified and applied to the development of English literature from Donne to Tennyson. In a revealing example of what he often did with Gourmont's ideas Eliot took a highly provocative but undeveloped observation and built it into a relatively fully developed theory illuminating a wide range of literary experience.

There has been some argument about the extent and kind of relationship that existed between the Symbolist and Imagist movements, but in the eyes of many Imagist writers, Symbolism was their immediate forebear and Gourmont their prophet. This is reflected in Amy Lowell's essay on Gourmont in her *Six French Poets* and even more pointedly in the introduction to her anthology *Some Imagist Poets,* in which she quotes directly from Gourmont's preface to his *Livres des masques.* Similarly, T. E. Hulme, one of the founders of Imagism, echoes Gourmont's conviction that style is a product of the whole man and that the visual image, directly rendered, is the basis of poetic creation. Much in Hulme's *Speculations* appears to be paraphrased from *Le Problème du style,* as does much in John Middleton Murry's *The Problem of Style,* which begins with a discussion of Gourmont's ideas. And another facet of Gourmont's work—his drawing on the authority of contemporary science to justify his theories of art—can be seen as foreshadowing the aesthetics of I. A. Richards and Suzanne Langer. A juxtaposing of certain passages from Gourmont and from the two later critics reveals surprising similarities.[1]

1. For a fuller discussion see my *Remy de Gourmont: His Ideas and Influence in England and America* (Southern Illinois University Press, 1963) and Karl Uitti's *La Passion littéraire de Remy de Gourmont* (Princeton University Press, 1962).

The first group of essays in this volume presents Gourmont's study of the historical interrelationship of language and ideas. Although his writings on style, critical theory, and the creative process offer one of the richest and most stimulating bodies of thought of recent times, his essays on the "dissociation of ideas" are perhaps the most original. To be sure, the notion of dissociation had been in the air for some time—the work of Nietzsche, J. S. Mill, Jules de Gaultier, and Jules Renard had in one way or another made reference to dissociative methods—but Gourmont made the most cogent and explicit statement of this ingenious intellectual process and provided the most notable examples. The impact of these essays on American thinking was considerable. Some writers, like Joseph Wood Krutch, reacted hostilely and accused Gourmont of being a "nihilist," a strictly negative thinker at a time when the world needed constructive thought. Others, like Kenneth Burke, defended Gourmont's method of analysis as being the essential prelude to any constructive synthesis. This controversy serves to point up a real problem in reading Gourmont: it is true that he appears singularly negative. He does state that he considers his business to be one of "sowing doubts," and he insists that "truth tyrannizes," whereas "doubt liberates." Nevertheless, he also insists that what passes for "truth" among the common run of men are hand-me-down clichés having little application to the immediate needs of the individual man; these consecrated structures of superannuated thought are to be razed in order that new "truths," corresponding to current and individual realities, may be constructed from the debris. Gourmont was more than willing to play the role of the bomb-throwing syndicalist in intellectual realms, but not all his works are negative. The essays on the dissociation of ideas are intentionally destructive, but many of the others, especially those advancing the cause of Symbolist writers, are almost evangelical.

Gourmont's essays do not always make easy reading. They are lively, often impertinent, rarely tempered by modesty, and usually clear, but sometimes irritatingly obscure. Gourmont writes in a "mixed" style. He states facts and opinions simply and flatly, then moves to an elaborate, extended metaphor. He suddenly shifts from prosaic simplicity to a game of cat-and-mouse with his reader. Obvious facts are often spelled out, while the most complex ideas are left tantalizingly in midair, undeveloped, unexplained, or couched in an elusive bit of poetic imagery. This, according to Gourmont's view of things, is as it should be. As a member of the Symbolist school of "suggestion" and "evocation" as distinct from "statement," Gourmont wishes to be explicit only in what he denounces; he wants to indicate the direction he thinks constructive thought should follow, but to leave the ultimate construction to the individual reader. It is his firmest belief that one must "create" his own truths in accordance with his own needs, his own "physiology," and that it is the function of the critic to make this possible by freeing the reader from intellectual and moral shackles—by freeing him, after the manner of Lucretius, from fear of "false gods," but not imposing a new set of dogmas. And so he is willing to make great demands on his readers, to engage their minds in the creative process, to insist on their collaboration in the "completion" of a train of thought. He was not interested in founding a "school" or inculcating a faith; he was concerned only to create an atmosphere of intellectual freedom in which the individual could respond openly and sincerely to the dictates of his own sensibility. And this, he feels sure, will result in a far greater sense of community among men than will habitual obeisance to the hollow abstractions that comprise the majority of inherited "truths."

It is worth noting, however, that while Gourmont's writings were of great importance in the development of modern literature, it was the *man* himself that many writers admired above all. Ezra Pound and Richard Aldington spoke for most of their associates when they praised Gourmont's uncompromising devotion to the life of the mind; he was the friend of earnest young intellectuals and a dedicated defender of new literary movements. They acclaimed his independence of mind on social and moral matters, his courageous stand against the literary establishment, his championing of experimental poets who were being scorned by conventionally minded critics. He was, for his young followers, the complete man of letters who embodied in his life and works an ideal felt to be fast passing away. For Aldington, perhaps his most devoted disciple, he was "almost the last of the true critics."

Gourmont died of a stroke in September 1915. He had come on bad days during the war, for he was entirely dependent on his writing for his support, and most of his publishing outlets had closed down. He was generously helped during his last months by American and English friends, Richard Aldington and Amy Lowell in particular. Ezra Pound wrote, "Gourmont is dead, and the world's light is darkened." Eulogies, tributes, and commemorative pieces appeared in the *Egoist* and *Criterion* in England and in the *Dial* and *Little Review* in America. The *Little Review* brought out a special "Remy de Gourmont Number" in 1919, and for some years translations and commentaries appeared regularly in the little magazines. Then Gourmont slipped into undeserved obscurity.

Some of these essays have been translated before by William Aspenwall Bradley in 1921 and Richard Aldington in 1929. Many are here translated for the first time. I would like to acknowledge the work of my two predecessors, against whose versions I was able to check my own interpretations of some of Gourmont's more difficult passages; and I wish to thank Professors Alexander Fischler and Carrol Coates of Harpur College for their assistance. Thanks are also due the State University of New York Research Foundation for a summer research grant and typing aid.

Harpur College, State University of New York at Binghamton

PART I

The Dissociation of Ideas

The Dissociation of Ideas

There are two ways of thinking. Either you accept current ideas and associations of ideas, just as they are, or you undertake to form new associations or, what is rarer, original associations of ideas. An intelligence capable of such efforts is, more or less, according to the degree, abundance, and variety of other gifts, a creative intelligence. It is a matter of either conceiving new relationships among old ideas and images, or of separating old ideas, old images united by tradition, and considering them one by one, being free to rework them and arrange an infinite number of new couplings which a new operation will disunite once again until new ties, always fragile and equivocal, are formed. In the realm of facts and experience these operations would be limited by the resistance of matter and the intolerance of physical laws. In the purely intellectual realm they must submit to logic; but as logic itself is an intellectual structure, it is almost infinitely accommodating. In truth, the association and dissociation of ideas (or of images—an idea is only a worn image) evolve along meandering lines that are impossible to determine and even whose general direction is difficult to follow. There are no ideas so remote, no images so incongruous, that an easy freedom of association cannot join them at least for the moment. Victor Hugo, seeing a cable wrapped in rags at a point where it bore on a sharp edge, saw at the same moment the knees of tragic actresses which are padded against the dramatic falls of the fifth act;[1] and two such disparate things—a cable anchored on a rock and the knees of an actress—are evoked, as we read, in a parallelism that intrigues us because the knees and the rope are both "furred,"[2] the one above and the other below, at the bend; because the elbow made by a cable thrown in such a way rather resembles a bent leg, because Giliatt's situation is perfectly tragic,[3] and finally because, even while perceiving the logic of these comparisons, we perceive no less well their delicious absurdity.

Such associations are necessarily the most fugitive, unless the language should adopt them and make them into those figures of speech with which it loves to enrich itself. It should occasion no surprise if the bend in a cable were called the "knee." In any event, the two images are always ready to be divorced. Divorce is permanent ruler in the world of ideas, which is the world of free love. Simple folk are sometimes scandalized by it. Whoever first dared to speak of the "mouth" or the "muzzle" of a cannon, according to which term is the older, was no doubt accused of either preciousness or grossness. If it is improper to speak of the knee of a rope, yet it is quite acceptable to refer to the "elbow" of a pipe or the "pot-belly" of a bottle. But these examples are given only as elementary types of a mechanism whose practice is more familiar to us than its theory. We will leave aside all those images that are still alive in order to consider only the ideas, that is to say, those tenacious and fugitive shadows that fluster about eternally bewildered in men's minds.

Some associations of ideas are so durable that they appear eternal, so closely linked that they resemble those double stars the naked eye seeks in vain to separate. They are usually called "commonplaces." This expression, relic of an old rhetorical term, *loci communes sermonis,* has assumed, especially since the development of intellectual individualism, a pejorative meaning that it was far from possessing originally or even as late as the seventeenth century. The meaning of "commonplace" has also been narrowed, as well as debased, until it has become a variant of banality, of the already-seen and already-understood, and for the mass of men with imprecise minds, "commonplace" is now one of the synonyms of cliché. But cliché refers to words, commonplace to ideas. Cliché describes the form or the letter, commonplace the substance or spirit. To confuse them is to confuse the thought with the expression of the thought. The cliché is immediately perceivable; the commonplace very often escapes notice if decked out in original dress. There are few examples, in any literature, of new ideas expressed in original form. The most critical mind must often be content with one or the other of these pleasures, only too happy when it is not deprived of both at once, which is not too rarely the case.

A commonplace is something more and something less than a banality: it is banal, but sometimes unavoidably so. It is banal but so universally accepted that it therefore comes to be called a truth. The majority of truths which travel the world (truths are great travelers) may be regarded as commonplaces, that is, associations of words common to a large number of men, almost none of whom would dare deliberately to break them up. Man, in spite of his tendency toward mendacity, has a great respect for what he calls the truth. Truth is his staff in his voyage through life; commonplaces are the bread in his bag and the wine in his jug. Deprived of the truth of commonplaces, men would find themselves without defense, without support, and without nourishment. They have such a need for truths that they adopt new ones without abandoning the old, and so the mind of civilized man is a museum of contradictory truths. This disturbs him not at all, because he is a "successive." He ruminates his truths one after the other. He thinks as he eats. We would vomit in horror, if someone presented to us, on a large single platter, the various foods, the mixtures of soup, wine, coffee, from the meats to the fruits, which usually comprise our "successive" repasts. Our horror would be just as great if we were shown the repugnant amalgam of contradictory truths lodged in our minds. Some few analytical intelligences have attempted in vain to draw up an objective inventory of their own contradictions. To every objection offered by the reason, sentiment opposes an immediately valid excuse; because, sentiments, as M. Ribot has pointed out, are what are strongest in us, representing as they do permanence and continuity. An inventory of the contradictions of others, when it is a matter of one man in particular, is no less difficult to make. We run up against a hypocrisy whose very social role is to veil and dissimulate the too strident clash of our variegated convictions. We therefore must interrogate all men—that is, the human entity—or at least sufficiently numerous groups of men that the cynicism of some might compensate for the hypocrisy of others.

In the lower animal regions and the vegetable world, one of the ways of creating life is budding. Scission is likewise seen to take place in the world of ideas, but the result, instead of being a new life, is a new abstraction. All general grammars or elementary treatises on logic teach how abstractions are formed. They neglect to show how they are not formed—that is, why a certain commonplace persists in living on without a posterity. It is a rather delicate question, but it would lead to some interesting remarks in a chapter called "Refractory commonplaces, or the impossibility of dissociating certain ideas." It would perhaps be useful to examine first how ideas become associated and for what purpose. The method of this operation is very simple. Its principle is analogy. The elements of some analogies are very remote; others are so close that they are within the grasp of everyone.

Many commonplaces have an historical origin: two ideas were united one day under the influence of events and that union has been more or less durable. Europe, having seen with its own eyes the agony and death of Byzantium, coupled the two ideas, Byzantium-Decadence, which has become a commonplace, an incontestable truth for all men who read and write, and necessarily for all others—for those who cannot verify the truths offered them. This association of ideas was extended from Byzantium to the entire Roman Empire which, for respectable and learned historians, is nothing but a succession of decadences. We read recently in a serious journal: "If the despotic form of government had a particular virtue, conducive to the creation of good armies, would not the establishment of the Empire have been an era of development in the military power of the Romans? It was, to the contrary, the signal for debacle and collapse." This commonplace of Christian origin has been popularized in modern times, as everyone knows, by Montesquieu and Gibbon; but it has been authoritatively dissociated by M. Gaston Paris and is now nothing but nonsense. But, since its genealogy is well known and we have seen it live and die, it can serve as example and explain to us rather well the nature of a great historical truth.

The secret purpose of a commonplace is, in fact, to express a truth. Isolated ideas only express facts or abstractions. To have a truth there must be two factors; there must be—it is the commonest mode of generation—a fact and an abstraction. Nearly every truth, nearly every commonplace, can be resolved into these two elements.

In conjunction with a commonplace, one could nearly always use the word "truth," thus defined once and for all as a commonplace that is not yet dissociated, the dissociation being analogous to what one calls analysis in chemistry. Chemical analysis questions neither the existence nor the qualities of the substance that it dissociates into diverse elements, often dissociable in their turn. It confines itself to freeing those elements and offering them to a synthesis which, by varying the proportions, by invoking new elements, will obtain, if it likes, entirely new substances. With the débris of a truth, one can make another truth "identically contrary," a task which would be only a game, but still an excellent one, like all exercises which render the intelligence supple and lead toward that state of disdainful nobility toward which it should aspire.

There are, however, truths which one never dreams of analyzing or denying. They are incontestable, either because they have been provided by the secular experience of humanity, or because they form part of the axioms of science. The preacher who proclaimed from the pulpit, before Louis XIV, "We all die, Gentlemen!" proffered a truth which the scowling of the king was not intended seriously to challenge. It is nevertheless one of those which have undoubtedly been most difficult to establish and which even now are not yet universally accepted. The Aryan races did not, all at once, link these two ideas, the idea of death and the idea of necessity, and many of the black races have still not reached that stage. For the black man, there is no natural death, no necessary death. At each decease he consults the witch-doctor in order to learn the author of that secret and magical crime. We are still somewhat of that state of mind, and each premature death of a celebrated man immediately starts rumors of poisoning, of mysterious murder. Everyone remembers the legends born of the deaths of Gambetta and Félix Faure. They are naturally related to those that excited the end of the nineteenth century, even more than those deeds, no doubt rare, which darkened the Italian sixteenth century. Stendhal, in his Roman anecdotes, makes too much of that poison superstition which must still, even in our day, claim more than one judicial victim.

Man associates ideas not according to logic or verifiable exactitude, but according to his pleasure and interests. It is for this reason that most truths are nothing but prejudices. Those that are the least open to question are also those that he has always sought to combat cunningly by the ruse of silence. The same inertia is opposed to the work of dissociation seen operating slowly on certain truths.

The degree of dissociation of moral commonplaces seems rather closely correlated with the degree of intellectual civilization. Here, too, it is a question of a kind of struggle, not of individuals, but of

peoples formed into nations, against obvious facts which, in aug-
menting the intensity of the individual life, thereby diminish, as experience shows, the intensity of collective life and strength. There is
no doubt that a man might derive great personal benefit, of considerable advantage to his integral development, from immorality
itself, from rebellion against decalogued prejudices; but a collectiv-
ity of individuals who are too strong and too independent of each
other will as a group be only a mediocre people. Then we see the
social instinct enter into conflict with the individual instinct, and societies professing, as societies, a morality that any one of its intelligent members, followed by a very large part of the group, would
judge empty, antiquated, or tyrannical.

We find a rather curious illustration of these principles in examining the present state of sexual morality. This morality, peculiar to
Christian peoples, is based on the very close association of two ideas,
the idea of carnal pleasure and the idea of reproduction. Anyone,
man or people, who has not dissociated these two ideas has not applied the freedom of his mind to the elements of that truth—to the
notion that outside of the strictly generative act performed under
the protection of religious or civil laws (the second is only a parody
of the first, in our essentially Christian civilizations), sexual relations are sins, errors, faults, weaknesses. Whoever consciously adopts
this rule, sanctioned by statute-books, obviously belongs to a still
rudimentary civilization. Since the highest civilization is one in
which the individual is the freest, the most exempt from obligations,
this proposition would be challengeable only if one took it as a
provocation to libertinism, or as a depreciation of asceticism.
Whether it is moral or immoral is of no importance here. If exact, it
should be revealed by the first glance at the facts. Nothing is easier.
A statistical table of European births will convince the most stub-
born minds that there is a very close connection, a connection of
cause and effect, between a people's intellectuality and their fecundity. It is the same for individuals and social groups. It is through
intellectual weakness that proletarian families are overflowing with
progeny. In the slums we see unfortunates who, having produced a
dozen children, are astonished at the inclemency of life. These poor
people, who lack even the excuse of religious beliefs, have not yet
learned to dissociate the idea of carnal pleasure from the idea of
procreation. To them the first determines the other, and their ac-

tions obey a childish and almost animal mentality. A man who has achieved a truly human intellectual status limits his offspring to suit himself. It is one of his privileges, but it is also one that he may acquire only to die of it.

Fortunate as this particular dissociation might be for the individual, it is, in fact, much less so for a whole people. Nevertheless, it will favor the further development of civilization in maintaining on earth those gaps necessary for man's evolution.

It was not until rather late that the Greeks succeeded in separating the idea of woman and that of procreation, but they had much earlier dissociated the idea of procreation from the idea of physical pleasure. When they ceased to consider woman as exclusively an instrument of procreation, the reign of the courtesans began. The Greeks, moreover, seemed to have always had an exceedingly vague sexual morality, which did not prevent them from cutting a certain figure in history.

Christianity could not, without denying itself, encourage the dissociation of the idea of carnal pleasure from that of procreation, but on the other hand it did successfully provoke—and this was one of the great conquests of humanity—the dissociation of the idea of love from that of physical pleasure. The Egyptians were so far from being able to understand such a dissociation that the love of brother and sister was to them nothing if it were not consummated in sexual union. One finds, among the lower classes of our large cities, many willing Egyptians in this respect. The various kinds of incest that sometimes come to our attention attest to the fact that an analogous state of mind is not absolutely incompatible with a certain intellectual culture. The peculiarly Christian form of chaste love, freed from any idea of physical pleasure, is divine love, such as one sees flourishing in the mystical exaltation of contemplatives. It is a truly pure love, since it corresponds to nothing definable; it is intelligence adoring itself in the infinite idea which it creates of itself. Whatever sensuality may be involved derives from the very nature of the human body and from the law of the interdependence of bodily organs. It should not be considered, therefore, in any study that is not physiological. What we rather ineptly call Platonic love is also a Christian creation. It is, in fact, a passionate friendship, as lively and jealous as physical love, but freed from the idea of carnal pleasure, just as the latter was freed from the idea of procreation.

This ideal state of human affections is the first stage on the way to asceticism, and one could define asceticism as the state of mind in which all ideas are dissociated.

With the decline of Christian influence, this first stage of asceticism has become a less and less frequented resting-place, and asceticism itself, become equally rare, is often reached by another route. In our own time, the idea of love is very closely related to that of physical pleasure, and the moralists are busy reestablishing its primitive association with the idea of procreation. It is a rather curious retrogression.

One could undertake a psychological history of the human race by determining the exact degree of dissociation which characterized, in the course of the centuries, a certain number of truths that right-thinking people agree to call primordial. This method should even be the basis, and this investigation the very goal, of history. Since everything, in man, is founded on the intelligence, everything in history ought to be founded on psychology. The facts would be justified, if they admitted of explanations that were neither diplomatic nor strategic. What was the association of ideas, or the truth not yet dissociated, which favored the accomplishment of the mission Joan of Arc thought she received from heaven? To answer this, we would have to discover the ideas capable of being united in both French and English minds, or a truth which was at that time indisputably accepted by all Christians. Joan of Arc was considered by both her friends and her enemies to be in possession of a supernatural power. To the English she was a very potent sorceress; the opinion was unanimous and the evidence abundant. But for her partisans? Also a sorceress, no doubt, or rather a magician. But magic was not necessarily diabolical. The supernatural beings hovering in people's imaginations were neither angels or demons, but Powers which could be subjected to the intelligence of man. The magician was a good sorcerer: otherwise would such a man of science and sanctity as Albertus Magnus have been credited with magic? Both the soldier that followed Joan of Arc and the soldier that fought her, sorceress or magician, very probably formed ideas of her identical in their dreadful obscurity. But if the English cried out the name of sorceress, the French repressed the name of magician, perhaps for the same cause that protected for such a long time, through such marvellous adventures, the usurper Ta-Kiang, as recounted in Judith Gautier's admirable *Dragon Impérial*.

What idea, in any given era, did each class of society form of the soldier? Would there not be, in the answer to this question, an entire course in history? In approaching our own time, we should ask at what moment, in the average mind, the idea of honor and the idea of the military were conjoined. Is it a survival of the aristocratic conception of the army? Was the association formed as a result of events of thirty years ago,[4] when the people undertook to exalt the soldiery for their own encouragement? This idea of honor must be understood, for it includes several others: the ideas of valor, of disinterestedness, of discipline, of sacrifice, of heroism, of probity, of loyalty, of candor, of good humor, of straight-forwardness, of simplicity, etc. We would find in this word, in the final analysis, a summary of the qualities of which the French race believes itself to be the expression. To determine its origin would be to determine thereby the time when the French began to consider themselves a compendium of all the manly virtues. In France, in spite of recent objections, the military has remained the very type of the man of honor. The two ideas are very strongly united; they form a truth which is scarcely disputed at the present time except by mentalities of minor authority or questionable sincerity. Its dissociation therefore is not very far along, as regards the nation as a whole. However, it was, for a brief psychological moment at least, completely operative in certain minds. It involved, from the strictly intellectual point of view, a considerable effort of abstraction which we cannot help admiring when we objectively consider how the cerebral machine functions. No doubt the result attained was not the product of normal reasoning. The dissociation was accomplished in a fit of fever. It was unconscious and transitory, but it was accomplished, and that is what is important for the observer. The idea of honor with all its implications became separated from the idea of the military, which is, in this instance, the factual idea, the female idea ready to receive all modifiers, and we can perceive that, if there were a certain logical relation between the two ideas, it was not a necessary one. That is the decisive point. A truth is dead whenever one can point out that the relationships which unite its elements are relationships of habit and not of necessity; and since the death of a truth is a great boon to mankind, that dissociation might have been exceedingly important if it had been definitive, if it had remained stable. Unfortunately, following that effort toward the pure idea, the old mental habits regained their sway. The former modifying element was immediately replaced by an element in no way new, less logical than the old one, and even less necessary. It seemed that the operation had miscarried. Ideas were associated as before, identical to their predecessors, except that one of the elements had been turned inside out like an old glove: honor had been replaced by dishonor, with all the adventitious ideas belonging to the former element now transformed into cowardice, double-dealing, lack of discipline, falseness, duplicity, wickedness, etc. This new association of ideas may have had a destructive value, but it is of no intellectual interest.

The upshot of this story is that ideas which seem to us the clearest, the most obvious—the most palpable, so to speak— nevertheless lack the power to impose themselves in all their nakedness on common minds. In order to assimilate the idea of the army, the contemporary mind must surround it with elements that have only a chance or currently fashionable correlation with the principal idea. Doubtless we could not ask a humble politician to conceive as simple an idea of the army as Napoleon had: a sword. Very simple ideas are only within the grasp of very complicated minds. It seems nevertheless that it would not be absurd to conceive of the army as merely the externalized strength of a nation, and then to require of that particular strength only those qualities that we ask of strength in general. But perhaps this is too simple?

What an ideal opportunity we have today to study the mechanism of association and dissociation of ideas! We frequently talk about ideas; we write of the evolution of ideas. Yet no word is vaguer or more ill-defined. Naive writers hold forth on the Idea, as such. There are cooperative societies that set out suddenly in quest of the Idea. There are people who are devoted to the Idea, who suffer for the Idea, who dream of the Idea, who live with their eyes fixed on the Idea. But just what the object of these maunderings is I have never been able to understand. Used by itself in this way, the word is perhaps a corruption of the word Ideal; perhaps this qualification is to be understood? Is it the chance débris of Hegel's philosophy deposited, by the slow march of the great social glacier, in certain minds where it rolls and rattles around like a rock? No one knows. Used in its relative form, the word is not much clearer in ordinary phraseologies. We too readily forget not only the primitive meaning of the word and the fact that an idea is only an image arrived at the stage of abstraction, or notion, but also that a notion, to be entitled to the name of idea, must be innocent of all compromise with the contingent. A notion that has achieved the status of an idea has become indisputable: it is a cipher, a sign, one of the letters of the alphabet of thought. There are not true or false ideas. The idea is necessarily true; an arguable idea is an idea amalgamated with concrete notions, that is to say, a truth. The task of dissociation tends precisely to detach the truth from its fragile portion in order to render the idea pure, single, and consequently unassailable. But if we never used words except according to their unique and absolute meaning, connected discourse would be most difficult. We must allow them a bit of that vagueness and flexibility with which usage has endowed them and, especially, not insist too much on the gap that separates the abstract from the concrete. There is an intermediary state between ice and running water—when water begins to fashion itself into needles, when it still cracks and yields under the hand plunged into it. Perhaps we should not even ask that the words in philosophical handbooks abandon all rights to ambiguity?

The idea of the army, which provoked serious polemics and was liberated just for a moment only to be obscured anew, is closely involved with the concrete and cannot be spoken of without detailed references to the reality. The idea of justice, to the contrary, can be considered in and of itself, *in abstracto*. In the inquiry that M. Ribot made on the subject of general ideas, nearly all those who heard the word Justice pronounced, saw, in the mind's eye, the legendary lady and her scales. We find, in this traditional representation of an abstract idea, a notion of the very origin of the idea.

The idea of justice is, in fact, only the idea of equilibrium. Justice is the dead point in a sequence of acts, the ideal point where contrary forces neutralize each other to produce inertia. Life which had passed by this dead point of absolute justice could live no longer, since the idea of life, being identical with the idea of the conflict of forces, is necessarily the idea of justice. The reign of justice could only be the reign of silence and petrification: mouths cease to speak—futile organs of stupefied brains—and arms, gestures arrested in the frozen air, write no more. Theologians situated justice beyond this world, in eternity. There alone can it be conceived and, without danger to life, exercise once and for all its tyranny which knows only one kind of sentence, the sentence of death. The idea of justice, then, clearly joins the series of ideas that are indisputable and undemonstrable. We can make nothing of it in its pure state, for we must associate it with some factual element or else cease completely to use a word which corresponds only to some inconceivable entity. To tell the truth, the idea of justice is probably dissociated here for the first time. In its name men sometimes invoke the idea of punishment, which is very familiar to them, and sometimes the idea of nonpunishment—a neutral idea, a mere shadow of the former. It is a matter of punishing the guilty and of not disturbing the innocent, all of which immediately implies, if the distinction is to be seen clearly, a definition of guilt and a definition of innocence. This is difficult, these words of our moral dictionary no longer having any but a fleeting and entirely relative significance. And why, we might ask, should a guilty man be punished? It seems, to the contrary, that the innocent one, whom we suppose a sane and normal man, might be much more capable of enduring punishment than the guilty one, who is a diseased and weak man. Why should we not punish, instead of the thief, who has his excuses, the imbecile who allows himself to be robbed? That would constitute our justice if, instead of being a theological conception, it were still, as it was in Sparta, an imitation of nature. Nothing exists except by virtue of a disequilibrium, an injustice. All existence is a theft paid for by other existences; no life flowers except on a cemetery. If the human race would itself be the auxiliary and no longer the negation of natural laws, it would take care to protect the strong against the coalition of the weak and let the people serve as footstools for the aristocrats. It appears, to the contrary, that what is now understood by justice means, along with the punishment of the guilty, the extermination of the strong; and along with the nonpunishment of the innocent, the exaltation of the humble. The origin of this complex, bastard, and hypocritical idea must therefore be sought in the Gospels, in the "a blight on the rich" of the Hebrew demagogues. Thus understood, the idea of justice appears contaminated at once by hatred and by envy. It no longer contains any of its original meaning, and we cannot undertake its analysis without danger of being duped by the common meaning of the words. However, we can, with a little care, discern the fact that the depreciation of this useful term derives from a confusion of the idea of law with the idea of punishment. The day that the word justice came to mean sometimes criminal justice and sometimes civil justice, people confused these two practical notions, and the founders of people's institutions, incapable of a serious effort at dissociation, aggravated a misunderstanding which, moreover, served their interests. Therefore the real idea of justice appears, finally, as entirely nonexistent in the very word which figures in humanity's vocabulary. The word is resolved, by analysis, into elements that are still exceedingly complex, wherein one can distinguish the idea of law and the idea of punishment. But there is so little logic in that singular coupling that we would tend to doubt the accuracy of our analysis, if social facts did not supply the proof.

Here we could examine this question: do abstract words really exist for the people, for the average man? It is hardly probable. It even seems that, according to the prevailing degree of intellectual culture, the same word achieves only graduated levels of abstraction. The pure idea is more or less contaminated by the concern of personal, class, or group interests, and the word justice thus disguises, for example, all sorts of special and limited meanings under which its supreme significance, overwhelmed, disappears.

Whenever an idea is dissociated and is put, quite naked, into circulation, it takes on in its voyage around the world all sorts of parasitic growths. Sometimes the primary organism vanishes, completely devoured by the self-serving colonies that developed on it. A highly amusing example of this deviation of ideas was given recently by a company of house-painters at the ceremony called the "triumph of the republic." These workmen paraded a banner on which their demands for social justice were summed up in this cry: "Down with Ripolin!" If we knew that Ripolin is a prepared paint that anyone can apply on woodwork, then we can fully understand the sincerity and ingenuousness of this slogan. Here Ripolin represents injustice and oppression. It is the enemy, the devil himself. We all have our Ripolin with which we color, in our own interests, abstract ideas which otherwise would be of no personal use to us.

The idea of liberty, as presented to us by politicians, is one of these incoherent motleys. When we hear the word liberty, we rarely think of anything but political liberty, and it seems as if all liberties that a civilized man might enjoy are summed up in that ambiguous term. Moreover, it is the same with the pure idea of liberty as it is with the pure idea of justice; it can be of no service to us in the ordinary course of life. Neither man nor nature is free, any more than man or nature is just. The reason has no grasp of such ideas. To express them is to assert them, but they necessarily falsify all arguments into which they are introduced. Reduced to its social sense, the idea of liberty is still imperfectly dissociated. No general idea of liberty exists, and it is difficult to form one of it, since the liberty of one individual is only exercised at the expense of the liberty of another. In the past, liberty was called privilege. Everything considered, it is perhaps its true name. Even today, one of our relative liberties, the freedom of the press, is an assortment of privileges. Privilege also is the freedom of speech granted to attorneys, and that given to trade unions, and, tomorrow, the liberty of association currently being proposed. The idea of liberty is perhaps only the emphatic deformation of the idea of privilege. The Latins, who made considerable use of the word liberty, understood it as the privilege of the Roman citizen.

We can see that there is often an enormous disparity between the vulgar sense of a word and its real significance in the depths of obscure verbal consciousnesses, either because several associated ideas are expressed by a single word, or because the primitive idea has disappeared under the invasion of a secondary idea. One can therefore write, especially if it is a matter of generalities, whole series of phrases having, at the same time, an overt meaning and a secret meaning. Words, which are signs, are nearly always ciphers as well. The unconscious conventional language is very much in use, and there are even matters where it is the only one used. But ciphering implies deciphering. Even the most sincere writing is difficult to understand, and even the author himself can often go astray, because the meanings of words vary not only from one man to another, but from one moment to another in the same man. Language is thus a great source of deception. It evolves in the realm of abstraction, while life evolves in the realm of the most concrete reality. Between speech and the things speech is meant to designate, there is the distance between a landscape and the description of a landscape. And we must further bear in mind that the landscapes we depict are known to us, most of the time, only through words which are, in turn, reflections of previous words. Yet we understand one another. It is a miracle which I have no intention of analyzing at the moment. It will be more to our purpose, to complete this sketch, which is only a method, to undertake the examination of the very modern ideas of art and beauty.

I am ignorant of their origins, but they come later than the classical languages which lacked any fixed and precise words to express them, although the ancients were able to enjoy as well, if not better, the reality those words contain. They are intertwined. The idea of art is dependent on the idea of beauty, but the latter idea itself is nothing other than that of harmony, and the idea of harmony is reducible to the idea of logic. The beautiful is what is in its place. Whence derive the feelings of pleasure that beauty gives us. Or rather, beauty is a logic which is perceived as pleasure. If we admit that, we will immediately understand why the idea of beauty, in feminist societies, nearly always confines itself to the idea of feminine beauty. Beauty is a woman. There we have an interesting subject for analysis, but the question is rather complicated. First of all, we would have to demonstrate that woman is not more beautiful than man; that, situated on the same plane in nature, constructed on the same model, made of the same flesh, she would appear, to a sensitive intelligence outside of humanity, exactly the female of man, exactly what, for men, a filly is to a colt. And, observing at closer range, this Martian who wished to learn something about the aesthetics of terrestrial forms would notice that, if there exists a difference of beauty between a man and a woman of the same race, same caste, and same age, the difference is almost always in favor of the man; and that if, moreover, neither the man nor the woman is entirely beautiful, the defects of the human race are more accentuated in the woman, where the two-fold protuberance of the belly and the buttocks—a sexual attraction, no doubt—awkwardly warps the double line of the silhouette. The curve of the breasts is nearly inflected under the influence of the back, with its round-shouldered tendency. The nudes of Cranach ingenuously confess these eternal imperfections of the female. Another fault which artists of taste instinctively remedy is the shortness of the legs, so accentuated in photographs of nude women. This cold anatomy of feminine beauty has often been made, so it is useless to insist—all the more as its verification, unfortunately, is only too easy. But if womanly beauty is so open to criticism, how is it that it remains, in spite of everything, unchallengeable—that it can become for us the very basis and leaven of the idea of beauty? It is a sexual illusion. The idea of beauty is not a pure idea; it is intimately connected with the idea of carnal pleasure. Stendhal obscurely perceived this line of reasoning when he defined beauty as "a promise of happiness." Beauty is a woman, even for women themselves, who have carried their docility in regard to men to the point of adopting this aphorism which they are capable of understanding only in the form of extreme sensual perversion. We know, however, that women do have a particular insipid kind of beauty, which men have naturally branded "doll-like." If women were sincere, they would themselves long ago have inflicted an equally pejorative name on this type of feminine beauty by which man is the most willingly seduced.

This identification of women with beauty has gone so far today that we have had innocently proposed to us "the apotheosis of woman." This means the glorification of beauty with all the Stendhalian promises contained in the word in its current erotic sense. Beauty is a woman and a woman is beauty. The caricaturists accentuate the general sentiment when they invariably couple a woman, whom they strive to make beautiful, with a man whose ugliness they push to the basest vulgarity—in spite of the fact that pretty women are so exceedingly rare in real life, and that after the age of thirty the woman is almost always inferior in plastic beauty, age for age, to her husband or lover. It is true that this inferiority is no easier to demonstrate than it is to feel, and that this reasoning remains ineffectual, once the page is finished, for the reader as well as for the writer. And this is most fortunate.

The idea of beauty has never been dissociated except by aestheticians. The common run of men accepts Stendhal's definition, which is tantamount to saying that the idea does not exist and that it has been totally swallowed up by the idea of happiness, of sexual happiness, the happiness given by a woman. That is why the cult of beauty is suspect among moralists who have analyzed the value of certain abstract words. They translate it into the cult of lust, and they would be right if this last term did not imply a rather stupid insult to one of man's most natural tendencies. The inevitable result is that in opposing the excessive apotheosis of woman they have infringed on the rights of art. Since art is the expression of beauty and beauty can be understood only in the form of the material elements of the true idea it contains, art has become almost uniquely feminine. Beauty is woman, and also art is woman. But this is less absolute. The notion of art is even rather clear, for both the artists and the elite: the idea of art has been extremely well liberated. There exists a pure art which is solely concerned with its own self-realization. No definition should even be given of it. It could not be done except by relating the idea of art to ideas which are foreign to it and which would tend to obscure and sully it.

Previous to this dissociation, which is recent and whose origin is known, the idea of art was tied to various ideas which are normally foreign to it—the idea of morality, the idea of utility, the idea of education. Art was the edifying illustration introduced into the catechisms of religion or philosophy; this was the conception of the last two centuries. We freed ourselves of this yoke, but there are those who would now like to reimpose it on our necks. The idea of art is once again sullied with the idea of utility; art is labeled social by the modern preachers. It is also called democratic—well-chosen labels, if intended to mean the total negation of its principal function. To accept art because it can render individuals or masses more moral is to accept roses because we can extract from them some useful remedy for eye ailments. This is to confuse two series of notions which any proper exercise of intelligence would place on different planes. Plastic arts have a language, but it is not translatable into words and phrases. The work of art is addressed to the aesthetic sense and to it alone. Anything else it might say for the perception of our other faculties is not worth listening to. Nevertheless, it is this expendable element that interests the preachers of social art. They are the majority and, as we are ruled by the law of the majority, their triumph appears assured. Perhaps the idea of art will prove to have been dissociated only for a very few years and by a very few intellects.

There are, then, numerous ideas that men have never used in their pure state, either because they have not yet been dissociated, or because that dissociation was unable to achieve the necessary stability. There are also numerous ideas that exist in a dissociated state, or that we can provisionally consider as such, but which have a particular affinity for other ideas in whose company we very often find them. There are still others who seem to resist certain associations, even though they very frequently correspond to the same facts of reality. Here are some examples of these attractions and repulsions chosen from the most interesting realm of commonplaces, or truths.

Flags were originally religious tokens, like the oriflamme of Saint-Denis, and their symbolic utility has remained at least as great as their real utility. But how, apart from war, did they become symbols of the idea of country? This is easier to explain by facts than by abstract logic. Today, in nearly every country, the idea of country and the idea of flag are invincibly associated. The two words are even interchangeable. But this is a matter of symbolism as much as association of ideas. Insistence on it would lead us to the language of colors, the counterpart of the language of flowers, but even more unstable and arbitrary. If it is amusing that the blue of the French flag is the devout color of the Holy Virgin and the children of Mary, it is not less so that the pious purple of Saint-Denis' robe has become a symbol of revolution. Just like the atoms of Epicurus, ideas cling to each other however they can, by chance encounters, collisions, and accidents.

Certain associations, though very recently formed, have rapidly acquired a singular authority, such as those of education and intelligence, of education and morality. Now, this is especially the case if education is taken to be merely one of the special forms of memory or a literal knowledge of the commonplaces of the Commandments. But the absurdity of these forced relations is very clearly seen in regard to women: indeed they seem to get a kind of instruction these days which, far from stimulating their intelligence, tends to stupefy it. Since they have been educated seriously, they no longer have the least influence in politics or literature: in this regard we can compare our last thirty years with the last thirty years of the ancien régime. These two associations of ideas have, nonetheless, become veritable commonplaces—truths which it is as useless to expose as to combat. They are to be added to all those which clutter the books and the degenerate brain lobes of mankind, those old and venerable truths such as: virtue-reward, vice-punishment, God-goodness, crime-remorse, duty-happiness, authority-respect, unhappiness-punishment, future-progress, and a thousand others, some of which, however absurd, are useful to mankind.

One could make an equally long list of ideas that men refuse to associate, while delighting in the most disconcerting debauches. We have given above the explanation of this mulish attitude: it is because men's principal occupation is the search for happiness, and because they are more concerned with reason according to their interests than to logic. Hence the universal aversion to connecting the idea of nothingness with the idea of death. Although the first idea is obviously contained in the second, humanity persists in considering them separately. It opposes their union with all its strength. It untiringly drives a chimerical wedge between them with resounding blows from the hammer of hope. This is the most beautiful example of illogicality that we can give ourselves and the best proof that, in serious matters as in trivial, it is sentiment that always triumphs over reason.

Is it a great thing to know that? Perhaps.

—November 1899

Success and the Idea of Beauty

In one of his *Paradoxes,* where he sometimes shows a little of Heine's irony and Schopenhauer's wit, Max Nordau has designed a Machiavellian plan for a school of success. The reverse of usual morality would be taught there: not virtue, but the art of arriving. This school exists: it is life itself. Precocious eyes and ears absorb its teachings from the time of adolescence; young men devote themselves to success as others do to the priesthood or to glory. Are they unreasonable? No. And contemptible? Why? Writing, singing, sculpting are all acts. Thinking, even in the silence of the night and in the depths of a dungeon, is an act. Now, what act does not have as its end its own accomplishment? The reasoner who has convinced himself will necessarily wish to convince others, and the poet who admires himself will wish to evoke enthusiasm in others. Those who are content with an intimate or limited approbation are perhaps the wise ones, but they will never be counted among the strong. Even if he is timid or disdainful, the dreamer desires the glory of dreaming, and he would dream with delight before throngs rapturously contemplating his eyes lost in an ocean of dreams and nonsense. That would be success. Success has something precise about it that calms and nourishes. It is a feast. It is a fact. It is the ultimate goal.

Success is a fact in itself independent of the work or the act that accompanies it. The assassin who succeeds in his crime, step by step, experiences other joys than that of quenched avidity. He finds, in short, that success has made him right; and with all pursuit thrown off the track, we understand very well the state of mind that Barbey d'Aurevilly dared to describe. However, crime, unless it is political, only rarely receives public applause in our civilizations, as it does among the Dyaks of Borneo or the subjects of the Old Man of the Mountain. That is why, despite the celebrated irony, we do not consider assassination to be "one of the fine arts." It should at least be classed in that category of art whose one and only end is success and which prizes most what it is called at the end rather than at the beginning. But that is not at all the subject of this essay, which is indeed serious and whose words will be carefully weighed. It will be concerned solely with works of art and particularly those belonging to literature.

Success is, then, a fact, but, for the category of facts that concerns us, it is a contingent fact. Success does not change the essence of the act itself. In this respect I would gladly compare success to consciousness, a flame which burns in us and illuminates our actions and thoughts, but which has no more influence on their nature than its shadow has, on a moonlit night, on the movement of a passing train. No act is determined by consciousness. Success does not create a work, but it brings it to light, and in such a way that something of it will remain almost forever in men's memories. One does not become Racine by having been applauded under the house-lights, and one remains Racine even if *Phèdre* were played six nights in a row before darkened seats.[1] But one becomes Pradon, and that is considerable. To be Pradon, through the centuries, is to live by an obscure and unpleasant glory, sad and futile. No doubt, but scarcely less precarious than what we call real life. Pradon is, at the same time, ridiculous and illustrious. We cannot recount Racine's career without involving Pradon's name. We study his works in order to understand that renown of a day that has been prolonged through so many morrows. There is no doubt of it: Pradon had almost no talent, although he was rather adroit in his trade as a dramatic constructor. He was, as the journalists say, a man of the theater. One observer even went so far as to claim that to have a perfect *Phèdre,* it would have to be written by Racine on a plan by Pradon.[2] It is absurd, but every success has a cause. The cabal explains nothing. The Duchess of Bouillon would not have risked the battle on a worthless card. Pradon was known. His tragedy of *Pyrame et Thisbé* had been applauded. Ten years after *Phèdre,* and without a cabal, his *Régulus* was praised to the skies. He was, then, destined for a moderate reputation, such as that which *Solyman,* for example, earned its author, the Abbé Abeille, about the same time.

Was it fortunate for this mediocre poet to have encountered the duchess of Bouillon on his path? Anticipating our modern ways, that terrible woman bought up all the seats of two theaters, filling one and leaving the other empty. In our time, she might have bought up the newspapers as well, but no one knows how much she paid for the chatter of newsmongers and pamphleteers. It was one of the most beautiful strokes of its kind, for it succeeded marvellously. But what did it gain Pradon? After much abuse, an ocean of posthumous abuse. Not a day passes that some professor does not treat him like a Damiens or a Ravaillac.[3] Does immortality compensate for that? Is a shameful immortality preferable to the darkness of night? First of all, we must dismiss the shame and ignore the abuse. All success ignites the flames of hatred and thickens the descending smoke. It is of no importance. Hatred is an opinion, as are the abuses and words that cast infamy. Success is a fact. The duchess of Bouillon could not change the essential value of each of the two *Phèdres*[4] any more than one can transmute "base lead" into "pure gold"; but she was able to veil the gold and gild the lead. She was able to force posterity to repeat the name of her favorite. That was her work. It is beautiful and memorable. At that time, no one knew which of these two similarly framed pictures he was supposed to admire. The friends of Pradon were as powerful as those of Racine. One had Boileau; the other had Sanlecque, his sometimes fortunate rival. But the authority of Boileau gave way before that of Mme de Houlières, representing polite society and the literary coteries. It happened that the War of the Sonnets put even wit on the side of Pradon, for the wit of the Duke de Nevers retains, even today, the most engaging malice. Molière, who detested Racine and had earlier lent his theater to a parody of *Andromaque,* no doubt would have backed Pradon. Friends of good literature were spared this scandal by his death. It was therefore around a reasonable illusion that a crystalization of success was formed, and the elegant wits did not have to blush for their part in it. It is a pious lie of historians of French literature to claim that the true public avenged Racine for the desert organized by Mme de Bouillon. The boxes of the Hôtel de Bourgogne had been hired for six days, while Racine's *Phèdre* played only seven times. The public had understood: it responded to success like dogs to the whistle.

Success, even when organized by fraudulent means, exerts a

powerful attraction on crowds, even literate ones. Surely the theater public, in 1677, was considerably superior in intelligence, knowledge, and taste to the average public today, and nevertheless we see it attracted to decidedly mediocre plays and disdaining the finest. It is because success, especially theatrical success, can result spontaneously from a chance occurrence—the pleasing face of an actress, a fine gesture, a well-placed applause, the whims or feelings of a small group of spectators. The herd follows, since all assemblages of men are herds, and history counts another name and another date.

The Americans—those of the North, for in the South they have more finesse—never hesitate before success. What is the dramatic poem whose success has surpassed even the enthusiasm for the *Cid* and *Hernani?* It is *Cyrano de Bergerac.* Therefore it is something to be admired, and they see that it is learned by heart, along with *l'Aiglon,* in the schools where, themselves illiterate, they cultivate learned wives. To restate my true opinion, I do not find this unreasonable. Let us not confuse history, which is a completed novel, or is at least to be continued, with the present time, which appears fragmentary to us, like one edition of a newspaper torn into a thousand scraps of paper. How are these to be arranged, and according to what order? We have not the slightest idea. Our judgments of today, those which seem the wisest and sanest, will appear ridiculous in twenty years, because we lacked the patience to reconstitute the entire page, or because fire or wind made off with some of the tiny squares. In this fog of our ideas, success glows like an electric moon. Something undeniable shines forth—which professors of philosophy call a criterion. But may we call it merely a fact, as a flower is a fact, or a shower, or a conflagration? And what could they oppose to that fact to contradict it? Practically nothing—the result of some judgment, some man's notion of literary beauty. Yet this opposition is not at all radical, since, in principle, beauty is in no way excluded from chances of success. But no bets should be placed on beauty—it would be imprudent to back her on even terms. But there are some examples in history of a most beautiful work also being the one that men have most celebrated. Then success is worthy of adoration, like the sun which comes to ripen the harvest, like the storm which fills the rivulets and fountains. What is a beautiful book of which not a single known copy remains? What was the armless Venus before M. de Marcellus called her up from the abysses? Success is similar to daylight and, once again, if it does not create the work, it finishes it, by tearing away its enveloping veil of shadows.

There is another consideration which enhances still further the value of success: if the end of art is to please, the greater the total number of its conquests the better this end will be fulfilled. Art surely has a function, since it exists; it satisfies one of the needs of our nature. To say that this need is precisely artistic taste is to say that coffee or tobacco are loved because they satisfy the taste men have for coffee or tobacco. It is to say nothing at all, not even non-sense; it is to offer utterly meaningless words. Things in life do not correspond with such simplicity, like that amiable relationship be-tween a pot and its cover. Let us leave such questions to the Chris-tian philosophy of final causes. The end of art being to please, suc-cess is at least a beginning of proof in favor of the work. To please—it is a very complex idea: we will see later what it involves, but the word can serve us provisionally. Therefore a certain work pleases. A tower is suddenly erected to the passionate plaudits of the crowd. That is the fact. The tower should be demolished. That is not easy, since, by a singular magic, nearly all the battering rams directed at it are transformed into buttresses which add their weight to the solidity of the monument. It must be proven to that fortress that it does not exist; and to the crowd that its admiration has not moved all those stones, that it is lying, hallucinated, or imbecile. But this cannot be done. They find it beautiful. What to respond to them, if not: yes, it is beautiful.

The priest takes a wafer from the corporeal and raises it to the dignity of Divinity. He places it in the monstrance and shows it to the people, who during this ceremony kneel, bow their heads, pray, and believe. The work that success exalts is chosen no less by chance than the wafer by the fingers of the priest; and its divinity, from the moment it is chosen, is no less certain. We must respect the decrees of destiny. We must not oppose popular piety.

II

However, there exists, it is said, an aesthetic. There are even several of them. But we will suppose that there is only one, and that— always in principle—it has good reasons for opposing success, what-ever it may be. If we grant the existence of an aesthetic, we are obliged to recognize that there is also an absolute beauty and that works are judged beautiful in proportion to their resemblance to that vague and accommodating ideal. It is this aesthetic—admitting its existence for the moment—that is now to be laid open and subjected to the scalpel.

The sensibility which either yields to success, or provokes it, is extremely interesting, but perhaps it will be permissible not to scorn completely and out of hand the sensibility which is opposed to success and denies that the successful work is, therefore, a beautiful work. These two sensibilities, equally spontaneous, are not equally pure. The second is very mixed. The aesthetic by which it is summed up—as fragile as morality—is a mixture of beliefs, traditions, arguments, habits, conceptions; it involves some respect, fear, and an obscure appetite for novelty. "With new thoughts we will make old verses." The old-new—that is what all aesthetics advocate; for an élite or caste must be flattered according to its particular nerves and knowledge. The judgment of the artist in matters of art is an amalgam of sensations and superstitions. The ingenuous crowd has only sensations. Its judgment is not aesthetic. It is not even a judgment. It is the naive avowal of pleasure. It necessarily follows that only the aesthetic caste is qualified to judge the beauty of works and to endow them with this quality. The crowd creates success; the caste creates beauty. It is all the same, if you like, since there is no hierarchy in sensations or acts and everything is in motion. It is the same, yet different. Here, then, we have established a point. In matters of art, the opinion of the sensibility is opposed to the opinion of the intelligence. The sensibility cares only for pleasure. If to that pleasure is joined an intellectual element, we have an aesthetic. The crowd can say: that pleases me, therefore it is beautiful. It cannot say: it pleases me and nevertheless it is not beautiful; or: it displeases me, and nevertheless it is beautiful. The crowd, as a crowd, never lies. Aesthetic judgment is one of the most complex forms of lying.[5]

It is quite evident that there is no such thing as absolute beauty, any more than absolute truth, justice, or love. The beauty of poets, the truth of philosophers, the justice of sociologists, the love of theologians are just so many abstractions which can only enter the realm of our senses—and then very ineptly—when shaped by the sculptor's chisel. Like ideas conceived in the future or in the past, they express a certain concordance between our present sensations

and the general state of our intelligence. We feel this especially regarding truth, which is a sensation not contradicted by our intelligence; but any other intelligence may contradict it, or it can be contradicted by sensations of a different intensity or different order.

The idea of beauty has an emotional origin and is related to the
idea of procreation. The female who is to become a mother must
conform to the racial type; that is, she must be beautiful.[6] The
woman is less demanding, perhaps because the man transmits only
a small part of himself to his descendants. The first standard of
beauty was, then, woman, and, in general, the human body. For an
animal or an object to be beautiful, it must have something of the
human in its form, in its character. A countryside can be described
in terms almost all of which are applicable to womanly beauty.
Marble has her whiteness; and sapphires are her eyes, and coral her
lips. We have here a complete vocabulary of clichés. To be sure,
some of them should be corrected, and it should be noted that it is
ebony that is black like black hair and the swan that has a woman's
neck. Beauty is indeed so sexual that the only incontestable works of
art are those that simply show the human body in its nudity. Greek
statuary, by its perseverance in remaining purely sexual, has put itself above all discussion for all eternity. It is beautiful because it is a
beautiful human body, one with which any man or woman would
wish to be united for the perpetuation of the race.

But another and more obscure fact, although no less certain,
suggests that the idea of beauty may be connected to the very idea of
sexuality by yet another route. That is that all human emotions,
whatever their order, nature, or intensity, arouse a more or less
marked response in the genital nervous system. Sexual pathology
has brought this to light. Perfumes as well as the sight or odor of
blood, noise and heat, intellectual and muscular toil, repose and
fatigue, intoxication or abstinence—the most contradictory sensations are all favorable to the sexual impulse. Others, such as fear,
cold, and vexation also react on a neighboring and intricate center
of the genital system. Look at the first chapter of *En Ménage,*
where M. Huysmans describes the effect produced on a gentle and
nervous person by the discovery of a lover in his wife's abode.
Among the emotions most surely aroused in any organism of the
slightest sensitivity, the aesthetic emotions must be placed in the first
rank. And thus they return to their source. Whatever leads to love

seems beautiful; whatever seems beautiful leads to love. There is undeniable interlacing. One loves a woman because she is beautiful; and one thinks her beautiful because one loves her. It is the same with everything that permits associations of sexual ideas and all emotions that react on the genital system.

But it is not at all necessary that a work of art present a sensual scene. In order to awaken ideas of love, it is sufficient that it be beautiful, captivating. It arouses passion. But where will we seek the seat of that passion? The brain is only a center of transmission; it is not a terminus. It was a happy and praiseworthy error to have made man's brain the absolute center of man; but it is an error. The only natural end of man is reproduction. If there were another end to his activities, he would no longer be an animal, and we fall back into Christianity, to be confronted once again by the soul and its demerits and all the jargon of the spiritualist quacks. We become conscious of emotion at the very moment of its passing, but it does nothing but pass, leaving its image, and it descends into the loins. This manner of speaking is perhaps figurative, and, moreover, I do not have in mind intense and strongly localized excitements. I mean only to say that aesthetic emotion puts a person in a state favorable to receiving erotic emotion. This state is brought about in some by music, in others by painting or drama. I know a man—of a certain age, to be sure—who could escape sexual desire by leafing through albums of engravings. The opposite case would no doubt be less paradoxical: the aesthetic emotion is the one from which man allows himself most easily to be distracted by love—so easy, almost inevitable, is the transition. This intimate union of art and love is, moreover, the sole explanation for art. Without it, without that genital echo, it would not have been born and would not have been perpetuated. There is nothing useless in the profound human habits: everything which endures is therefore necessary. Art is the accomplice of love. Take love away, and there is no more art. Take art away, and love is scarcely anything but a physiological need.

But here it is less a question of art than of its emotional power, and under the name of art must be classed everything in the nature of spectacle or sport, all diversions enjoyed in public, or with regard to which one communicates his impressions to himself. Fireworks can thrill quite as much as a tragedy; the sole hierarchy is one of intensity. Now there is no doubt that the success of a work of art greatly increases its emotional impact on the general run of men. From this derives, for the crowd, that very natural belief that every successful work is beautiful, and that failure and scorn are always deserved. In short, what the elite calls beauty the people call success; but they have learned from the aristocrats this word that is really bereft of meaning for them, and they use it to enhance the quality of their pleasures. This is not in the least illegitimate, success and beauty having a common origin in the emotions, the sole difference being the difference between the nervous systems in which they evolved. And, moreover, very few men are capable of an original aesthetic emotion. Most of those who do experience it only obey, like the crowd, the suggestion of an expert, a commandment from their memories, the influence of their environment, or the current fashion. There is passing beauty as precarious as a faddish success. A work of art extolled by today's aesthetic caste will be scorned by tomorrow's, and it will perhaps vanish sooner than the work neglected by caste and acclaimed by the people. For success is a fact whose importance grows with the dust it stirs up, with the number of faithful that come to join the retinue. The emotions of the elite and the emotions of the people are destined for the same terminus. Nature, which does not make leaps, does not make choices. It is a matter of making children. The sense of smell (or an analogous sense) of the emperor moth is so highly developed that a female larva of this rare butterfly attracts, on the very day of its hatching, a host of males where, on the previous evening, not one could be seen. This acuteness would be absurd if the emperor moth employed it only to choose the most delicate food among a group of flowers, or, in some fashion or other, to enhance its pleasure and its mental improvement, the cultivation of its intelligence. But it is an aid to the emperor moth in making love. It is its aesthetic sense.

There are human natures, however, less diffuse or more refractory, in which the emotions do not react upon the center of the major sensibility, either because the center is atrophied, or because the emotional current has, in its course, encountered an obstacle, a dike, an impenetrable barrier. Let us use, without prejudging the aptness of the analogy, some of the most common and striking comparisons. An electric current is sent through a wire for the purpose of creating a movement. The wire falls, and is supported by a piece of wood, and instead of movement it produces heat: the train

burns, when we wanted to make it roll. The emotion, en route towards the genital sense that it is meant to awaken, encounters a center of resistance. It is broken, it twists back on itself, but it is stuck
there; and all the emotions of the same order that pass through the
same center will have the same fate. A wheel was to be turned, and
we have fire-works; the species was to be preserved, and the idea of
beauty was born. Aesthetic emotion, even in its purest and most disinterested form, is therefore only a deviation of the genital emotion.
Aphrodite, who enticed us into her cult, troubles us no more. The
woman has faded away. Noble forms remain, pleasing lines—but a
horse is also beautiful, and a lion, and an ox. A fortunate short cir-
cuit which has allowed us to reflect, to compare, to judge! The current hurls us on toward the sister of the goddess. Now it turns us
from her, for she is less beautiful! It might be supposed that it is in
the intellectual region that the emotional current has become
diffused, thus forming that mixture of emotion and intelligence
which gives us the aesthetic sense. Intelligence is an accident; genius
is a catastrophe. We must carefully avoid even dreaming of a social
state where health, equilibrium, equity, moderation, order would
reign uniformly, where catastrophes would be impossible and accidents very rare. Human intelligence is certainly the consequence of
what we naively call evil. If the threads did not become cut and
knotted, if emotion always attained its goal, men would be stronger
and more beautiful and their houses as perfect as anthills. Only, the
world would not exist.

III

Before returning to our point of departure, here is a résumé: Two
sorts of emotions share in the formation of the aesthetic sense: emotions of a genital nature, and all the other emotions, whatever they
might be, in proportions that vary infinitely with each man. The first
are those that we feel at the perfect representation of our racial type.
Apollo is beautiful because he is the human male in all his purity.
For the majority of men, every adventitious idea being rigorously
excluded, the sight of this marble is pleasing because it evokes desire, either directly or, according to the sex, by counterevocation. We
recall the words of Stendhal: beauty is the promise of happiness.
The sensualist philosophy which sanctions this definition was not
stupid. We will have to return to it, with science as a point of sup-

port. In short, the word "beauty" was invented for the purpose of describing the "promise of happiness." And this word has been successively applied to everything which offers men the realization of one of their increasingly more numerous and complex desires. Later, emotional need being very highly developed, it was applied to all causes of emotions, even terrible and bloody. But emotions of any nature, which comprise the very life of man, have one purpose—like the sense of smell of the emperor moth. They penetrate us to remind us that our one duty as living creatures is to preserve the species. Whichever sense they act on first, they rebound from there toward the center of the general sensibility. I am thinking of those romantic lovers, enveloped by the storm, possessing one another furiously, or of the gentle emotion of Tibullus, *quam juvat immites*. . . . The horrible, stupid, savage tragedies that delighted the Greeks and the French of the ancien régime were philters, and nothing more. If great poets (like women, the great poets have neither taste nor a sense of disgust) had not taken the trouble of rethinking the stories of Orestes, Thyestes, Polynices, we would judge them to be the delirium of an infantile, or a degenerate, society. There is not one tragedy of Racine's that has not been played a hundred times in criminal courts by loathsome performers. You will find, if you care to, in the special treatises by Ball and Binet, and in certain popular works, the transformation of any sensation whatsoever into a sexual act. Here, there are no categories—the field is unlimited. We see men for whom the odor of rotten apples gives rise to powerful and necessarily sexual emotions. Schiller always kept a supply in the drawer of his work table; but, as he possessed a refractory passage where emotional currents were in large part broken up, he made verses, after having breathed rotten apples, instead of making love.

We have here, then, a whole class of men in whom the emotions, arrested halfway, are transformed—in a most obscure and yet dynamic way—into intelligence, aesthetic taste, religiosity, morality, or cruelty, according to the milieu and circumstances. We can even say that this transformation, large or small, occurs in all men. It also happens that the emotions react almost equally in all directions, a considerable part flying toward the genital centers, while enough is left along the way to produce a great philosopher, a great artist, or a great criminal. Love seems particularly allied to cruelty, whether by its absence or excess. The nemesis of cruelty is exactly that of sexual love. Duchenne of Boulogne proved that by his experiments. In types like Torquemada or Robespierre, emotions do not terminate in the genital senses. They run up against an obstacle which inclines them toward another center; instead of being transformed into the need for reproduction, they are transformed into the need for destruction. But there is the Neronian type and the Sadic type in whom sexuality and cruelty are stimulated at the same time and intertwined. And there are men capable of stronger emotional shocks than other men. Though divided and distributed toward two goals, the current remains strong enough to produce extremely intense acts. The same phenomenon appears, though in a more amiable form, when intellectual power is exercised at the same time as genital power. Every man capable of emotion is capable of love and of cruelty at the same time, stemming perhaps from intellectuality, perhaps from religiosity. But it sometimes happens that the emotional current is entirely absorbed by one of the human activities. Then we have one of the extreme types, the other extreme being furnished by men of great emotional receptivity and consequently of a great diversity of aptitudes.

But let us remain in the realm of average humanity and the question of aesthetics. According to the extent to which the emotional current is diverted, we will have, for example, a spectator who retains from a tragedy all that it offers in the way of pure or strong beauty, who will depart in a state of intellectual emotion, less aware of the murder than of the curve of the arm that struck the blow, less aware of the curses and terrors than of the musical form that limited and enveloped them, and made them live. We will also have a spectator who, despite some glimmers of intellectual emotion, leaves the theater very much as he leaves a boxing-match or bull-fight. Here we have the extremes. The one, viewing a perfect statue, enjoys the grace of its lines and thinks: what a beautiful work! The other exclaims to himself: what a beautiful woman! Between these two types there is a whole spectrum of shadings. For the average type the idea of beauty scarcely exists. He will judge the work according to the intensity or quality of his emotion. It will please him or leave him cold, and that is all. It is the average type who determines success in art. The average type must be pleased; he must be moved.

The representatives of the aesthetic caste also judge a work of art by the emotion that they experience, but this emotion is a very special order: it is aesthetic emotion. For them those works alone that are capable of arousing the emotion, the aesthetic thrill, belong to art, to the category of beauty. Thus are excluded from art all utilitarian, moralizing, social works possessing any purpose whatsoever outside this precise and exclusive goal—aesthetic emotion. Also excluded are works of too sexual a nature, whose appeal to sexual activity is too direct, though they too respond—but with an excessive clarity—to the primary idea that men have had of artistic beauty. Thus is formed that aesthetic category which, eternally unstable, ranging from realism to idealism (a certain idealism), from sentimentality to brutality, from religiosity to sensualism, remains, nonetheless, a closed garden.

Art, therefore, is what arouses a pure emotion, that is to say, without vibrations outside a limited group of cells. It is what conduces neither to virtue, nor to patriotism, nor to debauchery, nor to peace or war, nor to laughter or tears, nor to anything that is not art itself. Art is impassive, and, as an old Italian poet has said of love, *non piange né ride.* There is nothing about it either rational, or just, or consistent with any truth. It is a matter of the manners and customs of an intellectual caste. Born of an imperfection of the nervous system, the idea of beauty has picked up, on the way, all sorts of rules, prejudices, beliefs, habits, and it has created a canon whose form, without being absolute, does not vary at a given moment except between certain limits. The restriction is necessary. All refined men of a period understand each other regarding the idea of beauty. Today, for example, there are touchstones: Verlaine, Mallarmé, Rodin, Monet, Nietzsche. To confess that you are not moved by the *Hands,* by *Hérodiade,* by *Eve,* by the *Cathedrals,* by *Zarathustra,* is to confess that you are deficient in aesthetic sense. But works of quite a different tone were admired in the past by the same group of men. From Ronsard to Victor Hugo, the principle of beauty was sought in imitation. They imitated the Ancients, the Italians, the Spanish, the English. But during the last century, the principle became originality, and even that resulted, some years ago, in an excess of false notes, but also in a music less flat, on the whole, than that which had for such a long time wearied the muses. Not that they imitated any less, but they did it under the illusion of creating anew, and illusion is almost always fertile. France, moreover, is the country where the idea of beauty has undergone the most variations, being populated with eager and curious men, always alive to what is happening and ready to make the acquaintance of everything strange and new, and feeling free to laugh if the novelty does not happen to suit their temperament.

Our aesthetic sense, then, has its caprices. But while historically variable, it is solid enough at any given moment. There is an aesthetic caste today; there is always one, and the history of French literature is hardly anything more than the *catalogue raisonné* of the works successively chosen by this caste. Successes are created in the streets, but glory comes from the coteries. As there are no examples to the contrary, this must indeed be admitted as a fact; also this, that coteries become disgusted with those glories that escape them and start running the streets. A fact, being always logical, is always legitimate, but one can oppose it with the repugnance of one's own sensibility or of a group of sensibilities. That is what the crowd does when led by certain educated mediocrities, good lawyers all, since they hate the house which they are fighting and which does not recognize them. We see, then, the often obscure reputation established by the aesthetic caste incessantly opposed by the celebrities of success. It is easy to fool the people by showing them, on the one hand, the poor solitary lamp; and on the other, the harsh glare of globes and the violent brilliance of tulips. But the people hardly need encouragement; they gravitate naturally toward what dazzles them. That is also a fact, and it is also legitimate. The public, led by cunning shepherds, is wrong to despise the confused glitter of stars; but the aesthetic caste is wrong to laugh at the pleasures of the people. It is wrong also to monopolize certain words and to refuse the name of work of art to compositions which have exactly the same purpose as those which they themselves admire—arousing the emotions. It is a question of quality, not of essence. They suffer less from seeing a poor work applauded than a good work scorned. The aesthetic caste's judgment, so apt in scenting false art, suddenly weakens and grows angry when a partisan of popular taste does not bow before its predilections.

It is always a mistake to appeal to justice, but it is idiocy to appeal for justice from a social group. We must forsake all that and shut ourselves up in an opinion as in a tower. It would be easier to cut the throats of a hundred fanatical admirers of *Quo Vadis* than to convert them, and much less fatiguing. Literary justice is an absurdity. It supposes an equality of emotions in men of different physiological categories. A work is beautiful to anyone whose emotions it stirs. The sensibility of the populace as well as that of the coteries is incorruptible. It is as incorruptible as the sense of taste and smell. In the past they believed in Taste, in and for itself—an absolute Taste which one worshipped in a temple. Nothing is more ridiculous, or more tyrannical. Let us leave men to freely seek their own pleasures. Some want their entrails wrenched; some want to vent their spleen; others want to be pierced to the heart. There must be different instruments for each of these operations. Art is a form of surgery whose case is well-equipped—a pharmacopoeia filled with vials of every shape and smell.

One talks very seriously—that is, without laughing—about initiating the people to art. In less vague terms, corresponding to a certain scientific reality, it is a matter of so fashioning the physiology of the common run of men that emotions, instead of reaching the genital center, might be diffused toward the aesthetic center. Hardly the least of undertakings! The poor people! How one makes a game of them, and how stupid their intellectual masters are, in all their good intentions! They actually believe that the taste for painting, music, and poetry can be learned like spelling and geography! And suppose it could be, and suppose a few admirations were imparted to some workers? What does it matter that the people do not admire what we admire? They would have the same right to demand that we share in their enthusiasms. There is no absolute aesthetic standard. What is beautiful is what moves us, but we can be moved only according to our emotional receptivity and the state of our nervous system. Insensitivity to what we call beauty, which becomes a very complex idea the moment we leave the human form, would seem, on the whole, merely to be evidence of a healthy organism, a normal brain, where the nervous currents go directly to their goal without deviations. But this seems to be a rare state. All men are capable of receiving certain aesthetic emotions, and all are eager for them; but almost none care about the quality of that emotion. The important thing is to be moved. No monument since the cathedrals, or perhaps since the pyramids, has moved the aesthetic sensibility of humanity as much as the Eiffel Tower. Confronted with all that scrap iron stacked on high, stupidity itself became lyrical, foolishness meditated, asininity dreamed. And from those heights showered down, as it were, a storm of emotions. Some tried to divert it, but it was too late. Success had arrived. The more a work is the object of admiration, the more beautiful it becomes to the mob. It becomes beautiful, and almost a living creature. It gives off emotional waves that come to break like surf on a drunken and gasping people. The entire organism celebrates; and, stupid and beautiful, the genius of the species smiles in the shadows.

Such is the social role of art. It is immense. There is an Australian bird that builds, for a nest, a large cabin which it strews with all the bright pebbles it can find. The male, in the middle of this mosaic, dances a grave minuet before its agitated companion—and that is art, surprised in its obscure birth, at the moment when it is closely related to the expansion of genital instinct. A red pebble stirs a bird's emotion, and this emotion heightens its desire. Such is the social role of art. The people have to admire—and here I mean, by people, all humanity—they have to experience aesthetic emotions. Their nerves must tremble with long vibrations, and their loves must be rich and complicated: but what does it matter where the cloud comes from, provided it rains!

I have wished only to demonstrate the legitimacy of every aesthetic emotion, whatever its source, and of every success, whatever its quality; but I will be readily believed if I confess that I keep my preference for a certain form of art, a certain expression of beauty. But in this respect I depart from the common sentiment—I believe it is fruitless to generalize on opinions, to teach admirations. Forcing an admiration is as wicked as forcing an entrance. Each man must grant himself the emotions that he needs and the morality that suits him. Apuleius' ass wanted to browse among the roses because then he would immediately regain human form. It is a good idea to browse among roses. It is one method of deliverance.

—From *Le Chemin de velours,* 1901

Glory and the Idea of Immortality

The idea of glory is not one of the most difficult to analyze. It can be identified with the general idea of immortality, of which it is only one of the secondary and more naive forms. It differs from the general idea only by the substitution of vanity for pride. In the latter we have the idea of duration fortified by the pride of a being who believes himself to be of immortal importance but quietly consents to enjoy, without fuss, an absolute perennity. In the idea of glory, however, vanity replaces pride and brushes aside the idea of the absolute, or declaring itself incapable of attaining it, fastens on a desire of eternity, no doubt, but an objective eternity, perceptible to others, a rather ostentatious eternity which loses in general worldly reputation what an absolute immortality gains in profundity and proud humility.

Abstract words poorly define an abstract idea; it is better to rely on common opinion. We all know what glory is; every writer imagines literary glory for himself. Nothing is clearer than these kinds of illusions; nothing is clearer than desire or love. Definitions, for which dictionaries alone have an obligation, contain of reality what a badly retrieved fishnet contains of the obscure and swarming life in the sea where it awaits its prey—some seaweed tangled about and some scrawny creatures waving their translucent limbs, and all sorts of snails, and bivalves that a mechanical sensibility clamps shut. But reality, which was a sizable fish, has, with a flip of its tail, slipped overboard. In general, clear and distinct phrases have no meaning whatever—they are affirmative gestures that suggest dutiful acquiescence, and that is all. The human mind is so complex and things are so tangled up with each other that, to explain a blade of straw, one would have to take to pieces an entire universe. In no language is there a single legitimate word on which a lucid intelligence could not build a psychological treatise, a history of the world, a novel, a poem, a drama, according to the day and the temperature. A definition is a sack of flour compressed into a thimble. What can we do with it, unless we are Antarctic explorers? It is more to the point to put a pinch of that flour under a microscope and to search the bran patiently for the living starch. In what is left after we analyze the idea of immortality, the idea of glory will shine forth like a brilliant sparkle of gold.

Man still believes himself to be the ultimate work of the creative force. Darwin, corroborating the Bible, had the human couple emerge from limbo only on the sixth day. And the most reputable scientists hold the same view, which gives rise to those dubious writings in which the questionable accord of Science and Faith is celebrated. But Darwinism is destined to fade away before more precise notions. Tomorrow we will not hold to the belief that the creativity of the world, having organized the inferior species without moral ideas, invented man in order to deposit in his brain a principle which it had gotten along very well without, itself, in the course of its preparatory labors. If man is no longer the latest arrival among creatures, if man is indeed an ancient animal in the history of life, if the flower of the vital tree is not Adam, but the Dove, then the entire metaphysic of morality is going to crumble. What! After that masterpiece, Man, He (or She, according to which empty word one professes) is going to lower himself to create a mere bird? What? the stork after Abraham's ancestor! Yet it is so. The work of M. Quinton no longer allows us to doubt it. It becomes certain that human intelligence, far from being the end of creation, is only an accident of it, and that moral ideas are only parasitical vegetations born of an excess of nutrition. The phenomena of intelligence, moral conscience, and all the titles of nobility enumerated on parchment, no doubt could have appeared in any other species. Birds, whose evolution is not completed, should perhaps not be exempted. Their arterial system is considerably superior to that of man— simpler and more solid. They can eat without suspending their breathing; they steal, they speak, they can recite the Rights of Man and the Nicene Creed—supreme activities of many men. But the bird, chronological king of creation, has remained up till now, and

despite its improvements, an animal. The bird species does not appear superior, in intelligence, to the mammalian species, in which
Man figures as an inexplicable exception. Intelligence could therefore be considered a final end only if each of the animal species were
rigorously determined and fixed. That is the opinion, at least provisionally, of M. Quinton. The species, since they are species, since the
individuals that comprise them reproduce themselves in beings
identical to themselves—the species, as defined by these very syllables—*spe-cies*—can disappear, but they can no longer change. Man
has most certainly passed through various stages in which he was
not a man, but from the day that man produced a man, humanity
was immutable. It is therefore possible that human intelligence, instead of being an accident, a derogation, might have been determined, from the beginning, like the human hands and feet, like
human hair. It would therefore have, in the universe, a normal and
logical role, and its very excess—genius—would be no more than a
superabundance of vital energy. But there remains the stupidity of
birds to be explained: could it be evidence of the intellectual degeneration of the creative energies? A more probable opinion is that intelligence is an excrescence like the oak-apple! What insect has
given us that bite? We will never know.

Whether intelligence is, as Taine believed, a normal product of
the brain, or whether it is a malady, is of little importance, especially
since any blemish that is transmitted intact from generation to generation ends by losing its pathological characteristics. It becomes an
integral and normal part of the organism.[1] However, its accidental
origin is corroborated by this: an excellent instrument for making a
priori combinations, the intelligence is—especially, one could say—
inept at perceiving reality. Metaphysics, religions, and morals are all
the result of this infirmity. Since the external world can reach our
consciousness only by scrupulously embracing all the folds and
curves of the pocket, it turns out that in believing we have an image
of the world we have only an image of ourselves. Certain rectifica-
tions are possible; analysis of the phenomena of vision brings us to
admit that. By comparison of our sensations and ideas with what
we can grasp of the sensations and ideas of others, we manage to
determine probable averages—but, above all, negative averages. For
it is easier to draw up a list of nontruths than a list of truths. To
affirm that a certain religion is false no longer indicates a great bold-

ness of mind or even a great amount of mind. The truth of any religion is no longer a subject of controversy except for various European clergymen who make a living by it or for those belated rationalists who are always on the lookout, like their master Kant, for the propitious and lucrative time for opportune conversions. But to the naive question posed by those who, like the nature of the seventeenth century, abhorred a vacuum: "What will you replace it with?" nobody can answer. It is enough, and a worthy thing, to have transmuted a truth into a nontruth. The supreme business of the critic is not even, as Pierre Bayle proclaimed it was, to sow doubts. He must go farther—he must destroy. The intelligence is an excellent instrument of negation. It is time to use it, and to cease wishing to erect palaces with pickaxes and torches.

The history of the idea of immortality is a good example of our congenital inability to perceive reality other than reformed and reworked by judgment. The idea of immortality was born of the belief in the double. During sleep, and while the body is inert, there is a part of man that moves, travels, fights, eats, enjoys or suffers, exercises all functions of life. That part of man, his double, his astral body, survives the decomposition of the material body whose usages and needs it conserves. Such, no doubt, is the origin of the belief in what has been called, since the days of Hellenism, the immortality of the soul. The Egyptian religion, at an even more ancient stage, was based on the theory of the double: it was for the doubles and not for souls that one placed real nourishment, and later on symbolic food, in tombs. But the Egyptian religion was already charged with the idea of justice, of equilibrium: the doubles were weighed in the scales of good and evil; the metaphysic of morality had obscured the primitive idea of immortality, which is nothing more than the pure idea of indefinite duration.

For theologians and philosophers, if there still are any who profess these honest doctrines, and for the common run of men, the idea of immortality or future life is intimately linked with the idea of justice. Eternal happiness is a compensation accorded to human sufferings. There are also—but for theologians alone—personal torments, by which the lapses of the priestly orders are punished; and these torments represent for the good an increase or reward and a guarantee against promiscuity. It is an aristocratic selection, but based on the idea of good and evil instead of on the idea of strength and weakness. These strange inversions of values enraged Nietzche, but one must accept them at least as the transitory consequences of the sensibility of civilized man. Primitive man, whose nerves are more steady and whose intelligence is passive, feels suffering, though dully, but does not feel injustice, which is moral suffering. In order to find a similar state, we must bypass the middle regions and interrogate a Goethe, a Taine, or a Nietzsche—the men whose intelligence, by very excess, has finally conquered and repelled the supplications of pity and the sentimental temptations of justice. If the idea of immortality were born in a superior intelligence, it would not have differed from the brutal conceptions of primitive humanity except in its being more logical.

M. Marillier has collected and organized, from among noncivilized beliefs, everything that concerned the survival of the soul.[2] This compilation of facts shows that the idea of justice has in no way influenced the idea of immortality. Few discoveries may be more important for the history of human beliefs. The idea of immortality was originally, as M. Marillier boldly points out, a purely scientific idea; it is the enlargement and prolongation of a fact, poorly observed, but a fact. Future life is a continuation of present life, and it entails the same practices, the same pleasures, the same vexations. This world has, it too, its double: the other world. There, in the other world, the wicked and the good, the strong and the weak perpetuate their condition. There life, without change in the relation of its elements, is sometimes more agreeable; sometimes, under the same conditions, it is worse. But whether the future life is considered better or worse, it is the same for all. If better, it is perfect equality in the mediocre pleasures which are the common ideal among civilized man as well as savages. The tribes of New Guinea, anemic through constant hunger, dream of eating unlimited sago throughout all eternity. Since even in this egalitarian paradise, one will find some vague idea of compensation and therefore of justice, one should look further—to Java, where paradise, no doubt because of an excessive toll, was accessible only to the rich; to those resigned tribes, where the kings, priests, and nobles were alone saved; to Borneo, where the hereafter, divided into seven circles, corresponded to the seven divisions of the social hierarchy. In one corner of that great island "every person that a man kills in this world becomes his slave in the other." We see a paradise clearly based on the idea of strength and a belief that rather laughs at the categorical imperative. Not only is the weakling not "compensated," but his weakness and suffering can, at the whim of the strong, be carried into infinity; and the killer acquires an immortal form. Some societies having poetry, art, and laughter still live with such a morality. One can be saddened by it but not surprised, for it is evident that here we see a terrible element of resistance against foreigners. That has its drawbacks: from time to time, in Borneo, a group of young Dyaks who have not as yet killed, descend on a village and kill. Having thus gained eternal life and a slave, they become more peaceful. Among the Shans, if one is destroyed by an elephant, he is deprived of paradise; if eaten by a tiger, he becomes a tiger. Women who die in childbed become ghouls and haunt tombs, their feet reversed, heels foremost. In the Marianas, there is a paradise and a hell. A violent death leads to hell, a natural death to paradise: these people were from all eternity destined for slavery. In another region of Oceania, the fate of a soul is decided by the defunct one's family by a roll of the dice: odd means annihilation; even means eternal happiness. In Tahiti the blind souls, on leaving the body, wander at random towards an open field where there are two stones: one, if touched first, bestows eternal life; the other, eternal death. Here we have the nearly sublime absurdity: it is as grandiose and terrible as predestination. Saint Augustine located it in the night that precedes birth; the Tahitians situated it in the shadows after death. Protestantism, to which the poor folk have since become addicted, has not greatly changed their beliefs. In general, the greatest effort of a religious or philosophical novice is to put last what is found at the beginning and vice versa.

By linking itself to the idea of immortality, the idea of justice has, then, considerably deranged its original character. It has even contaminated the idea of terrestrial immortality—the idea of glory.

II

How glory, at first reserved for the kings and warriors whose praises were sung by the poets, has come to be attributed to the poets themselves rather than to the heroes of their poems, is a fact of civilization whose exact origin would not have a great deal of interest. It would be more interesting to learn in consequence of what modification of mores or what aggrandizement of egoism and vanity the idea of perennity of name and work came to be linked to the complicated idea of justice. At what period of Greek civilization did an Athenian dramatist, whose work had been scoffed at by the people, have the audacity to appeal to posterity? Do we know of any ancient texts wherein such recriminations can be read? Sensibility has increased to such an extent that today there exist no scorned poetasters who do not dream of the justice of future generations. The *exegi monumentum* of Horace and Malherbe is democratized, but how can one believe that the vanity of authors has ever had a beginning? The fact must be admitted, however, if we are to hold with the logic of successive developments of human character. Originally literary glory was nothing more than the feeling of the future duration of a present reputation—a legitimate feeling which accords well enough with the facts, for absolute failures are almost as rare as solid revivals. At the moment, it is a scientific probability. Aeschylus believed that the relation that existed between his *Suppliants* and public opinion would remain constant throughout the ages. Aeschylus was right, but not if he had the same hopes for his *Danaids* and *Egyptians*. Yet, Pratinas saw himself as one of the future rivals of Aeschylus, and now Pratinas is no more than a name, and scarcely that. The idea of glory, even in its most ancient and most legitimate form, would seem, therefore, to contain the idea of justice, at least by preterition, since its nonrealization suggests the idea of injustice. But we must not judge the men of so ancient a civilization according to our own sensibility. Pratinas would, perhaps, have submitted to destiny; he would, perhaps, have called a fact, pure and simple, what we are pleased to call injustice.

The idea of justice, being as it is subject to variations of sensibility, is one of the least stable of ideas. Most of the facts which today we rank in the category of injustice, the Greeks relegated to the category of destiny. For others, which we discard under the name of misfortunes or fatality, they strove to find remedies. In principle, whenever people restrict the "destiny" category for the benefit of the "injustice" category, it is because they are beginning to confess their own decadence. The extreme state of sensibility to injustice is expressed by the gag of Zaina, who breathed only through a veil in order not to destroy any life[3]—a state of intellectual degradation towards which European humanity, whose vegetarian mystics were the precursors of the sentimental socialists, is also marching. Do we not already have "inferior brothers" and do we not hear ourselves praising machines that spare animals the exercise of their muscles? To cry over the slave who turns the wheel, or over the poet who sings in the wilderness, is a sign of depravity: for the slave who turns the wheel loves life more than he suffers from his labor, and the poet who croaks like a frog in his hole finds his song to be an agreeable physiological exercise.

The physical laws promulgated or established by scientists are admissions of ignorance. When we cannot explain a mechanism, we claim that its movements operate by virtue of a law. Bodies fall by virtue of the law of gravity. This has precisely the same value, in the realm of the serious, as the comic *virtus dormitiva*. Categories are the confession of impotence. To throw a fact into the abyss "destiny" or the drawer "injustice" is to renounce the exercise of the most natural analytical faculties. The *Lusiads* were saved because Camoëns knew very well how to swim and Newton's first treatise on light and color was lost because his small dog, Diamond, overturned a lantern. Looked at in this light, the two events no longer belong in either the "Providence" category or the "Fatality" category. They are unqualifiable facts—facts such as are produced by the thousands without our finding in them pretexts for enthusiasm or wrath. That Aeschylus has survived and Pratinas is dead are accidents like those that occur in war. Some of them are more scandalous than others, but none of them should be judged according to the sterile notion of a distributive justice. If justice is wounded because Florus keeps afloat in the shipwreck in which Varius and Calvus perish, it is justice which is wrong. It was out of place there.

However, since it has attached itself to the idea of paradise, the idea of justice has become a parasite on the idea of glory. For the immortality for which Tahiti gambled heads or tails has been substituted, with the best of intentions, a providential immortality; but, with regard to glory at least, we know that Providence, even if it does not draw the names of the elect by lot, is determined by motives that it would probably not dare to acknowledge. However unjust man might be, by nature or preference, he is less unjust than the God who created him: thus chaste men produce obscene literature, as Ausonius has pertinently remarked; thus the work of the true genius is always inferior to the brain that gave it birth. Civilization has put a little method, provisionally, into glory.

Even in the spiritual realm, men have almost always been at odds with the decisions of their gods. Most of the saints of yesteryear were created by the people in spite of the priests. In the course of the centuries the catalog of saints and the catalog of great men have drawn so apart that soon they will no longer have a single name in common. Nearly all the venerated men of this century, nearly all of those whose clay contains veins or traces of gold, were outcasts. We live in the time of Prometheus. When Providence alone governed the earth, during the interregnum of mankind, she caused such slaughters that intelligence nearly perished. In the year 950, the son of one of Aurillac's serfs, the young Gerbert, summed up almost an entire European tradition. He was, all by himself, civilization. What a moment in history! Men, through an admirable instinct, made him their master: he was the Pope Sylvester II. When he died, they began to build, on that column that had sustained the world, the legend that was to culminate in the *Faust* of Goethe. Such is glory—that Gerbert is unknown. But he is not unknown like Pythagoras; for one could write of his life, and his writings have been preserved. If Gerbert is not one of our great men today, he might well be tomorrow; he has kept intact all his possibilities for resurrection. That is because—to leave for the moment the paradoxical idea of Providence—there have been almost no changes in our civilization since Gerbert's time.

When the Christians arrived in power, they preserved, other than what was spared by chance, only those books necessary for school instruction. There remained of Antiquity what would have remained of the seventeenth century if the professors of the old University, together with the Jesuits and the Minims, had had the power of life and death over books. Adding La Fontaine to Boileau's catalog, they would have burned the rest. The Christians burned much, despite their professions of love: and what they did not burn they revised. It is to them that we owe the image, almost burlesqued, of a chaste Virgin. The authentic incompletion of the *Aeneid* was a good pretext for deletions and erasures. The booksellers charged with the duty were, moreover, unintelligent and lazy. But the major cause of the disappearance of almost all pagan literature was more general. The day arrived when it was considered to be of no interest. From the time of the first centuries, its circle had begun to shrink. How could a Saint Cecilia enjoy Gallus? This delicious and heroic Roman woman (who was found last century couched in dust in her bloody robe) changed her heart when she changed religion. Women ceased to read Gallus, and Gallus has perished almost totally.

In the interesting book he published on this subject,[4] M. Stapfer has not taken into account some changes in civilization. To explain the loss of so many ancient books, he has thought only of the element of chance. Chance is a mask, and it is precisely the task of the historian to lift it or tear it. From the sixth century to our own time there has been one partial modification of our civilization —in the fifteenth century. Around that time, ancient literature began to move the reading public no longer: its novels, miracles, and stories seemed suddenly old. They were no longer copied or re-cited, and rarely printed—a single manuscript preserved *Aucassin et Nicolette,* which is something like the Daphnis and Chloë of the Middle Ages. Accidents frighten the poet—and even the critic, who is colder and more rigorously logical—the moment anyone tries to separate the sentimental idea of justice from the purely historical idea of literary survival. Up till now, and I again refer to the conservationist role of modern civilization, the printing press has protected writers from destruction, but the serious role of printing has affected as yet only four centuries. This remote invention will appear some day as contemporary with both Rabelais and Victor Hugo. When the time will have elapsed between ourselves and a given moment in the future equal to that which separates us from the birth of Aeschylus, in two thousand, three hundred, and seventy-five years, what influence will the printing press have had on the conservation of books? Perhaps none. Everything which will not be worth the trouble of reprinting, that is to say everything except a few fortunate fragments, will have disappeared, and the more rapidly since the material substance of books has become more flimsy. Even the discovery of durable paper would not be a sure cause of survival, because of the temptation to use such excessively strong paper for a thousand other purposes. Thus the cost of the parchment often determined the sacrifice of a manuscript; thus gold art objects go necessarily into the smelting pot when styles have changed. The material which would best preserve books would resist deterioration, but be fragile, a bit brittle, so as to be good for nothing outside of its binding. Would not such a discovery be a curse?

Up to now, the printing press has been a memorable blessing for the work of the last four centuries and for what remained undamaged, around 1450, of earlier work, as well as for what has been retrieved from the dust since then. We need not rely on opinions from earlier days. The books are there, and whether they are rare or common, we can discover and read them. We find ourselves the surprised and lenient judges of the glory and opprobrium that Boileau awarded his contemporaries. Martial discredited poets who might have been a Saint-Amant or a Scudéry; but we have, under our very eyes, parts of the Dossier of the Satires, and no professor who is friend to good manners and eternal principles can ever impose his mediocre hatreds. A man of intellect once remarked that Boileau treated writers who displeased him somewhat as we treat known murderers or seducers of young girls; but thanks to the unforeseen permanence of books, this abuse is of no more significance for judges today than vituperation of a lawyer. I have Sanlecque within reach of my hand, and even Cottin and Coras. If they are mediocre, I will decide according to my free personal impression.

A catalog of lost books has been published.[5] Their number amounts to five or six hundred, and yet, to reach that figure, it was necessary to count certain works that have merely strayed and some editions that were reprinted several times. And were there among these lost books any pages truly deserving of tears? It is hardly probable, judging from the epitaphs on these tombs. One doubts that they included any *Maxims* or *Phèdres,* or even other *Alarics: Herménégilde,* tragedy, by Gaspard Olivier (1601); the *Poétiques trophées* of Jean Figon de Montélimard (1556); or the *Courtisan amoureux* (1582), or the *Friant dessert des femmes mondaines* (1643). But who knows? The *Coupe-Cul des moines,* however, or the *Seringue spirituelle* inspires mild regrets, and similarly the *Estranges et espouvantables amours d'un diable déguisé en gentilhomme et d'une demoiselle de Bretagne.* A more obvious loss is that of several *Almanachs* written by Rabelais, but that does not matter too much. The fact that feverish fingers prematurely wore out the first editions of *Astrée,* some *Aventures du baron de Foeneste,* and some *Odes* by Ronsard [6] only proves the immediate success of those works which were never out of the hands of the curious for more than a half century, and one could say as much for the original editions of Alexander Dumas' first novels, which cannot be classed, for the most part, among lost books. But the fact that we can read the inscriptions in a cemetery proves at least that the dead thus identified had a name and a glory, however transitory. The true lost books are those whose titles no one can even guess today. That anonymous dust would no doubt fill a sizable ossuary, but with lost manuscripts one could build a necropolis.

It is unlikely that much more than a hundredth part of French literature of the Middle Ages has survived changing fashions. Nearly all the theater has disappeared. The number of authors must have been immense in a time when the writer was his own editor, the poet his own reciter, the dramatist his own actor. In a certain sense, the printing press was a hindrance to the practice of letters. It exercised a selectivity and cast contempt on writings that had not succeeded in being printed. This situation still obtains, but is attenuated by the low cost of mechanical typography. The invention that threatens us now—a home printing apparatus—would multiply by three or four times the number of new books, and we would find ourselves in the situation of the Middle Ages: everyone who is the least literate—and others, as is the case today—would venture his little lucubration which he would pass out to his friends before offering it to the public. All progress ends by negating itself. Having arrived at its maximum expansion, it tends to reestablish the primitive state which it was intended to replace.

The change in civilization, from antiquity to the Middle Ages, was intellectual and emotional rather than material. The same occupations were perpetuated under the same primitive conditions. The bookstore in the times of Rutebeuf was one which sold, all fresh and full of life, the odes of Horace. In both periods, which were equally periods of abundance, literature was equally plentiful. But almost nothing of it remains today. All of Latin poetry, from Ennius to Sidonius Apollinaris, is contained in two folio volumes,[7] but almost all the second volume is devoted to Christian poets. The Greeks were no better treated. Antony made a gift to Cleopatra of the library at Pergamos, which consisted of two hundred thousand Greek works in single copies; whereas Greek literature in the Didot edition contains sixty-one volumes. If we add an occasional treatise by Aristotle, Herodas, Bacchylides, we will not greatly increase the number of pages. What happened to literature was like what happens to a decimated army: you bury the dead and make heroes of the survivors. We can judge their absolute value, but not the relative value of what remains. Here we find Pratinas once again. He teaches us that glory is a fact.

III

Glory is a fact pure and simple, and not a fact of justice. There is no exact relation between a writer's merit (we confine ourselves to the question of literary glory) and his reputation among men. In order to reward the survival of a book after four hundred years, following the whims of chance and, if you will, of injustice, critics have devised a hierarchical system which divides writers into castes, from the idiot to the genius. This has an air of seriousness and solidity, but it is arbitrary, since aesthetic or moral judgments are nothing but generalized sensations. And so literary judgment becomes involved, to the point of confusion, with religious judgment.

Earthly immortality and the other, which functions ideally beyond real life, are conceptions of the same order and born of a single cause: the impossibility for thought to think of itself as nonexistent. Descartes merely posed a physiological axiom and a human truth so absolute that it might well have been composed by the most ancient and humble people. "I think, therefore I am" is the translation into words of a cellular state. Every living brain thinks the same, though perhaps unconsciously. Every minute lived is an eternity; it has neither beginning nor end. It is what it is, and it is absolute. However, the disaccord between cerebral truth and material truth is complete. The organ dies by which man thinks himself immortal, and the absolute is conquered by reality. The disaccord is complete, obvious, undeniable. Yet it is inexplicable. Confronted by such a contradiction, the hypothesis of dualism takes on a certain force, and moreover the laboratory affirms the essential difference between muscular work and cerebral work. The bending of a forearm, and even of a phalanx, releases a certain amount of carbonic acid. Cerebral activity, all the muscles being in repose, registers no trace of combustion. That is not to say that the organs of thought are immaterial. One can touch them, weigh and measure them, but they are of a peculiar materiality whose vital reactions are as yet unknown to us. Inexplicable in theory, the disaccord between thought and flesh is explained, in fact, by a difference at least of molecular structure. There are two states of being, each having but a superficial knowledge of the other, and the flesh is going to be dissolved that thought might think itself eternal.

There are, then, two immortalities: the subjective immortality which man awards himself willingly and even necessarily, and the objective immortality—which Pratinas was denied—the one which is a fact. The first, religious or literary—in the light of what we have just said of it, and in the absence of precise analyses—allows only of philosophical, that is, vague, consideration, whereas objective immortality is a subject of less abstract discussion. One could, with a little good will, bring all history within its scope, but French literature provides a sufficiently long and brilliant cavalcade.

Words, from the moment they gather beneath their wings a certain amount of perceptible reality, willingly yield up their formula. Glory is life in the memory of men. But of what men, and what life?

M. Stapfer has attempted to enumerate those works which, from the sixteenth to the eighteenth centuries, have lasted—in the sense that "lasted" is used in professional critical language. This chapter, wittily entitled (with a somewhat Jansenist wit) "the little number of elect," would be brief if it were only a catalog. In short —and one can admit it provisionally—of all the French writers of the last three centuries, twenty-five or thirty have achieved what might be called glory, but of these thirty, the majority are scarcely more than names. What life and of what men? M. Stapfer has in mind works that a Frenchman of today, "of average culture," might consider glancing at some rainy day. But it is impossible to make a serious analysis if one allows, in his reasoning, the use of such expressions as "average culture." A man of "average culture" might indeed find pleasure in Saint-Simon and not possess a Pascal, nor a Bossuet, nor a Corneille, nor a Malherbe. One can read and reread Pascal and have little taste for Rabelais. But these lovers of difficult reading are professors, ecclesiastics, lawyers—men who, even if they do not themselves write, have a professional interest in literature and feel an obligation to keep in contact with the classic period of French literature. And where did they learn that Boileau is a better poet than Théophile or Tristan? In school, for it is through the school that literary glory is sustained in the bored memory of heedless generations. There is no "average culture" that can be felt and figured by a flexible curve, but there are programs. Villiers de l'Isle-

Adam invented a "Glory Machine." At the Ministry of Public Instruction there is a room where, on the door, should be read: "Bureau of Glory." It is there that the Superior Council meets to elaborate its program of studies. This program is the "crammer" that produces "average culture." Any names absent from this program will be forever unknown to the generations for which it will be the paternal guide. But the conscience of an educator cannot impose on children a knowledge of writers whose morality is not universally admitted. Molière was exceedingly immoral in his time, and that is what caused his success with a public which had to choose, in its repentent days, between the more eloquent and the more clever preachers. And it is to the extent that Molière has become less understood, little by little, that he has become a moralist. As the sensibilities of successive generations have become increasingly differentiated from that of the seventeenth century, coarseness has lost some of its rank odor, to the point where we find delicacy in sallies which, if couched in today's terms, would cause us considerable embarrassment. Molière, much more brutal in depth than on the surface, enjoys what one could call "acquired morality." It is an inevitable phenomenon of accommodation. It was necessary either to sacrifice Molière or to demonstrate the beauty of his philosophic genius.

His words, which are only words, "For the love of humanity," have been hollowed out and belabored by commentators like an ivory ball which, in a lathe, ends up as a network of concentric circles: it is only a baby's rattle. How can one reconcile les *Femmes savantes* and Feminism? It would be a curious performance very interesting to follow. In her *Réflexions sur les femmes,* so penetrating and so beautifully expressed, Mme de Lambert says that this comedy, besides being odious, made the education of girls appear improper, immodest, a kind of obscenity: whence the mad craze for purely sensual pleasures to which women inclined, as they had no other resources than luxury and love. The best way around this problem is to consider the idea of feminism and the idea of *Femmes savantes* separately and to carp at the word "savant," which has recently taken on a very precise meaning. The savant, in the seventeenth century, meant not only one interested in the sciences, but also in literature; one with a mind eager for novelties, who discussed vortices without neglecting Vaugelas. Mme de Sévigné was a "femme savante," as was Ninon. No doubt it was necessary to save

Molière; it was worth the trouble. But could it not have been done with more honesty and clarity?

The same bringing into focus, applied to Rabelais and Montaigne, has been less successful. Rabelais, above all, has discouraged the most stubbornly naive of moralists, and, since they could not harvest virtuous sheaves in his abbey of good pleasure, they rank Pantagruel among the vague precursors of modern ideas, which has no appreciable meaning, modern ideas being so exceedingly contradictory. La Fontaine lent himself to the caprices of moralists with that indifference to good and evil which was the property of his uniquely sensual temperament; and, as for Racine, whose work would be shocking if it were not expressed in a language as cold and abstract as algebra, the Jansenist devotion of his later days permits us to find pious intonations even in his most delirious chantings of sensuality and cruelty.[8] Why has not this same solicitude been shown a Saint-Amand or a Théophile? We find there the influence of Boileau, who is still dangerous to contradict when seeking a certain quality of reputation. Happy to find their task limited and determined by a celebrated authority, educators end their catalog of glories as soon as it attains a decent length. Their enterprise involved moral rather than literary criticism. One book alone—the *Fables,* for example—could have served as an album wherein they could have deposited the artful aphorisms of the old catechism. The ideal of the educator is the Koran, whose pages contain at once an example of writing, a model of style, a religious code, and a handbook of morals.

We can therefore conclude that, in reality, there is no literary glory. Great writers are held up for our admiration not as writers, but as moralists. Literary glory is an illusion.

However, while keeping for instructional purposes some of the greater French geniuses, historians of literature have been obliged to offer motives for their choices, to feign artistic preoccupations. A Nisard wrote a history of French literature which was concerned almost entirely with morality. Such a preoccupation is noble but too exclusive. The common handbooks adroitly intermix the two orders. Naturally a child does not understand clearly whether La Fontaine is prescribed to him as a great poet or as a simple, good-natured man who teaches prudence, like the author of *Philémon et Baucis* or a precursor of Franklin. Armed with the four rules of literature, the professors have examined various talents and classified them. They have awarded prizes and honorable mentions. There is the first order and then the others ranked down to the fourth and fifth order. French literature has become as hierarchically arranged as an apartment house. "Villon," one of the classifiers told me one day, "is not of the first order." Admiration must have its shadings according to the seven notes on the university scale. Serious flutists excel at this game.

It is not a question of challenging the awards of glory nor of proposing a different list. Such as it is, this practice serves its purpose; it can have the usefulness of the arbitrary classifications in botany. It is not a matter of amending it; it is a matter of tearing it up. That Racine is a better poet than Tristan l'Hermite and that *Iphigénie* is superior to *Marianne* are two propositions unequally true; for we could just as well have taken for comparison the following, which is by Racine:

> Que c'est une chose charmante
> De voir cet étang gracieux
> Où, comme en un lit précieux,
> L'onde est toujours calme et dormante!

> Quelles richesses admirables
> N'ont point ces nageurs marquetés,
> Ces poissons aux dos argentés,
> Sur leurs écailles agréables! [9]

with this, which is by Tristan:

> Auprès de cette grotte sombre
> Où l'on respire un air si doux,
> L'onde lutte avec les cailloux,
> Et la lumière avecque l'ombre.

> Ces flots, las de l'exercice
> Qu'ils ont fait dessus ce gravier
> Se reposent dans ce vivier,
> Où mourut autrefois Narcisse.

> L'ombre de cette fleur vermeille
> Et celle de ces jons pendans

Paraissent estre la-dedans
Les songes de l'eau qui someille.[10]

I am well aware that I am here comparing the best of Tristan
with the worst of Racine, but, all the same, if Racine has his park,
Tristan has his garden, and he does very well in it. Let us tear up
the list of awards, then, in order that we might be ignorant of the
fact that Tristan l'Hermite is a poet "whose versification is ridiculous," [11] so that the pleasure that we might take in meeting him will
not be spoiled in advance, and so that we might dare to say to his
muse, with him:

Fay moi boire aux creux de tes mains
Si l'eau n'en dissout point la neige.

This is the drawback to comparative methods. Critics, having
elected as ideal the great poet of a century, then evaluate the others
only as precursors or disciples.[12] They judge writers according to
what they are not, often because they failed to understand an author's peculiar genius and failed to interrogate him themselves. In
truth, Pratinas is better treated: he enjoys a silence.

But he is dead, and it is a question of living. Living—what life
and in the memory of what men? Life is a physical fact. A book is
not dead that exists as a volume in a library, and perhaps it is a
more enviable glory to be unknown in the manner of Théophile
than to be celebrated in the manner of Jean-Baptiste Rousseau?
Glory, when it is only that of a classic, is perhaps one of the more
lasting forms of humiliation. To have dreamed of stirring men and
women to great passions, and to be no more than the dull task that
keeps a bored schoolboy imprisoned! But are there any universal
reputations that are not classic? Very few, and they have yet another
blemish. It is only for what they contain of the improper that one
reads the preposterous novels of Restif,[13] the syphilitic stories of
Voltaire, and that tedious *Manon Lescaut,* so ineptly adapted from
the English. Books of former days no longer have a public, if by
public we must mean disinterested men who read solely for pleasure
and enjoy what a book contains of art and thought; but they still
have readers, and all have some.

No book is dead except the lost book. All the others live, and
almost the same life; and the more ancient they are, the more that

life, in becoming more precious, becomes more intense. Literary glory is nominal; literary life is personal. There is no poet of the prodigious seventeenth century who is not revived, each day, in the pious hands of some curious reader. Bossuet is not more leafed through than the *Recueil* of Pierre du Marteau; [14] and, all things considered, the *Plainte du cheval Pégase aux chevaux de la petite ecurie, par Monsieur de Benserade* is more agreeable and less dangerous reading than the *Discours sur l'histoire universelle.* Is pompous moralizing so superior to lighthearted burlesque? Every plant on the mountain is of equal interest to the artless botanist. For him the euphorbia is not celebrated or the borage ridiculous (it has, moreover, the most beautiful eyes in the world), and he fills his bag till it refuses another blade of grass. Literary glory is an invention for the use of children preparing for examinations. It matters little to the explorer of the mind of the past that this pleasing verse is by an unknown writer or that powerful thought is by one of the despised. A man and his work—they are of such different interest! The man is a physiology that had no value except in the milieu in which it evolved. The work, whatever it might be, can preserve, through the centuries, an abstract power. But we must not exaggerate this power or make of it a tyranny. A thought is scarcely anything other than a dried flower; but the man has perished and the flower remains in its herbarium. It is the witness of a vanished life, the sign of an annihilated sensibility.

When, in the Gallery of Apollo, we gaze at those onyxes and corundums in shapes of conches and cups, those golden works engraved with flowers, and those violent enamels, do we, before daring to enjoy them, ask the name of the maker of such jewels? However, the question would be vain. The work lives and the name is dead. What matters the name!

"I, who do not wish for glory," wrote Flaubert. He was speaking of posterity, of those future and consequently nonexistent times, to which so many mediocre energies sacrifice the only reality—the present hour. For as none of Flaubert's books could survive on the pretext of teaching morality, Flaubert was wise. He did not desire, and could not have desired, glory, unless *Madame Bovary* should somehow retain its equivocal reputation during the next century and become inscribed, in schoolboys' tradition, among the celebrated bad books. That is hardly likely, since *Mademoiselle de Maupin* has already become painful reading. But what we cannot say for the future, either of Flaubert or of any writer of the last half of the century, we can say for the past. Gautier and Flaubert knew glory—the glory they granted themselves in invincible consciousness of their own genius. Glory is a sensation of life and strength; a wood-sprite would taste it in a tree trunk.

How amusing it is to hear the eloquent professor who declares: "This book will not last." But no book lasts, and yet all books last. Does anyone know *Palemon, fable bocagère et pastorale,* by the Sieur Frenicle? [15] Well, that book has lasted because I just read it, and because I resurrect one of its verses, which is not ugly:

O que j'eus de plaisir à la voir toute nue!

It is time that man learns to resign himself to the void, and even to enjoy this idea whose sweetness is incomparable. Writers should be an example to people by resolutely abandoning their vainglorious hopes. They will leave a name that will ornament the catalogs for some centuries and some works that will last as long as the material on which they are printed. It is a rare privilege, for which they ought to be willing to silence their complaints. And even if that illusory eternity should be refused them, as well as all present glory, why should that diminish their activity? It is to the passerby and not to future humanity that the wild cherry tree offers its fruit; and even if no one passes, just as in the springtime it is covered with snow, it will take on its purple when summer arrives. Life is a personal, immediate fact, which slips away the very moment it is felt. To wish to connect that minute to the coming centuries is to reason badly, for the present alone exists, and we must keep within the limits of logic in order to remain men. Let us be a bit less primitive and not figure that the next century will be the "double" of the present one or that our works will keep the position they occupy today, or a worse one. The way we understand *Bérénice* today would offend Racine, and Molière would gladly blow out the candles on those evenings when the *Misanthrope* is so boring. Books have only one season. Trees, shrubs, or lowly grass die having sometimes sown their likenesses, and the true glory would be to provoke a work whose shadow would engulf oneself. That would be true glory because it would return to the most noble conditions of life. The witnesses of the past are never anything but paradoxes. They began to languish a few years, or even less, after their birth, and in their old age they drag themselves, sad and wrinkled, among men who no longer understand them nor love them. To wish for immortality is to wish to live eternally in the state of Swift's Struldbrugs.

"Such are the details given me regarding the Immortals of this country . . ."—and yet man's emotions continue to rebel against the idea of annihilation, and the writer trembles at the idea of perennial obscurity. Our sensibilities need a tiny light shining in the distance, among the trees that line our view. It reassures the muscles, and it calms the pulse.

—From *Le Chemin de velours,* 1900

Stéphane Mallarmé
and
the Idea of Decadence

Decadence: A very convenient word for ignorant peda-
gogues; a vague word behind which we shelter our laziness
and lack of curiosity regarding the law.
          —Baudelaire: letter to Jules Janin

I

Abruptly, around 1885, the idea of decadence appeared in French
literature. After having served to glorify or to ridicule a whole
group of poets, it came to rest, as it were, on a single head. Stéphane
Mallarmé was the prince of this ironical and almost insulting
realm—as it would have been if the word had been understood and
used in its true sense. But, by an eccentricity which is a Latin trait,
the academic world, in keeping with its usual but unhealthy horror
of new tendencies, so labeled the fever for originality which tormented a generation. M. Mallarmé, held responsible for the acts of
rebellion he encouraged, appeared, to the innocent ass-drivers who
accompany but do not guide a caravan, as a redoubtable Aladdin,
assassin of the sound principles of universal imitation.

These principles are, to be sure, habits of a thoroughly literary
nature. They have been flourishing now for nearly three centuries,
and even the most celebrated rebels have scarcely shaken them and
have certainly never uprooted them. Since the aftermath of the Romantic insolences, the poet has been stifled and forced to crawl
under the ancient greenwood which furnishes the schoolmasters'
rods.

These are also thoroughly Latin habits. The Romans, so long as
they were Romans only, knew nothing of individualism. Their civilization provides the spectacle and idea of a beautiful social animal-

ity. For them, emulation aimed at similarity, just as for us it aims at dissimilarity. As soon as they had five or six poets—successful offshoots of Hellenic grafting—they refused to admit any others, and it is very possibly true that, their social and racial instincts dominating their instincts for freedom and individuality, no poet of original inspiration was born to them for four or five centuries. They had their emperor and they had Virgil, and they obeyed both equally until the Christian revolt and the barbarian invasion joined hands over the Capitol. Literary freedom, like all others, is born of the union of consciousness and strength. We should consider memorable the day when Saint Ambrose, in writing his pious songs, failed to follow Horace's principles, for it clearly signaled the birth of a new mentality.

Just as the political history of the Romans has furnished us with the conception of historical decadence, so the history of their literature has furnished us with the conception of *literary* decadence—the double face of the same conception, for it is easy to point out the coincidence of the two movements, and easy to establish the belief that their developments were necessarily connected. Montesquieu's fame derives from his having been the particular dupe of this illusion.

Savages are very reluctant to admit the possibility of natural death. For them every death is a murder. They have not the least sense of law; they live in a world of accidents. It is a state of mind which we have agreed to call inferior; and so it is, though the notion of a rigid law might be as false and dangerous as its negation. The only absolutely necessary laws are natural laws; they can neither vary nor change. In the case of political and social evolution, not only are there no necessary laws, but there are not even any very general laws. Either these laws, being confused with the facts which they explain, are nothing but wise and honorable assertions, or else they affirm, emphatically, the very principle of evolution. Therefore empires are born, grow, and die. Social combinations are unstable; in different periods human groups have different cohesive forces. New affinities appear and are propagated. Here we have material for a treatise on social mechanics, if the writer did not insist too rigorously on squaring his philosophy with the reality of unexpected catastrophes. For the unexpected must be left a place which sometimes becomes the throne whence irony flashes and laughs. The idea of decadence is, then, merely the idea of natural death. Historians admit no other. To explain the taking of Byzantium by the Turks, they make us listen to the babble of theological quarrels and the crack of Blue's whip in the circus. Longchamps leads to Sedan, no doubt, but Epsom leads to Waterloo as well. The long decadence of expiring empires is one of the most remarkable illusions of history. If certain empires died of sickness or old age, the majority of them, on the contrary, perished a violent death, in the plenitude of their physical power, in the full force of their intellectual vigor.

Moreover, intelligence is personal, and no reasonable relationship can be established between the strength of a people and the genius of a man. Neither Greek literature nor the literatures of the middle ages correspond to any stable and powerful political forces, whether Greek, Italian, or French; and it is precisely now, when their political power has become nil, that the Scandinavian kingdoms find themselves adorned with original talents. Perhaps it would be nearer the truth to say that political decadence is the condition most favorable for intellectual flowering. It is when a Gustavus Adolphus and a Charles XII are no longer possible that an Ibsen and a Björnson appear. In the same way, the fall of Napoleon seemed a signal for nature to clothe herself again joyously in green and to put forth her most magnificent growths. Goethe was the contemporary of his country's ruin. But, in order to exercise and satisfy our tendencies toward historical skepticism, we must not fail to oppose to these examples the evidence of those doubly glorious periods of which the pompous century of Louis XIV is the venerated model. After doing this, however, a few moments' reflexion will bring us to an opinion rather different from the one found and passed along in textbooks and conversation.

Bossuet was the first to conceive of judging universal history— or what he naively regarded as such—according to the principles of Biblical Judaism. He saw the collapse of all those empires on which Jehovah had laid his heavy hand. This is the idea of decadence explained by that of punishment. Montesquieu's more complicated philosophy is perhaps even more puerile: it is only with a kind of disgust that we cite a historian who has the decadence of Rome begin with the dawn of those admirable centuries of peace which were probably the only happy epoch of civilized humanity. The meaning of the words must be closely examined. Then it will be perceived that they contain no sense whatever and that memorable writers used them all their lives without understanding them. But however questionable or at least vague the general idea of decadence might be, it is clear and distinct compared with the more restricted notion of literary decadence.

From Racine to Vigny, France produced no great poet. It is a fact, and such a period is most certainly a period of literary decadence. It is not necessary, however, to go beyond the fact itself, nor to attribute to it an absurd character of logic and necessity. Poetry was asleep during the eighteenth century, through a lack of poets; but this failing was not the result of an excessively rich flowering earlier. It was what it was, and nothing more. If we give it the name of decadence, we admit a sort of mysterious organism—a being, a woman, Poetry, which is born, reproduces, and dies at almost regular intervals, in accordance with the habits of human generations—an agreeable conception, a subject for a dissertation or lecture, but one to be omitted from a discussion which aims only at the anatomy of an idea.

The poetry of the eighteenth century was characterized by the spirit of imitation. The century was Roman by virtue of this spirit. It imitated with zest, grace, tenderness, irony, stupidity. It imitated conscientiously. It was "Chinese" as well as Roman. There were "models." The word was imperative. It was not a matter of a poet's expressing the impression life made on him; he had to observe Racine and scale the mountain. A singular psychology! The same philosopher who had undermined the idea of respect in politics patched it up and whitewashed it anew in literature. There were critics; while Goethe was writing *Werthers,* they were comparing Gilbert and Boileau. It was a debasement. Must we seek a cause for it? It would be futile. To attempt to explain why no poet was born in France for a hundred years, with the exception of Delille [1] and Chénier, would lead necessarily to explaining the birth of Ronsard, Théophile, and Racine as well. We know nothing about it, and nothing can be known. Stripped of its mysticism, its necessity, of all its historical genealogy, the idea of literary decadence is reduced to a purely negative idea, to the simple idea of absence. That is so naive that one scarcely dares to mention it, but when superior intellects default in any given period, the proliferation of mediocrities makes itself obviously and actively felt, and, since the mediocre man is an imitator, periods which have been justly labeled decadent are nothing more than periods of imitation. In the final analysis, the idea of decadence is identical to the idea of imitation.

II

Nevertheless, in the case of Mallarmé and a literary group, the idea of decadence has been assimilated to its exact opposite—the idea of innovation. Such judgments have made a sharp impression on us, men of our own time, because, doubtless, we were ourselves implicated and were foolishly flouted by "right-minded" critics. They were, however, nothing but the latest version, clumsy and threadbare, of those decrees by which the sages of all times have tried to curse and crush the new serpents who break out of their shells under the ironic eye of their old mother. Diabolical Intelligence laughs at exorcisms, and the holy water of the University has never been able to sterilize it any more than that of the Church. In the past a man rose up—shield of the faith—against novelties and heresies— the Jesuit. Today it is too often the Professor who rises up as champion of the rules. Here again we find the antinomy which surprises us in Voltaire and the Voltairians of yesterday: the same man, courageous in matters of justice or political liberty, falters and recoils when it is a matter of literary novelty or freedom. When, coming to Tolstoi and Ibsen, he alludes to their glory, he adds (in a note): "Are these reputations—especially Ibsen's—firmly established? The question whether the author of *Ghosts* is a mystifier or a genius is as yet undecided." [2] Such, when confronted with the unknown, with the not yet seen or read, is the attitude of a writer who, in the very volume here quoted, proves that he has an admirable independence of judgment. It is unnecessary to add that, in his pages, the "decadents" are ridiculed at every turn. How, after this, can we be surprised at the heavy-handed raillery of lesser minds? Any new way of stating eternal human truths is at first scandalous for most men—especially men who are too well educated. They register some kind of alarm. In order to regain their assurance, they have recourse to negation, to insults or derision. It is the natural attitude of the human animal confronting physical danger. But how does one ever come to regard as a peril every real innovation in art

or literature? Why, above all, is this association one of the special
maladies of our time—and one of the gravest, since it tends to restrict movement and deny life?

For years Delacroix and Puvis de Chavannes, so different in
their genius, were joked about and rejected by the juries. Underly-
ing obviously contradictory pretexts we find a single explanation:
originality. The guardians of art feel themselves threatened by a
work of art in which they can perceive almost nothing deriving
from earlier methods, and which they cannot immediately relate to
something known and already understood. They respond to this
provocation each according to his own temperament. The formulae
also change with the times: in the eighteenth century, nonimitation
was considered a lapse in taste, and that was a serious matter at a
time when Voltaire was erecting a temple, which was merely a
miniature, to that waggish god. For ten years, and up to a few
weeks ago, writers and artists who refused to plagiarize from the
masters were branded as either decadents or symbolists. This latter
insult prevailed in the end, being verbally more obscure and consequently easier to handle. It contains, moreover, exactly the same
abhorrent idea of nonimitation.

As was said long ago, well before M. Taine developed his social
philosophy: "Imitation rules the world of men, just as gravitation
the world of things." This law is very evident in the realm of art
and literature. Literary history is, in sum, nothing but the chart of a
succession of intellectual epidemics. Some were brief. Fashions
change or endure according to caprices impossible to foresee and
difficult to determine. Shakespeare had no immediate influence.
Honoré d'Urfé, during his life and for a half-century after his
death, was the master and inspiration of all romantic fiction. He
might have reigned longer had it not been for *La Princesse de
Clèves,* the clandestine work of a *grande dame.* The seventeenth
century, part of whose literature was merely translation and imitation, was not hostile, however, to moderate and prudent novelties.
The reason is that, if it would have been shameful not to imitate the
ancients—or, strange to say, the Spaniards, but only they!—in their
fables and phrases (Racine trembled for having written *Bajazet*),
it was an honorable thing to be able to give classic borrowings an
air of freshness and novelty.

However, this literature itself very quickly became classic.

There was thus a second source of imitation, and as it was more accessible, it soon came to be almost the sole spring where successive generations came to drink and pray and water their ink. Boileau, before his death, saw himself deified. Voltaire, from the moment he could read, read Boileau. The principle of imitation was to reign supreme thenceforward in French literature.

If we do not count certain exceptions—however memorable—this principle has remained very powerful and so well understood, with the spread of education, that a critic has only to invoke it for a shamefaced reader to reject any new work which he found refreshing. Thus the columnists have succeeded in preventing Ibsen's work from being accepted in France. Thus verse dramas, works of imitation par excellence, now are successful even on the boulevards! These theatrical events, which advertising always exaggerates, are good illustrations of a theory.

The idea of imitation, then, has become the very idea of art and literature. It is no more possible today to conceive of a new novel which is not the counterpart or sequel of a preceding novel than it is to conceive of rhymeless verse or verse whose syllables have not been, one by one, scrupulously scanned. When such innovations were nevertheless produced, suddenly altering the customary aspect of the literary landscape, there was a commotion among the experts. To conceal their discomfiture, they began to laugh (third method). Then they handed down judgments: since these things, these pieces of poetry and prose, were not designed in imitation of the latest models of the works celebrated in the handbooks, they must spring from an abnormal source, something not familiar to us—but what? There were attempts at explanation by way of pre-Raphaelitism, but they were not convincing. They were even a bit ridiculous, so profound and invulnerable was the ignorance on all sides. But about this time there appeared a book which suddenly enlightened all minds. A parallel was inexorably established between the new poets and the obscure versifiers of the Roman decadence praised by Des Esseintes.[3] The reaction was unanimous, and the very ones thus disparaged accepted the label as a distinction. Once the principle was admitted, comparisons abounded. Since no one—and perhaps not even des Esseintes himself—had read the depreciated poets, it was a simple matter for some journalist to compare Sidonius Apollinaris, of whom we knew nothing, with Stéphane Mallarmé, whom he did not understand. Neither Sidonius Apollinaris nor Mallarmé is a decadent, since each possesses, in different degrees, his own originality; but for that very reason the word was justly applied to the poet of *L'Après-midi d'un faune,* for it signified very obscurely, in the minds of the very ones who used it, something little known, difficult, rare, precious, unexpected, new.

If, on the contrary, one wanted to restore to the idea of literary decadence its real and really cruel meaning, I suspect it would no longer be Mallarmé, Laforgue, or any symbolist who is still writing today, who would be named. The decadent of Latin literature is neither Ammianus Marcellinus nor Saint Augustine, each of whom fashioned a new language in his own manner, nor is it St. Ambrose, who created the hymn, nor Prudentius, who conceived a literary genre, the lyrical biography.[4] We are beginning to take a more indulgent attitude toward Latin literature of the second period. Tired, perhaps, of ridiculing it without reading it, we have begun to glance at it a bit. Before long, we will be admitting this simple notion— that there is no such thing, in itself, as a good Latin or a bad Latin; that languages are alive and their changes are not necessarily corruptions; that a man could have genius in the sixth century as well as in the second, in the eleventh as well as in the eighteenth; that classical prejudices are an obstacle to the development of literary history and to total knowledge of the language itself. Had they been better understood, the poets in the library at Fontenay would not have served to christen a literary movement, unless the intention had been to compare idealistic with Christian innovators—an arduous and rather absurd undertaking.

III

Since I have wished here merely to attempt a historical (or anecdotal) analysis of an idea, and to indicate, by a rather extended example, how a word comes to have only the meaning which it is in our interest to give it, I do not think it is necessary to establish in minute detail the reasons for Mallarmé's meriting either hatred or ridicule.

Hatred is queen in the hierarchy of literary sentiments. Literature is, perhaps, along with religion, the abstract passion to which men react the most violently. To be sure, we have not yet seen any literary wars comparable to the religious wars of, let us say, the past;

but that is because literature has never yet descended suddenly to the level of the people. By the time it does reach them, it has lost its explosive force. It is a good distance from the opening night of *Hernani* to the day when Victor Hugo is sold in the illustrated magazines. However, it is rather easy to imagine a mobilization of German sentimentalism against English humor or French irony. It is because peoples do not know each other that they hate each other so little. An alliance characterized by a close fraternization inevitably ends with cannon shots.

The hatred that pursued Mallarmé was never very bitter, for men cannot hate seriously, even in literature, except when material interests come to add a little spice to the struggle for the ideal. But Mallarmé offered no surface for envy, and he took injustice and abuse as inevitable in the condition of genius. It was only the obvious superiority of his intellect, then, that was derided, on the pretext that he was obscure. Artists, even when depreciated by instinctive cabals, receive orders, earn money. Poets have the resource of long articles in the reviews and newspapers. Certain of them, like Théophile Gautier, earn their living by it, whereas Baudelaire succeeded badly at it, and Mallarmé worse still. It was, then, toward the poet stripped of every social adornment that the sarcasm was directed.

There is in the Louvre by chance, in an absurd collection, a certain marvel, an Andromeda, carved in ivory by Cellini. It is a terrified woman, all her flesh quivering with fright at being bound. Where can she flee? This is the poetry of Stéphane Mallarmé. The image is the more appropriate still, since, like the sculptor, the poet achieved nothing but some cups, vases, caskets, statuettes. He is not colossal, he is perfect. His poetry does not represent a vast treasure spread before the astonished crowd. It does not express common and forceful ideas which easily galvanize popular attention stupefied by toil. It is personal, infolded like flowers that fear the sunlight. Its perfume is only of the evening. Its thought lends itself only to the intimacy of another thought, cordial and sincere. Its modesty, excessive to be sure, is enveloped in too many veils; but there is much delicacy in that desire to flee the eyes and hands of popular appreciation. But flee—flee where? Mallarmé took refuge in obscurity as in a cloister. He interposed the wall of a cell between himself and the understanding of others; he wished to live alone with his pride. But that was the Mallarmé of the last years, when, hurt but not discouraged, he felt himself overtaken by the same disgust for futile phrases which had, in times past, afflicted Jean Racine— when he created, for his own use, a new syntax, when he used words in accordance with new and secret relationships. Stéphane Mallarmé wrote, relatively, a large amount, and the greater part of his work is unsullied by obscurity; but, if later and towards the end, beginning with the *Prose pour des Esseintes,* there are dubious phrases and irritating verses, only an inattentive and vulgar mind will dread undertaking the delicious conquest.

There are too few obscure writers in French. Thus we have accustomed ourselves like cowards to enjoying writing that is easy and soon to become elementary. Yet it was clarity that made the prestige of classical literatures and it is what makes them so clearly tiresome. Clear minds are ordinarily those which can see only one thing at a time. Whenever the brain is rich in sensations and ideas, it swirls like an eddy and its smooth surface is troubled at the moment of gushing forth. Let us prefer, like M. Doudan, marshlands swarming with life, to a glass of clear water. To be sure, we are thirsty at times. All right, then, we filter. It must fall from on high, rebound in cascades from stone to stone, in order to flow at last through the valley, within reach of all men and all livestock.

If, then, we were to undertake a definitive study of Stéphane Mallarmé, the question of obscurity would have to be treated solely from the standpoint of psychology, because there is never absolute, literal obscurity in a work written in good faith. A sensible interpretation is always possible. It will vary according to the evening hour, perhaps, as the clouds vary the shadows on the lawn; but the truth, here and everywhere, will be what our feelings of the passing hour make it be. Mallarmé's work is the most marvelous pretext for reverie which has yet been offered to men weary of so many heavy and useless affirmations. It is a poetry full of doubts, of shifting nuances and ambiguous perfumes, and it is perhaps the only poetry that will be able, henceforward, to give us pleasure. And if the word decadence really summed up all these autumnal, twilight charms, we should welcome it and even make it one of the keys of the viol. But it is dead, the master is dead, the penultimate is dead.

—From *La Culture des idées,* 1898

The Value of Education

Without being as widespread as it might be, or as it will be, education is very much in vogue. We live less and less, and we learn more and more. Sensibility is surrendering to intelligence. I saw a person laughed at because he gazed, with rapt pleasure, at a dead leaf. No one would have laughed to hear him mumble some technical terms about it. But there are other men who, without being ignorant of the handbooks, believe that true science should be felt first of all as a pleasure. But such is not the fashion. The fashion is to learn solely from books and from the lips of those who recite books.

Cornelius Agrippa, who possessed all the learning of his time, and more, amused himself by writing a "Paradox on the uncertainty, vanity, and abuse of the sciences." [1] It could be rewritten today, but on another note, for it is not necessary that a science be uncertain, vain, and abusive for it to be useless to anyone who cultivates it; and on the other hand, the certainty of a science, its importance and authenticity, do not confer on it the absolute right to intellectual dominion. We would even readily agree as to the absurdity of a debate on the certainty and uncertainty of the sciences. Some are highly contingent and problematical, but it is lightweight or prejudiced minds who call them so. The word science includes, by definition, the idea of objective truth, and we must abide by that, without further dispute, and even concede this objective truth, whatever repugnance we feel about the indissoluble union of two words which become, henceforth, ironical.

It is not, moreover, science which is in question, but the education of which science is the substance or pretext. What is the value of education? What sort of superiority can it confer on an average intelligence! If education is sometimes a ballast, is it not more often a burden? Is it not also, and even more often, a sack of salt that melts on the ass's shoulders with the first storms of life? And so on.

Education is of two kinds: it is either useful or ornamental. Even astrology can become a practical science if the astrologist earns his daily bread by it; but what good can it do a magistrate to know geometry, except perhaps to warp his mind? For an intelligent carpenter, everything that concerns his trade—drawing and archeology, even, and all notions of that kind—would be profitable. But of what possible use is aesthetic theory, except perhaps to hamper his activity? Education, when it does not find some application, some way to turn itself into profit, becomes an ingot sleeping under a glass case. It is useless, not very interesting, and devoid of beauty.

There is much talk, in certain political quarters, about integral education. This means, no doubt, that everything should be taught to everyone; also that a vague and universal idea would be of great benefit and comfort to any intellect whatsoever. But this kind of reasoning confuses substance with form. Intelligence, while it has a general and common form, takes a particular form in each man. Just as there are several kinds of memory, there are several kinds of intelligence; and each of these, modified by its own physiology, determines the individual intellect. Far from its being a good thing to teach everything to everybody, it seems clear that a given intelligence can receive, without danger to its structure, only those kinds of notions that enter it without effort. If we were accustomed to giving words only those relative meanings associated with them, integral education would mean any sort of instruction compatible with the unknown morphology of the brain. In most cases, the amount of that instruction would be reduced to nothing, for the majority of intelligences cannot be cultivated.

At least not by the methods currently being employed, which can be summed up by a single term: abstraction. In teaching circles they have come to admit that life can be known only in the form of discourse. Whether it is a matter of poetry or geography, the method is the same: a dissertation which sums up the subject and pretends to represent it. Finally, education has become a methodic cataloging of words, and classification has replaced knowledge.

The most intelligent and active man can assimilate only a very small number of direct and precise ideas. These are the only ones, however, that are truly profound. Teaching gives only instruction;

life gives knowledge. Instruction has at least this advantage: it is generalized and sublimated knowledge, and thus it can contain a large number of notions in a small package; but, in most minds, this overly condensed nourishment remains neutral and does not ferment. What is called general culture is most often nothing but a collection of mnemonic acquisitions, purely abstract, which the intelligence is incapable of projecting onto the plane of reality. Without an imagination that is alive and active in all directions, the ideas confided to the memory will wither away in its inert soil. Softening water and ripening sun are necessary for the germination of planted seeds.

It is better to know nothing than to know badly, or little, which amounts to the same thing. But do we know what ignorance is? We have to learn so many things in order to appreciate and understand it! Those who might enjoy ignorance, since they possess it, have too many illusions about themselves to find much free amusement in it, and those who would like to do so have left their first innocence too far behind. There have been moments in civilization when some men knew everything. It was not very much. Was it very much less than all the knowledge today? This relativism can make us reflect on the value of education. It will also serve to define it. Education is never anything but relative. It ought therefore to be practical.

M. Barrès, in his latest novel,[2] makes a deputy of Burdeau's type say, "Virtue, like patriotism, is a dangerous element to arouse in the masses." To these two abstractions should perhaps be added all the others, in order to decree a general ostracism of all ideas that have not been first defined. And this would not mean that virtues and patriotic sentiments must necessarily be proscribed, but only this: that nothing is worse for the health of the average intelligence than playing with abstract words, that false verbal science which is found to be inapplicable the moment one becomes involved in real life. It is not a matter of being virtuous. How do you realize a word that is the synthesis of several contradictory ideals? It is a matter of accommodating one's nature to moral traditions and to the vital conditions of one's environment. It is not a matter of being patriotic, but rather of defending, against strange animals, the purity of the fountain where one drinks. It is not a matter of knowing the abstract principle in which the large river of general ideas may find its source. It is a matter of making of one's life at once an act of faith

and of prudence. Above all, it is a matter of preserving enough simplicity to enjoy breathing the social air just as it is, and enough flexibility to obey without cowardice the elementary laws of life.

Life is a series of sensations connected by states of consciousness. If you do not have the kind of organism in which an abstract
notion, once it has been understood, redescends toward the senses; if
the word Beauty does not give you a visual sensation; if handling
ideas does not give you physical pleasure, almost like caressing a
shoulder or a fabric, then leave ideas alone. When a miller has no
corn to grind, he shuts his sluice-gates and sleeps, or goes for a
walk; but he would never dream of grinding on nothing and wear-
ing out mill-stones on thin air. Education is often nothing but the
sound of the wind in the sieves, and perceivable as words.

Education, from top to bottom, from the official to the popular
universities, from the village school to the Ecole Normale, is scarcely
anything other than a phrase-factory. The most serious of all these is
the primary school, where one learns to read and write, acquiring
not a science, but a new sense. If, from the other schools, one were
to cut out everything useless, inapplicable to life and to a certain
profession or trade, there would remain hardly enough material for
eighteen months of schooling. The great majority of people escape
the tortures of listening to the gentlemen who recite from books.
Children of the poor, freed from the scholastic prison, learn a trade,
which is an enhancement of the self, and begin to live at an age
when their rich brothers are laboring at the manipulation of words
which correspond to nothing real—tools which sculpt the eternal
void.[3] This is about to be remedied—here is an evening lecture
given at a popular university: "The Development of the Idea of
Justice in Antiquity." Supposing the improbable—that the professor
offered on this subject only some appreciations acceptable to a
healthy intelligence—of what possible use could such a discourse be
to a popular audience, and what could such an audience derive from
it that would be applicable to its humble existence? Surely less than
from those old-fashioned sermons which were not afraid to scorn
the people's vices and to frighten them out of their indulgence in
low pleasures. But the clergy of lay religion is grave and disdainful
of facts. Souls speak to souls. The ideal descends on the people. The
first Christians at least met both to pray and to eat together in a
fraternal spirit. After the meal, some stood up to make prophecies.

Modern prophets live only by abstractions, and it is this economical and ridiculous food that they are willing to share with their brothers.

The man who has slowly acquired a science, has, aside from the social advantages he may derive, conferred upon his organs of attention, by that very fact, a particular strength and agility. He possesses not only the desired science, but an entire hunting outfit in good condition and ready for new captures.

When he has learned a foreign language with care and patience, he can then learn related languages with considerably less toil. But if he has had recourse to some shortcut method, the acquisition no longer possesses its proper value and may even deteriorate rather rapidly. Water which has been quickly brought to a boil cools off with equal speed—a fact overlooked by the builders of public boilers. By the time it had crossed the street it was as cold as if it had come from a fresh spring. It is for the same reason that the rapid teaching by lectures is especially useless. One learns to believe and not to reason, which would still be a way of acting and living.

The baggage which constitutes education is made up almost entirely of beliefs. Literature and science are taught like a catechism. Life is the school of prudent doubt, whereas the official school is a pretentious church. Every professor is armed with an arsenal of aphorisms, and the adolescent who does not allow himself to be smitten to the heart is despised. This inversion of logical values is carried to the point where certain intellectual acts—like resistance to scientific faith, that Cartesian reserve—are considered evidence of unintelligence.

M. Jules de Gaultier has conceived a new Manichaeism whose prudent employment will prove very useful in clearing up certain questions.[4] To the vital instinct he opposes the instinct for knowledge; but one is not the good principle, any more than the other is the bad. They both have their role in the work of civilization; for if the instinct for knowledge develops the need to know at the expense of the forces that conserve vital energy, it permits the intelligence, at the same time, to better enjoy itself and the life of the senses. The spontaneous and unconscious genius of developing races does not refuse to obey either of these great instincts. Life does not exhaust its energy, which is immutable, but only the modes of energy which it has assumed. We tire of feeling before we tire of knowing. This is what Leibnitz naively expressed, and what has been repeated by all those whose minds are like vultures: "It is not necessary to live, but it is necessary to think." When this aphorism descends to the people, it means that a deteriorating vital instinct is beginning to give up the struggle. The glorious time of flowering may have arrived, but the plant is going to die once the flight of insects has fertilized it and the wind has carried its seeds towards the virgin soil.

An ignorant mass forms a magnificent reserve of life in a people. Our civilization has failed to recognize this: it is an immense field of little flowers which exhausts the earth's vitality for the sake of a useless resplendence.

Such ideas, even in the form of attenuated images, may seem barbarous to those who believe in the "benefits of education"; but it is beginning to be easier to find adjectives than arguments for reviving this ancient and nearly exhausted theme. Hearing so many journalists and deputies speak of education as if it were a sovereign elixir, one indeed feels that one has tasted it, in its true and good form, as synthesized in manuals and encyclopedias, but not in those detestable urns wherein the evil spirit of analysis is sleeping. True knowledge, the "gay knowledge," is singularly poisonous. It is as poisonous as it is beneficent. It contains as many doubts as there are specks of gold in Goldwasser. We never know where intoxication by this violent liquor can lead an intelligence which is neither very strong or very skeptical.

Compared with science, education is so slight a thing that it scarcely deserves a name. Of what value are elementary notions of chemistry when we think of the chemist who manipulates, composes and decomposes bodies, who counts molecules and weighs atoms? And of what importance is it that a hundred thousand bachelors of arts know the elements of air? But already they no longer know it. If they had been taught the nature of breath, perhaps they would have avoided two or three diseases, a predisposition to which, and whose germs, they have joyously transmitted to their children. It is necessary (despite the celebrated irony) that chemistry and chemical industries exist, but not that the first man who comes along be taught the obscure principles of a sham science. This is only one example, but it could be extended to nearly all the elements of general culture. An average brain today resembles those experimental gardens that cultivate specimens of all flora. Yet this garden can have its particular utility, whereas brains rich in a little of everything are good for nothing: the ground has not been transformed into a flower bed, but into a herbarium, and its arid plants are so mediocre and defective that they can be put to no decent use. The majority of the flower beds should at least have been reserved for a deep and passionate cultivation. This done, the dead corners of the garden would acquire once more a certain importance: they would serve as manure piles and compost pits to warm the heart of the living garden.

We do not claim, then, that general culture is useless. It is indispensable as an auxiliary and reserve, but as that alone, and only when that general and superficial culture coexists with one or more areas of intensive culture. Alone, it has no value. If we descend from the average level towards the little gardens of the people, we will see, in the place of rank but luxurious grass, only puny sprouts already frozen by life. All the natural flora has been weeded out, and what has been sown in its place in the poorly prepared, poorly cleared ground cannot possibly grow, lacking as it does both water and sun. The sole interest of these ridiculous little kitchen-gardens is an occasional large and beautiful tree, some chestnut or linden: it is a trade in which a man has resolutely developed himself. One of these trees alone is worth more than all the general cultures which have relegated it to a stony corner. It dominates them by its utility and beauty.

Man's purpose in life is to be a function. His days must be productive of a result. That is why we will eternally regret that the trades are being abolished, crumbling away in an extreme division of labor. Industrial civilization has deprived a very large number of men of the pleasure which they used to find in work. A high salary might make a man satisfied for having worked, but that does not provide satisfaction in the work itself—the joy of spending the present hour in the realization of an object. Industry has operated against the artisan in favor of the idler, and also in favor of capital and against labor. Any mechanical invention whatsoever has been more harmful to humanity than a century of war. The hedonic value of muscular activity has been so diminished that the only moments when workmen feel alive are those when ordinary men relax—the moments of repose; and they have necessarily tried to inflate these hours of negative sensation to the point of making them the whole pleasure of living: the means has been alcohol. In order to dry up this source of excitation, certain men of good intentions but unhealthy—that is, out of touch with reality—have thought to oppose the pleasure of drinking with the pleasure of learning. If such a task were not impossible, they would have replaced physiological intoxication with cerebral intoxication: and that would not be a very happy result. To follow a day of muscular toil with an evening of intellectual toil is to double the total fatigue without real profit to the man subjected to such a regime. Think of the poor chap who, after having spent ten hours pushing a plank of wood under the cruel teeth of a circular saw, comes back, after an indifferent meal, to hear a gentleman hold forth on the holiness of justice! But justice would demand that the preacher take turns with the artisan at pushing blocks of wood and at comfortably studying the fruitful principles of social charlatanism. Poor people who, with their instinctive need of priests, believe themselves victors because, having denied a dogma, they now applaud the moral of that same dogma, but deformed by hypocrisy and hatred! It is through education—a very ancient invention—that the clergy has dominated the people and the world. And it is still through education that lay sermonizers are determined to clip the last claws of the vital instinct.

For all these teachers desperately teach how not to live. In all good faith they infect the healthy section of the people with their own sickly habit of experiencing sensations only by reflection, of viewing in a mirror the life that they dare not encounter. The true end of this education is the imposition of a morality—a singular morality almost all of whose precepts are negative. By suppressing the will to live, to the profit of an unstable cerebrality, they fashion those enervated, obedient, and prudent generations which are the dream of third-rate tyrants. At the very moment when a race needs—if only to endure—all the energy of which its instinct is perhaps still the depository, they pour into it that same liquor, but spoiled and poisoned, with which the Roman apostles tamed the excess energies of the barbarians. We will suffer the same fate of those vanquished races if a protestantism—rationalist or religious—were to ever preempt the sovereign place of our traditional and pagan catholicism.

But how does one resist the temptation of giving precepts of conduct along with precepts of grammar? All we ask is that those precepts should not be depressants and that, to the contrary, adolescents might find them a stimulus to activity, to all kinds of activity. Education, in itself, is nothing. It is a torch which we can evaluate only by examining the surroundings by its light. For a torch is not useful because of its light, but because of the objects which its light illuminates. It is like an oven being methodically heated by kindling wood or faggots; but all that heat is nothing but a sterile blaze if it is not put to work, when its flames die down, baking the dough of the eternal bread.

Education is a means and not an end. It is painfully absurd to learn for the sake of learning, to burn for the sake of burning. The very song of the birds is not in vain. In periods of sexual calm, it is the rehearsal of the great concerts of love. Considered as the precise instrument for a future work, education can have a very great and even absolute importance. It can be the necessary condition for certain intellectual achievements. It will be the staff of the intelligence; but offered to a mediocre mentality, and directed only towards enlargement of memory, it has no power to regenerate sick cells. Rather, it will be their destruction; it will stupefy them. It will divert from the natural processes of life those activities which were intended merely for daily exercise. Education gives balance to unstable geniuses. It provides them with subjects for comparison and reflection. It provides, for geniuses already in equilibrium, a little of that discomfiture which is the source of irony. It is sometimes a support for certainty, sometimes the cause of a movement towards doubt. But it exerts influence only on intelligences in action, or capable of action.

It does not determine—it inclines. Above all, it does not create intelligence. We have constantly before our eyes examples of educated men, instructed in everything that is taught, who remain mediocrities, and who, though they have been writing for twenty years, have not even learned how to write. And then we have the others who know only one trade and who have read only their own lives: their lucidity sometimes shames even genius.

—From *Le Chemin de velours,* 1900

PART II

Language
and
the Creative Process

On Style or Writing

Et ideo confiteatur eorum stultitia, qui arte, scientiaque im-
munes, de solo ingenio confidentes, ad summa summe ca-
nenda prorumpunt; a tanta prosuntuositate desistant, et si
anseres naturali desidia sunt, nolint astripetam aquilam
imitari.

—Dante: *De vulgari eloquentia*

I

Depreciation of "writing," as an art, is a precaution taken from time
to time by worthless writers. They believe it valid gesture, but it is a
sign of their mediocrity and a confession of regret. It is surely not
without chagrin that the impotent man renounces the pretty woman
with the too limpid eyes, and there must be bitterness in the announced disdain of a man who confesses fundamental ignorance of
his craft or of the gift without which the practice of that craft is an
imposture. Nevertheless, some of these poor fellows glory in their
poverty. They claim that their ideas are so fine as not to need cloth-
ing, that the freshest and richest of images are only veils of vanity
thrown over the emptiness of thought—that what matters, after all,
is the substance and not the form, the spirit and not the letter, the
thing and not the word, and they can carry on like this indefinitely,
for they are armed with a host of chichés—facile but ineffective. We
should pity the first group and despise the second, and respond to
neither, except to say that there are two literatures and they belong
to each other.

Two literatures: this is a prudent and provisional manner of
speaking, in order that the mob might leave us alone, having its
share of the landscape and a view of the garden which it will never

enter. If there were not two literatures and two realms, it would be necessary to cut the throats immediately of nearly all French writers—it would be an unsavory business and one in which I would blush to take part. Let us leave it then. The boundary is established. There are two kinds of writers: writers who can write and those who cannot write—just as there are voiceless singers and singers who have voices.

The disdain for style appears to have been one of the conquests of 1789. At least, prior to the democratic era, it had always been taken for granted that writers who could not write were to be ridiculed. From Pisistratus to Louis XIV, the civilized world had been unanimous on this point: a writer must know how to write. The Greeks thought so, and the Romans loved fine style so much that they ended by writing very badly through wishing to write too well. Saint Ambrose esteemed eloquence to the point of regarding it as one of the gifts of the Holy Spirit, *vox donus Spiritus,* and Saint Hilaire of Poitiers, in the thirteenth chapter of his *Treatise on the Psalms,* does not hesitate to call bad style a sin. It cannot be from Roman Christianity, then, that we have derived our present indulgent attitude toward crude literature, but since Christianity is necessarily responsible for all modern aggressions against external beauty, one could suppose that the taste for bad style is one of the Protestant importations which, since the eighteenth century, have stained the soil of France: contempt for style and moral hypocrisy are Anglican vices.[1]

However, if the eighteenth century wrote badly, it did so unconsciously. It thought that Voltaire wrote well, especially in verse, and reproached Ducis only for the barbarousness of his models. It had an ideal. It did not admit that philosophy might be an excuse for bad literature. Everything was put into rhyme, from the treatises of Isaac Newton to garden manuals and cookbooks. This need to put art and fine language where they did not belong resulted in the adoption of a middling style, suitable for elevating all vulgar subjects and degrading all the others. With all good intentions, people of the eighteenth century ended by writing as if they, in all the history of the world, were the most refractory to art. England and France signed, at that time, a literary pact which was to last until the advent of Chateaubriand, whose *Génie du Christianisme*[2] was its solemn denunciation. Since the appearance of that book, which opens the century, there has been only one way for a writer to have talent, and that has been to know how to write—and no longer in the manner of Laharpe, but according to the examples of an un-vanquished tradition, as old as the first awakening of the sense of beauty in human intelligence.

But the eighteenth-century manner [3] responded too well to the natural tendencies of a democratic civilization. Neither Chateaubri-and nor Victor Hugo were able to counteract the organic law which precipitates the herd toward the green plain where there is grass, and where there will be nothing but dust, once the herd has moved on. It was soon considered useless to cultivate a landscape destined for devastation by the populace. There developed a literature with-out style, just as there are main thoroughfares without grass, without shade, without wayside fountains.

II

Writing is a trade, and I would rather see it put in its proper place in our vocabulary, between cobbling and carpentry, than isolated from other similar human activities. Thus set apart, its existence can be virtually denied under the pretext of according it special honor, and when so cut off from life's vital aspects it will die of its isola-tion. However, given a place in one of the symbolic niches along the great gallery, it suggests apprenticeship and the handling of tools. It repels impromptu vocations. It is severe and discouraging.

Writing is a craft, but style is not a science. "Style is the man," along with the other formula, proposed by Hello, that "style is in-violable," amount to the same thing: style is as personal as the color of eyes or the sound of the voice. One can learn the trade of writing, but one cannot learn to have a style. One can tint his style as one tints his hair, but it will have to be redone every morning and admit of no distractions. So little can be learned in the way of style that, in the course of a lifetime, one is often prone to unlearn: when the vital energies are diminished, one writes less well, and practice, which improves other gifts, often spoils this one.

Writing is very different from painting or modeling. To write or spell is to use a faculty necessarily common to all men—a primordial and unconscious faculty. We cannot analyze it apart from the complete anatomy of the intelligence. That is why all treatises on the art of writing, whether they number ten pages or ten thousand, are futile sketches. The question is so complex that one is at a loss how to approach it. It has so many sharp edges and is such a thicket of thorns and stickers that, instead of pushing straight into it, one goes around—and that is prudent.

To write, as Flaubert and the Goncourts understood it, is to exist, to differentiate oneself. To have a style is to speak, in the midst of the common language, a particular dialect, unique and inimitable, but in a way that it might be, at the same time, the language of everyone and the language of an individual. Style is self-evident. Studying its mechanism is useless to the point where uselessness becomes dangerous. Whatever can be reconstituted from the products of a distilled style bears the same resemblance to that style as a perfumed paper rose bears to a real rose.

Whatever the fundamental importance of a "written" work might be, possession of style enhances that importance. It was the opinion of Buffon that all the beauties found in a well-written work, "all the relations of which style is composed are so many truths fully as useful and perhaps more precious for the human spirit than those which comprise the subject matter." And this is also the common opinion, despite the common disdain, since books from the past which are still alive are alive only by virtue of their style. If the contrary were possible, a contemporary of Buffon like Boulanger, the author of *l'Antiquité dévoilée,* would not be unknown today, for there was nothing mediocre about him except his manner of writing. And is it not because he almost always lacked style that another contemporary, Diderot, has never enjoyed more than a few hours of reputation at a time, and that as soon as people stop talking about him, he is forgotten?

It is because of this incontestable preeminence of style that the invention of themes is of no great interest in literature. To write a good novel or a viable drama, one must either choose a subject so banal as to be absolutely nil, or imagine one so new that it would require genius to make anything of it—*Romeo and Juliet* or *Don Quixote.* Most of Shakespeare's tragedies are nothing more than a succession of metaphors embroidered on the canvas of the first story that happened along. Shakespeare invented only his verses and phrases: since the imagery was new, that novelty necessarily conferred life on the characters of the drama. If *Hamlet,* idea for idea, had been put to verse by Christopher Marlowe, it would be no more than an obscure and awkward tragedy which one would cite as an interesting sketch. M. de Maupassant, who invented most of his plots, is a lesser story-teller than Boccaccio, who invented none of his. Moreover, the invention of subjects is limited, though infinitely flexible. But a different age, a different story. M. Aicard, if he had genius, would not have translated *Othello;* he would have rewritten it, as the youthful Racine rewrote the tragedies of Euripides. Everything would have been said in the first hundred years of literature if man had not had style as a means of achieving variety. I am willing to grant that there might be thirty-six dramatic or novelistic situations, but a more general theory can, in fact, recognize only four. Man, taken as the center, has relationships: with himself, with other men, with the opposite sex, with the infinite—God or Nature. Any work of art necessarily falls into one of these four classes. But if there had been in the world only one solitary plot, and that had been *Daphnis et Chloë,* it would have been sufficient.

One of the excuses made by writers who do not know how to write is the diversity of genres. They believe that one genre calls for style and that another does not. A novel, they say, should not be written in the same tone as a poem. No doubt; but the absence of style results in the absence of tone as well, and when a book lacks writing, it lacks everything: it is invisible, or, as we say, it passes unnoticed. That is as it should be. Basically, there is only one genre— the poem; and perhaps there is only one medium—verse; for fine prose must have a rhythm which makes us doubt that it is merely prose. Buffon wrote only poems, as did Bossuet, Chateaubriand, and Flaubert. If *Les Epoques de la nature* arouses the admiration of scientists and philosophers, it is nonetheless a sumptuous epic. M. Brunetière has spoken with ingenuous boldness of the evolution of genres. He has shown that Bossuet's prose is merely one of the cuts in the great lyric forest where Victor Hugo was later a woodsman. But I prefer the idea that there are no genres or only one genre. This is, moreover, more in accord with the latest philosophies and science: the idea of evolution is going to give way to that of permanence, of perpetuity.

Can one learn to write? If it is a matter of style, this is to ask whether M. Zola, if he applied himself, could have become a Chateaubriand, or whether M. Quesnay de Beaurepaire, if he had taken pains, could have become a Rabelais: if the man who imitates precious marbles by spattering pine panels with a quick shake of his brush, could, properly guided, have painted the *Pauvre pêcheur,* or if the stone-cutter who shapes the sad façades of Parisian houses in the Corinthinan manner could not, after twenty lessons, have sculpted by chance *La Porte de l'enfer* or the tomb of Philippe Pot?

Can one learn to write? If it is a question of the elements of a trade, of what is taught to painters in the academies, one can learn all that. One can learn to write correctly in a neutral manner, just as engravers once worked in the "black manner." One can learn to write badly—that is to say, properly, and in such a way to win a prize for literary virtue. One can learn to write very well—which is another way to write very badly. How melancholy they are, those books which are well written—and nothing more!

III

M. Albalat has, then, published a handbook entitled *The Art of Writing Taught in Twenty Lessons.* If this manual had appeared in earlier times, it certainly would have become part of the library of M. Dumouchel, professor of literature, and he would have recommended it to his friends, Bouvard and Pécuchet: "Then they asked themselves of what, precisely, did style consist, and, thanks to the authors suggested by Dumouchel, they learned the secret of all the genres." However, these two old fellows would have found the remarks of M. Albalat a bit subtle. They would have been shocked to learn that *Télémaque* is poorly written and that Mérimée would profit from being condensed. They would reject M. Albalat and set about their history of the Duke of Angoulême without him.

I am not surprised at their resistance. Perhaps they sensed, in some obscure way, that the unconscious writer laughs at principles, at the art of epithets, and at the artifice of the three graduated preliminary drafts. If M. Albalat had known that intellectual toil, and in particular the toil of writing, is in large part independent of the authority of consciousness, he would have been less imprudent. He would not have divided a writer's qualities into two kinds: natural qualities and qualities which one can acquire. As if a quality, that is to say, a manner of being and feeling, were something external that can be added on like a color or an odor! One becomes what one is, and becomes it without willing it and in spite of every effort to oppose it. The most unflagging patience cannot change a blind imagination into a visual imagination; and the work of a man who sees the landscape whose aspect he transposes into literature is still better, however awkward, than it would be after retouching by a corrector whose vision is deficient or profoundly different. "But the master alone can give the forceful stroke." This discouraged Pécuchet. The master stroke in artistic writings, even the forceful stroke, is necessarily the very one that should not be emphasized. Otherwise, the stroke stresses the detail on which it is customary to place special value and not that which had struck the unskilled but sincere inner eye of the apprentice. M. Albalat makes an abstraction of that almost invariably unconscious vision, and he defines style as "the art of grasping the value of words and their interrelations." And talent, according to him, consists "not in making dry, lifeless use of words, but in discovering the nuances, the images, the sensations which result from their combination."

Here we are in the realm of pure verbalism, in the ideal region of signs. It is a matter of manipulating signs and arranging them in patterns which give the illusion of representing the world of sensations. Approached backwards in this way, the problem is insoluble. It may happen, since anything is possible, that such a combination of words will evoke life—even a determinate life—but most often it will remain inert. The forest becomes petrified. A criticism of style must begin with a criticism of the inner vision, by an essay on the formation of images. There are, to be sure, two chapters on images in M. Albalat's book, but they come at the end; and thus the mechanism of language is demonstrated in reverse, since the first step is the image and the last is the abstraction. A good analysis of the natural processes of style would begin with the sensation and end with the pure idea—so pure that it would correspond not only to nothing real, but to nothing imaginary either.

If there is an art of writing, it would be the very art of feeling, the art of seeing, the art of hearing, the art of using all the senses, either directly or imaginatively; and the serious, new method of a theory of style would be an attempt to show how those two separate worlds—the world of sensations and the world of words—manage to interpenetrate. There is the great mystery, since those two worlds lie infinitely far apart, that is to say, parallel. We are obliged to infer communication by some sort of wireless telegraphy. We observe that the needles on the two dials act in unison, and that is all. But this mutual dependence is actually far from being as complete and clear as in a mechanical device. In short, words and sensations are in accord only very rarely and very poorly. We have no sure way, except perhaps by silence, to express our thoughts. How many circumstances in life there are, where the eyes, the hands, the mute mouth, are much more eloquent than all our words! [4]

IV

M. Albalat's analysis is bad, then, because it is not scientific. Yet he has derived from it a practical method about which one can say that, if it will not produce an original writer—he is well aware of that himself—it might possibly attenuate the incoherence if not the mediocrity of speeches and writings to which custom obliges us to give some attention. That is, however, a matter of indifference to me. But even if this manual were more useless than I believe it to be, certain of its chapters would retain, nevertheless, some interesting documentation and exposition. The detail is excellent. We find, for example, some pages where it is demonstrated that the idea is closely linked to the form and that to change the form is to modify the idea: "It is meaningless to say of a piece of writing that the substance is good but the form is bad." These are sound principles, though the idea might exist as a residue of sensation, independent of the words and, above all, of a choice of words. But bare ideas, as naked as wandering larva, are of no interest whatever. It may be that such ideas belong to everybody. Perhaps all ideas are common property. But how different one of them, wandering about waiting to be evoked, will appear, according to the words that summon it from the shadows. What would Bossuet's ideas be worth, deprived of their purple? They are the ideas of any ordinary theology student, and if he were to propose them, people would recoil, embarrassed by stupidities which, couched in the *Sermons* and *Oraisons,* they found quite intoxicating. And the effect would be the same if, having listened complaisantly to Michelet's lyrical paradoxes, we were to come across them in the low discourse of some senator or in the sorry commentaries of the partisan press. That is why the Latin poets, including the greatest, Virgil, tend to disappear in translation, and become indistinguishable in the painful and pompous uniformity of normal school rhetoric. If Virgil had written in the style of M. Pessonneaux or M. Benoist, he would have been Pessonneaux or Benoist, and the monks would have scraped his verses off the parchment and substituted some worthy lease with a sure and durable interest.

A propos of these obvious truths, M. Albalat is pleased to refute M. Zola's opinion that "it is form that changes and passes the most quickly" and that "one achieves immortality by creating living creatures." To the extent that this last sentence can be interpreted at all, it would seem to mean this: what one calls life in art is independent of the form. But perhaps this is even less clear. Perhaps it has no meaning whatever. Hippolytus also, at the gates of Troezen, was "without form and color"—only he was dead. All that can be conceded to this theory is that a work of original beauty and original form, if it outlives its own century and, what is more, the language in which it was written, will be admired by men only as a subject of imitation, following the traditional injunction of educators. If the *Iliad* were to be discovered today in the ruins of Herculaneum, it would produce only some archeological sensations. It would interest us to exactly the same degree as the *Song of Roland*. But then a comparison of the two poems would show, more clearly than before, that they correspond to extremely different periods of civilization, since one is written entirely in images (a bit stiff, to be sure), while the other has so few that they have been counted.

There is, moreover, no necessary relation between the merit of a work and its span of life. Yet when a book does survive, the authors of "analyses and extracts conforming to the academic program" know very well how to prove its "inimitable" perfection and to resuscitate, for the purposes of a lecture, the mummy which then disappears back into its winding cloths. We must not confuse the idea of glory with the idea of beauty. The first is entirely dependent on revolutions of fashion and taste. The second is absolute to the extent of human sensations. One conforms to manners and customs; the other conforms to natural law.

Form passes, it is true, but it is hard to see how form could survive the matter which is its substance. If the beauty of a style becomes effaced or falls into dust, it is because the language has modified the aggregate of its molecules—words—as well as molecules themselves, and because this internal work has not been effected without swellings and disturbances. If Fra Angelico's frescos have "passed," it is not because time has rendered them less beautiful; it is because humidity has swollen the cement where the painting has become caked and dull. Languages swell and flake like cement; or rather they act like plane trees which can live only by constantly changing their bark and which, early each spring, shed on the surrounding moss the names of love engraved on their very flesh.

But what does the future matter? And what matters the approbation of men who will not be what we would have them be, if we were demiurges? What is this glory enjoyed by man the moment he takes leave of consciousness? It is time we learned to live in our present moment, to accommodate ourselves to the passing hour, however bad, and to leave to children this concern for the future, which is an intellectual weakness—though sometimes the naiveté of a man of genius. It is highly illogical to desire the immortality of works when we affirm and desire the immortality of souls. Dante's Virgil lived beyond life, his glory grown eternal. Of this dazzling conception there is little left but a tiny vain illusion which it would be better to extinguish completely.

That does not alter the fact, however, that we should write for men as if we wrote for angels, and thus realize, according to our calling and our nature, the greatest possible beauty, even though passing and perishable.

V

M. Albalat shows excellent judgment in suppressing those amusing distinctions which the old handbooks made between a flowery style and a simple style, between the sublime and the tempered. He is right in asserting that there are only two kinds of style: the banal and the original. If it were permissible to count the degrees from the mediocre to the worst, as well as from the passable to the perfect, the scale would be long in shades and colors. It is so far from the *Légende de Saint-Julien l'hospitalier* to a parliamentary oration that one really wonders if they involve the same language—if there were not two French languages and under them an infinity of dialects almost unintelligible to one another. Regarding political style, M. Marty-Laveaux [5] thinks that the people, having remained faithful in their speech to traditional language, understand such a style poorly and only in a general way, as if it were a foreign tongue which one understood a little but did not speak himself. He wrote this twenty-seven years ago, but the newspapers, more widely circulated today, have scarcely modified popular habits. One can rest assured that, in France, out of every three persons, one will read a newspaper only in part and then by chance, and another will not read it at all. In Paris people have certain notions regarding style. They have a taste for violence and wit. This explains the popularity—much more literary than political—of a journalist like M. Rochefort, in whom Parisians have for some time found their ancient ideal: the witty and wordy fire-eater.

M. Rochefort is, moreover, an original writer—one of those who should be cited first of all to show that substance is nothing without form. It is not necessary to read much beyond his regular article. Yet perhaps we are being fooled by him, just as we have been for a half-century, apparently, by Mérimée, from whom M. Albalat quotes a page as a specimen of the banal style! Going further, and playing his favorite game, he corrects Mérimée and proposes that we examine the two texts juxtaposed. Here is a sample:

> *Bien qu'elle ne fût pas insensible* au plaisir *ou à la vanité d'inspirer un sentiment sérieux* à un homme aussi léger *que l'était Max dans son opinion,* elle n'avait jamais pensé que cette affection pût devenir un *jour* dangereuse *pour son repos.*[6]

> Sensible au plaisir d'attirer sérieusement un homme aussi léger, elle n'avait jamais pensé que cette affection pût devenir dangereuse.

At least it cannot be denied that the severe professor's style is economical, since it eliminates almost one line out of every two. Subjected to this treatment, poor Mérimée, already far from fertile, would find himself reduced to the paternity of a few skimpy booklets, symbolic thenceforth of his legendary dryness! Having become the Justin of all the Pompeius Troguses, Albalat lays Lamartine out on his workbench to tone down, for example, *la finesse de sa peau rougissante comme à quinze ans sous les regards,* changing it to *sa fine peau de jeune fille rougissante.* What butchery! The words that M. Albalat crosses out are so far from being banal that they would, to the contrary, correct and resuscitate the flat commonplaces in the improved sentence. For Mérimée's surplusage expresses the very subtle observation made by a man who has studied numerous

women's faces—a man more tender than sensual, touched by modesty rather than by carnal prestige. Good or bad, style cannot be corrected. Style is inviolable.

M. Albalat offers some very amusing lists of clichés, but his
criticism sometimes lacks proportion. I cannot accept as clichés
"kindly warmth," "precocious perversity," "restrained emotion," "retreating forehead," "abundant hair," or even "bitter tears," for some
tears can be bitter and some tears can be sweet. It should also be
understood that an expression in the form of a cliché in one style
can be found in another style in the form of a renewed image. "Restrained emotion" is no more ridiculous than "dissimulated emotion." As for "retreating forehead," it is a scientific expression that is
highly accurate when properly employed. It is the same with some
of the others. If such locutions were to be banished, literature would
become an algebra which could be understood only after lengthy
analytical operations. If we object to them because they have been
overworked, then we would have to avoid all the usual words along
with all those that do not contain some mystery. But that would be
foolishness. The commonest words and most current expressions
surprise us. Finally, the true cliché, as I have previously explained,
may be recognized by this, that, while the image that it conveys, already faded, is halfway on the road to abstraction, it is not yet insig-
nificant enough to pass unnoticed and is ranked among those signs
which owe their lives and functions to the will of the intelligence.[7]
Very often, in the cliché, one of the words has kept a concrete sense,
and what makes us smile is not so much the expression's banality as
the coupling of a living word with one whose life has vanished.
This is very evident in such formulas as: "in the bosom of the
Academy," "consuming activity," "open his heart," "sadness was
painted on his face," "break the monotony," "embrace principles."
However, there are some clichés all of whose words seem alive: *une
rougeur colora ses joues;* [a redness (blush, flush) colored his
(her) cheeks] and others whose seem dead: *il était au comble de
ses voeux* [he was at the height of his desires]. But this last cliché
was formed at a time when the word *comble* was very much alive
and entirely concrete. It is because it still contains the residue of a
palpable image that its alliance with *voeux* offends us. In the former
example, the word *colorer* has become abstract, since the concrete
verb expressing this idea is *colorier,* and it goes badly with *rougeur*

and *joues*. I do not know just where a detailed work on this part of the language, in which the fermentation is still unfinished, would lead us. But no doubt one would end by demonstrating rather easily that in the true notion of the cliché incoherence has its place alongside of banality. For the practice of style, there would be material in such a study for reasoned opinions which M. Albalat might render fruitful.

VI

It is unfortunate that he disposed of the subject of periphrasis in a few lines. We expected an analysis of men's curious tendency to use a description to replace the word which is the sign of the designated thing. This malady—which is very ancient, since enigmas, or riddles, have been found on Babylonian cylinders (that of the wind nearly in the same terms as used by our children)—is perhaps the very origin of all poetry. If the secret of being a bore is to tell all, the secret of pleasing is to say just enough to be—not understood, but divined. Periphrasis, as it was handled by the didactic poets, is perhaps ridiculous only because of the lack of poetic power which it evidences, for there are plenty of agreeable ways to avoid naming what one wishes only to suggest. The true poet, master of his language, uses only periphrases at once so new and so clear in their shadowy light that any slightly sensual intelligence will prefer them to the too definite word. He wishes neither to describe nor to pique the curiosity, nor to show off his erudition. But whatever he does, he writes by periphrases, and it is not at all certain that all those he creates will retain their freshness for long. The periphrasis is a metaphor, and has the same life expectancy as a metaphor. It is a long way indeed from the vague and entirely musical periphrasis of Verlaine,

> Parfois aussi le dard d'un insecte jaloux
> Inquiétait le col des belles sous les branches,

to the mythological enigmas of a Lebrun, who calls the silkworm

L'amant des feuilles de Thisbé!

Here M. Albalat appropriately quotes the words of Buffon to the effect that nothing degrades a writer more than the trouble he takes "to express ordinary or commonplace things in an unusual or pompous manner. We pity him for having spent so much time making new combinations of syllables only to say what is said by everybody." Delille made himself famous by his taste for the didactic periphrase, but I believe that he has been ill-judged. It was not fear of the proper word that made him describe what he should have named; it was his rigid conception of poetry and the mediocrity of his talent. He was imprecise only because he lacked power, and he is very bad only when he is imprecise. But whether because of his method or his impotence, we are indebted to him for some amusing enigmas:

> Ces monstres qui de loin semblent un vaste écueil.[8]
> L'animal recouvert de son épaisse croûte,
> Celui dont la coquille est arrondie en voûte.
> L'équivoque habitant de la terre et des ondes.
> Et cet oiseau parleur que sa triste beauté
> Ne dédommage pas de sa stérilité.
> Et ces rameaux vivants, ces plantes populeuses,
> De deux règnes rivaux races miraculeuses.

It should not be thought, however, that *l'Homme des champs,* source of these charades, is an entirely contemptible poem. The Abbé Delille had his merits. When our ears, deprived of the pleasures of rhyme and rhythm, have become exhausted by current new versifications, we may recover a certain charm in the full and sonorous but by no means tiresome verses, and in landscapes which, though a bit severe, are broad and full of air:

> . . . Soit qu'une fraîche aurore
> Donne la vie aux fleurs qui s'empressent d'éclore,
> Soit que l'astre du monde, en achevant son tour,
> Jette languissamment les restes d'un beau jour.

VII

Nevertheless, M. Albalat asks how it is possible to be original and personal. His answer is not very clear. He counsels hard work and concludes that originality is the result of incessant effort. This is a highly regrettable illusion. Secondary qualities would no doubt be easier to acquire, but is conciseness, for example, an absolute quality? Should Rabelais and Victor Hugo, who were great word accumulators, be blamed just because M. de Pontmartin also has the habit of stringing together all the words that come into his head and piling up in the same sentence as many as twelve or fifteen epithets? The examples given by M. Albalat are highly amusing, but if Gargantua had not played, under the eye of Ponocrates, two hundred and sixteen different games, all very agreeable, it would have been most regrettable, though "the great rules of the art of writing are eternal."

Conciseness is sometimes the merit of dull imaginations. Harmony is a rarer and more decisive quality. I can find nothing to criticize in what M. Albalat says in this connection, unless it is that he believes too strongly in the necessary relations between the lightness and heaviness of a word, for example, and the idea that it expresses. This is an illusion born of habitual usage, and readily destroyed by analysis of sounds. As Villemain says, it is not only by imitation of the Greek or Latin *fremere* that we have made the word *frémir;* it is by the relation between the sound and the emotion expressed. *Horreur, terreur, doux, suave, rugir, soupirer, pesant, léger,* he says, come to us not only from Latin, but from an intimate sense which has recognized and adopted them as analogous to the impression produced by the object.[9] If Villemain, whose opinion M. Albalat has adopted, had been better versed in linguistics, he would doubtless have invoked the theory of roots, which at one time gave to his nonsense an appearance of scientific force. As it is, the celebrated orator's little paragraph would make a most agreeable subject for discussion. It is quite evident that if *suave* [sweet, bland] and *suaire* [winding-sheet, shroud] evoke impressions generally remote from each other, it is not because of the quality of their sound. In English the words *sweet* and *sweat* receive similar pronunciations. *Doux* [sweet, gentle] is not more *doux* than *toux* [cough] and the other monosyllables of the same tone. Is *rugir* [to roar] more violent than *rougir* [to turn red, blush] or *vagir* [to wail, cry, squeak]? *Léger* [lightweight] is a contraction of a five-syllable Latin word *leviarium.* If *légère* carries with its own meaning, does *mégère* [shrew, termagant] likewise? *Pesant* [weighing] is neither heavier nor lighter than *pensant* [thinking], and the two forms are, moreover, doublets of a single Latin original, *pensare.* As for *lourd* [heavy], it is *luridus,* which meant many things: yellow, wild, savage, stranger, peasant, heavy—such, no doubt, is its genealogy. *Lourd* is no heavier than *fauve* is cruel. And think of *mauve* and *velours* [velvet]. If the English *thin* contains the idea of *mince*, how is it that the opposite idea of *épais* is expressed by *thick?* Words are neutral sounds which the mind charges with whatever meaning it pleases. There are coincidences, chance agreements between certain sounds and certain ideas. There are *frémir, frayeur, froid, frileux, frisson.* No doubt, but there are also *frein, frère, frêle, frêne, fret, frime,* and twenty other analogous sonorities, each endowed with a very different meaning.

M. Albalat is more successful in the balance of the two chapters where he treats successively the harmony of words and sentences. He rightly calls the style of the Goncourts an "unwritten style." [10] This is even more strikingly true when applied to M. Loti: there are no longer any sentences. His pages are a tangle of parenthetical clauses. The tree has been felled, its branches lopped off; there is nothing to be done except make faggots of them.

Beginning with the ninth lesson, *L'Art d'écrire* becomes even more didactic. Here we find Invention, Disposition, and Elocution. I would find it most difficult to explain how M. Albalat succeeds in superimposing these three phases of literary composition, which are really only one. The *art of developing a subject* has been denied me by Providence. I leave all that to the subconscious. Nor do I know any more about *how one invents.* But I believe one invents by reversing Newton's method—that is, by not thinking about it at all; and as for *elocution,* I would be uneasy about putting my trust in the method of recasting. One does not recast—one remakes, and it is so depressing to do the same thing twice that I approve of those who let the stone fly at the first turn of the sling. But here is what proves the inanity of literary counsels: Théophile Gautier wrote the complicated pages of *Le Capitaine fracasse* day by day, on a printers table, among half-wrapped bundles of papers, in the stench of oil and ink; and it is said that Buffon recopied the *Epoques de la nature* eighteen times.[11] This discrepancy is of no importance whatever, since, as M. Albalat should have said, there are writers who make their corrections mentally, putting on paper only the sluggish or lively products of the subconscious, and there are others who need to see their work externalized, and to see it again and again, in order to correct it—that is, to understand it. Yet, even in the case of mental corrections, external revision is often profitable, provided that, as Condillac puts it, the writer knows how to stop,

how to bring his work to a conclusion.¹² Too often the demon of
the Better has tormented intellects and sterilized them; but it is true
that it is also a great misfortune not to be able to evaluate one's own
work. Who will dare to choose between the writer who does not
know what he is doing, and one who can stand back and watch
himself at work? There is Verlaine, and there is Mallarmé. One
must obey his own genius.

M. Albalat excels in definitions. "Description is the animated
painting of objects." He means that, in order to describe, one
should, like a painter, place himself before the landscape, whether
real or imaginary. Judging by the analysis he makes of a page of
Télémaque, it seems clear that Fénelon was endowed with a
highly mediocre visual imagination and an even more mediocre gift
of words. In the first twenty lines of the description of Calypso's
grotto, the word *doux* appears three times and the word *former* appears four. This has, indeed, become for us the very type of the
inexpressive style, but I persist in believing that it once had a certain
freshness and grace and that it legitimately appealed to the taste of
the times. When we smile at this opulence of gilded paper and
painted flowers—the ideal of an archbishop who had remained a
theology student—we forget that no one had described nature since
L'Astrée. Those sweet oranges, those syrups diluted with spring
water, were the refreshments of Paradise. It is cruel to compare
Fénelon, not only with Homer, but even with the Homer of
Leconte de Lisle. Translations too well done—those which one can
say possess literary literality—inevitably result, in fact, in transforming into concrete and lively images everything that in the original
had become abstraction. Did λευκοβραχίων mean one who had white
arms, or was it merely a worn-out epithet? Did λευκάκανθα suggest
an image such as a "white thornbush" or a neutral idea like "haw-
thorne," which has lost its representational value? We cannot say;
but to judge past languages by present ones, we must suppose that
the great majority of Homeric epithets had already become abstractions by Homer's time.¹³ It is feasible that foreigners might find in
a work like *Télémaque,* so superannuated for us, the same pleasure
that we find in the *Iliad* done in bas-relief by Leconte de Lisle. *Mille
fleurs naissantes émaillaient les tapis verts* is a cliché only when
read for the hundredth time. New, the image would be ingenious
and pictorial. The poems of Edgar Allan Poe, as translated by

Mallarmé, acquire a life at once mysterious and precise which they never had to a comparable extent in the original. And from Tennyson's *Mariana,* agreeable verses full of commonplaces and padding, grey in tone, Mallarmé made, by substituting the concrete for the abstract, a fresco of beautiful autumnal coloring. I make these observations merely by way of a preface to a theory of translation. They will suffice here to indicate that, where it is a question of style, comparison should be made only between texts in the same language and belonging to the same period. I have already explained the historical formation of clichés. Mallarmé lived to see, during his lifetime—and if he had lasted into our own, how he would have suffered!—some of his images, the most physical and lively of his children, couched, half dead, in the neuter verse and carbon-copy prose of more than one of his too fervent admirers.

It is very difficult, after fifty years, to appreciate the extent of a style's originality. One would have to have read all the notable books in the order of their publication. One can at least evaluate the present and also give some credence to the contemporary comments on a work. Barbey d'Aurevilly found in George Sand a profusion of *anges de la destinée* [angels of destiny], of *lampes de la foi* [lamps of faith], and of *coupes de miel* [honey cups], which were certainly not invented by her any more than the rest of her washed-out style; but "these decrepit tropes" would have been no better if she had conceived them. It seems obvious to me that the cup whose edges have been rubbed with honey goes back to the obscure days of pre-Hippocratic medicine. Clichés live such a long life! M. Albalat notes correctly that "there are images which one can renew and rejuvenate." There are many such, and among them some of the commonest; but I cannot see that, in calling the moon a "dull lamp," Leconte de Lisle has been especially successful in freshening up Lamartine's "golden lamp." M. Albalat, who gives evidence of wide reading, should attempt a catalog of images arranged by subjects: the moon, the stars, the rose, the dawn, and all the "poetic" words. Thus one would obtain a collection of a certain utility for the study of the psychology of words and the elementary emotions. Perhaps we should learn at last why the moon is so dear to poets. Meanwhile he has announced his next book: *The Formation of Style by the Assimilation of Authors;* and I suppose that, once the series is complete, everybody will write very well and that there will henceforth be a good medium style in literature, just as there is in painting and the other fine arts that the State so successfully protects. Why not an Academy Albalat, as well as an Academy Julian?

Here, then, is a book that lacks almost nothing except not having a purpose, except being a work of pure and disinterested analysis. But if it were to have an influence, if it were to multiply the number of honorable writers, it will have earned our maledictions. Instead of putting this handbook on literature and all the arts within the reach of everyone, it would be wiser to transport its secrets to some Himalayan peak. But there are no secrets. To be a writer, it is enough to have a natural talent for the trade, to practice that trade with perseverance, to learn a little more every morning, and to experience all human sensations. As for the art of "creating images," we must believe that it is absolutely independent of all literary culture, since the most beautiful images, the truest and boldest, are enclosed in our everyday words—time-honored work of the instinct, spontaneous flowering of the intellectual garden.

—From *La Culture des idées*, February 1899

Selections from The Problem of Style

The most important, or, if you wish, the longest chapter in this new collection of essays, belongs to a completely obsolete literary genre, the Refutation. Perhaps we have come to recognize that good books are irrefutable and that the bad ones refute themselves. That is fair enough, but it would be even more so if all books deserved one or the other of these extreme qualifications. There are many well made and seriously written, whose welcoming façades deceive one regarding the traps that lie within. The house has an honest air about it, and it is comfortable: you enter, you are pleased, and you remain awhile. If you want to leave, it is a prison.

I dislike prisons of any kind. That is why, having entered the house of M. Albalat, I have permitted myself to tear a few locks out by the roots. He will replace them, if it suits him, for, after all, he is master of his own house; and if he becomes angry with me, I will not insist, and will even ask him to excuse my indiscretion and bad humor.

For it is bad humor, rather than entirely good feelings of which I could be proud, that provokes me to this little enterprise. The confidence of a possessor of the truth moves me to laughter on some days and anger on others. It is as absurd to seek the truth—and to find it, when one has reached the age of reason—as it is to put one's shoes before the fireplace on Christmas eve. "At this time," I was told by one of the creators of a new science, "we cannot establish any theory, but we can demolish all those that will be established." We should try to remain always at this stage: the only fruitful quest is the quest for the nontrue.

Thus, and only thus, does criticism make a superior work. "My business is to sow doubts." This phrase of Pierre Bayle's contains an entire method and an entire morality. Truth is a tyranny—doubt liberates.

For the affirmations of M. Albalat, therefore, I have substituted doubts. This is less pleasant for the majority of men, who live by truths, just as cattle live by grass. But there are those who are not cattle: otherwise how would thoughts be generated in human organisms?

If art is important, if civilization is important, the problem of style is important. But it is insoluble in the sense that M. Albalat has wished to resolve it. One does not learn how to write, that is, to acquire a personal style; otherwise, nothing would be more common, and nothing is more rare. It is the pedagogical, and futile, side of the question. The real problem of style is a question of physiology. If it is impossible to establish the exact, necessary relation between a certain style and a certain sensibility, we can nevertheless affirm that a close dependence exists. We write, as we feel, as we think, with our entire body. Intelligence is only one mode of being of the sensibility, and not the most stable, still less the most voluntary.

In saying that this study belongs to the genre of Refutation, I did not at all mean to say that it is a true refutation. Its purpose, much less rigorous, is rather to develop five or six reasons for not believing in rhetorical recipes. But the fact is that, without the didactic works of M. Albalat, I would probably never have reflected on these questions. They were my point of departure, and I owe them much. But I will have given to the public more than I have borrowed. That should be my excuse.

There is almost nothing in the rest of the volume that is not related to the problem of style, whether it is a question of the origin or technique of Symbolist poetry, the destiny of the "art nouveau," or certain grammatical subtleties.

September 17, 1902

I. THE TWO KEYS TO THE COFFER

M. Albalat has just undertaken, once again, to guide us by the hand toward the conquest of style. He gives us a manual for the craft of writing, after having first published its theory.[1] This manual bears a redoubtable title, very much like those which, in olden days, one spelled out fearfully on books of wizard spells and on breastplates, or more recently on the bald foreheads of treatises on political economy. Here it is—formidable, an entire program, a world: *On the Formation of Style by the Assimilation of Authors*.[2]

There are a master and apprentices. The lesson begins and develops this principle: one must read. The whole world reads to be amused, to be informed—but that is not the point. One must read well. To read well is to read fruitfully. To read fruitfully is "to read authors whose style can teach us to write and to avoid those whose style does not teach us to write." For it is a matter of assimilating methods of procedure, and wherever there is no method, wherever the genius flowered in complete innocence of sensibility, reading would be nonproductive. Then what is the good of it? The simplicity of the reasoning will charm practical mentalities. It is, moreover, irrefutable. If there is an art of writing, and if that art can be learned, then one must frequent the schools where it is taught. It is with deductions of this clarity and force that M. Albalat has attracted to his lectures and books a faithful and grateful audience. Thus years ago Du Bellay—but in a different tone, to be sure, and for somewhat different reasons—urged an ardent group of young poets to go pillaging: "Therefore, Frenchmen, march courageously on that superb Roman city, and when you have stripped her of her useful spoils (as you have done more than once), decorate your temples and altars. . . . Move in on that story-telling Greece, and richly sow once more the famous Gallo-grecian nation. Pillage, without conscience, the sacred treasures of that Delphic temple. . . ." Du Bellay was only too well understood. M. Albalat, wishing, in his turn, to teach us the formation of style by the assimilation of Homeric methods—has his time come? Is he a herald or a scavenger-beetle?

Therefore—and still like Du Bellay who rejected all the old French literature that had educated Europe, to the profit of France —you should despise, you candidates for assimilation, all those useless writers whose company confers no benefits. You should not read Descartes—he has only ideas, and no visible style. His thought has a skin that clings to the flesh and no flowered robes. Nor that of Pascal: it is stark naked and often sweating with fever, yellowed by fasting, or suddenly red with blood that flees the heart and leaves it cold. It is naked as a soul. You will not read Pascal. Neither will you read the disdainful Retz, who is covered only with a transparent immodesty; nor any of those writers who embrace nature sometimes to the point of merging with her. It would be time lost. It would be more worthwhile, almost, to live and feel by oneself, to open one's eyes and ears, and exercise one's hands—a slow method that will teach the art of writing only to those who have the gift.

These naked writers have another fault, M. Albalat tells us. They lack taste. And taste is the key to the method.

What is taste?

"It is defined as a special discernment, a rapid judgment, an ability to distinguish certain relationships. . . ."

But I am reciting *Bouvard et Pécuchet*.[3] Let us start again. What is taste?

Nothing at all, this: *trahit sua quemque voluptas*. However one will arrive, in analyzing this notion, at the idea of beauty (Pécuchet also arrived there), and taste will be the tendency to feel certain emotions which awaken the idea of beauty. We know what analysis makes of this last idea. Beauty, to borrow from the transcendental mythology of M. Jules de Gaultier, is one of the traps set for us by the genius of the species. It is variable, except in its primitive form, which is the human body; and taste, an agent, varies according to what it must enjoy, by accommodation. There is always agreement, at any one time in literary evolution, between beauty and taste. This proves that they unquestionably modify each other in unison and intimately react on each other. However, M. Albalat believes that there exists an absolute taste, just as he takes as very probable the existence of an immutable beauty. But will he say so? He says so, and I am completely dazzled:

"Literary beauties are fixed."

He adds, it is true, that their forms are diverse. But just what, then, is this beauty-in-itself which haunts the minds of aestheticians, like the ghost of Hippolytus, formless and colorless? A word, and, to be precise, a collective word. We give the same name of literary beauty to exceedingly different sources of emotion—to the point of abusing the language. If *M. de Pourceaugnac* is a thing of beauty, what is *Le Lac*?[4] A thing of beauty. Let us admit, rather, that we have only one group of sounds to express fifty or sixty different and sometimes contradictory sensations. Used in isolation, without a defining clause, this group of sounds has no clearer meaning than some abstract prefix like *ante, cum,* or *pro.* It requires a complement. Then it will reflect both time and place, and the general formula will be stated thus: Literary beauties vary with kingdoms and epochs.

Nevertheless, M. Albalat, weary of riding the absolute, harnesses up this scrawny nag: there exists a dominant taste, and there also exist particular tastes. But one will neglect them, and even his own, in order to seek the speaking rose, taste-in-itself. The means of discovery is reading books "where there is talent." For it is by reading them that taste is formed. But since it is necessary to have taste in order to discern talent, I find myself enclosed in a circus-ring where the old nag would lead me around forever, if M. Albalat did not obligingly come to open the prison door. He takes my mount by the bridle, guides us and serves us refreshments. "One must," he tells us, "read numerous authors of the first, second, and third order." We will begin with the finest vintages in order to provide ourselves a criterium for tasting the others "who can then be read without peril." Good Lord! as poor François Villon said, that I might have had such a master "in the time of my mad youth"! I would not have contracted the bad habit of reading without discernment, without care for the three orders—reading even the tenth, and perhaps even the hundredth! Victor Hugo claimed to read only books which nobody else read. I have a tendency toward the same depravity. M. Albalat knows where that leads, as he knows all about belles lettres. But what of it? I have not observed that the books nobody reads are any more absurd than those everybody reads. And as for the fear of spoiling one's style, it would be a good thing for a Bembo, who used a factitious language. Style can become fatigued, like the man himself. It will age, just like the intelligence and sensibility of which it is the sign; but it will not change in personality, any more than will the individual—barring a psychological cataclysm. The digestive processes, a sojourn in the country or in Paris, sentimental affairs and their consequences, illnesses—these have considerably more influence on a true style than do bad readings. Style is a physiological product, and one of the most constant, though dependent on various vital functions.

"Literary people," M. Albalat tells us, "read in order to taste of talent. Men of learning read to learn, and women read in order to feel." But what kind of literary man is it that does not want to learn and does not enjoy feeling? Is it Goethe, by chance, or Sainte-Beuve, or Flaubert? Let us follow our master without further indiscrete questions. Tasting talent, it would seem, is assimilating art. And what is the good of that? Patience—we will find out. Assimilating art is the second key to the coffer. How to read good authors? M. Albalat advocates an amiable slowness and his own method, which is not to take notes, but to "underline with a pencil the passages to be retained." Here we have, in sum, a trait of character. M. Albalat loves to read. He does not love books.

II. THE DOUGH AND THE LEAVEN

Throughout this elegant treatise, we find imitation within a single literature perseveringly confused with imitation between two different literatures. So there is little worth preserving of what M. Albalat tells us about Virgil imitating Homer, Racine imitating Euripides, Corneille imitating Seneca. They all chose a master from a venerated literature, each according to his individual temperament. Classical French writers were students of the Latins and Greeks, as the Romantics were students of the English and German. But an innovation in literature, in art, in politics, in manners, can never come from within the same ethnic group. Every group, once formed, once individualized, is compelled to a uniform production, or at least a production systematized into fixed varieties. Race, terrain, climate—these determine the particular nature of its acts and works and limit its diversity. Man has the capacity for changing, but he cannot change spontaneously: a source of ferment from outside the dough is always necessary. Botanists, however, have granted the possibility of "spontaneous variation." If that means "variation without cause," it is absurd. If it implies a cause, the cause being necessarily exterior to the object, what we are really seeing in this expression is a confession of ignorance. Walled China changed exceedingly little in the course of the centuries, once its ossification was achieved. People who change the most are those who receive the most foreigners. Here the botanists would think of those plants that receive the most insects. England, several parts of whose organism seem immutable, is less visited, in most of its provinces, than central Africa or the Amazon basin. A stranger there panics the populace. The peasants of Coventry, a short time ago, believed an invasion of Boers was imminent. Australia, though scarcely formed, is in a state of degeneration, through lack of ferment; and if closed to immigration, the United States would decline into lassitude without the European travels of their upper classes, without the extreme diversity of climate and soils, and consequently the evolving races of that vast empire. Exchanges between people are as necessary to the revitalizing of every nation as social commerce is to the stimulation of individual energy. We have not acknowledged that necessity when we speak with regret of the influence of foreign literatures on our literature. There has not been a century, since the eleventh, when French thought has not been invigorated by a new fermentation. Its strength has been to bear painlessly so many successive effervescences and to appear, after each crisis, fresher and livelier. Similarly women (and men as well) are rejuvenated by a new love and find in almost uninterrupted succession of passions the very principle of their vital activity. In the twelfth century, it was Celtic legend—the cycle of the Round Table, to which *Tristan* is related—that renovated the *chanson de geste;* then Greek legend, *Eneas, Alexandre;* then courtly Provençal with Chrétien de Troyes. Later, there were the *fabliaux,* which came from afar, from the depths of the East; and up till the Renaissance, where it swelled into a torrent, the foreign influx did not cease to enrich, normally, our French literature, in allowing its continual renewal, the multiplying of young flowers on the old stem.

III. VISION AND EMOTION

The question of style does not fall within the province of grammarians unless they choose to be supported by solid psychophysiological ideas.

. . . .

To write well, to have style . . . is to paint. The master faculty of style is therefore the visual memory. If a writer does not see what he describes—countrysides and figures, movements and gestures— how could he have a style, that is, originality? . . . If, to the visual memory, the writer joins the emotive memory, and if he has the power, in evoking a material spectacle, of recovering exactly the emotional state which that spectacle had aroused in him, then he possesses, even if he is ignorant, the whole art of writing.

Without the visual memory, without that reservoir of images from which the imagination draws new and infinite combinations, there is no style, no artistic creation. It alone permits us not only to paint the different movements of life by means of verbal figures, but to transform immediately into visions every association of words, every second-hand metaphor, even every isolated word—in short, to give life to death. From this power came allegories, such as *The Shepherd of Hermas,* the *Consolation of Philosophy,* the *Vita Nuova,* the *Romance of the Rose,* the *Palace of Divine Love.* The styles of Michelet and Taine are the product of this very happy faculty of metamorphosing the abstract into the concrete, of making the very stone breathe and "the stars palpitate." Language is full of clichés which originally were bold images, happy discoveries of metaphorical power. All abstract words are the figuration of a material act: pondering is weighing . . . . Everything in spoken language is images; the smoothest conversation is a tissue of rougher metaphors than a page of Goncourt or Saint-Pol-Roux. These metaphors are called worn coins, and that is almost true. But, worn or new, they are coins, with an obverse which is the meaning on departure and a reverse which is the meaning on arrival. There are obverses and reverses so effaced that the most tyrannical imagination can no longer animate them. Nevertheless, many persons who make use of these coins by preference also make use of their eyes at least to classify the drab verbal riches heaped up in their memories. When the word *ocean* is mentioned, instead of a glaucous immensity, or a sandy beach or cliffs or any similar vision rising before them, they see—admirable simplification—the word itself written in space in printed letters, OCEAN. More advanced intellectually than the visuals, these privileged individuals are grouped at the negative pole of the magnet whose positive pole is occupied by the artists. A great step has been taken toward simplification; the world of things has been replaced by the world of signs. But the progress is greater still when the world of signs does not appear before our eyes in any perceptible form, when the words confined in the brain pass, as if by some distributing apparatus, directly from their pigeon-holes to the tip of the tongue or the pen, without any intervention of the consciousness or sensibility. It is marvelous, no less than the systematic agitation of an anthill or beehive. However, the visuals must, even in subconscious phrases, translate their vision exactly like a painter, and seek words and their combinations as a painter seeks colors and combinations of colors, whereas to the "mechanists" words and epithets come smoothly, fluently, all the labor of passing from the real to the idea and from the idea to the real having been done for them by previous writers. They willingly make use of everything consecrated by usage, of well-known phrases—rich in emotional ferment for having been dragged everywhere—of proverbs and commonplaces, everything that abbreviates, everything that sums up.

But, and here is the main point, there can be a true emotion in the beginning of a novel as trite as "It was on a radiant morning in spring." It affirms, without any possible contradiction, that the author is not a visual and is not an artist, but not that he is deficient in sensibility. To the contrary, he is an emotional par excellence! Only, incapable of incorporating his personal sensibility into original stylistic forms, he chooses phrases which, having moved him, he believes should also move his readers. It is pointless to suppose some calculation where there is only, in actuality, the ingenuous association of a word and a sentiment. Words have no meaning but through the sentiment which they convey and whose representation they are. Even geometric propositions become feelings, as Pascal has said, in one of those prodigious phrases which we have taken three centuries to understand. A theorem can be moving and, resolved, make the heart beat faster. It has become feeling, in the sense that it is no longer perceived except in association with a feeling; it can contain a world of desires, be an object of love. The most inert words can be vivified by the sensibility, can "become feelings." All those words abused by certain political philosophies—justice, truth, equality, democracy, liberty, and a hundred others—have value only through the sentimental quality attributed to them by those who use them. Not only does the content of the word become feeling for him who uses it, but also its very material form and the atmosphere which surrounds it. Every word, every figure of speech, even proverbs and clichés, become, for the emotive writer, nuclei of sentimental crystallizations. Possessing no garden, he buys flowers and dreams that he has plucked them. Untapped for creative purposes, his sensibility remains abundant; and moreover he does not give out any more of it than some small fragments around words he wishes to embalm. It remains intact—to be used for life, for love, and all the passions.

The writer with an abstract style is almost always a sentimentalist, at least a "sensitive." The artist-writer is almost never a sentimentalist and very rarely a sensitive. That is, he incorporates his entire sensibility into his style and has very little left over for life and its profound passions. The one takes a ready-made phrase or writes a facile phrase which, deceived by his own emotion, he thinks has an emotive value. The other, with words that are merely handfuls of clay, constructs the limbs of his work and erects a statue which, whether beautiful or ugly, heavy or winged, will yet keep in its attitude some of the life of the hands that shaped it. Nevertheless, the vulgar will feel more emotion from the banal phrase than from the original phrase; and this will be the counterproof: to the reader who draws his emotions from the very substance of what he reads is opposed the reader who only feels what he reads to the extent that he can apply it to his own life, to his own griefs and hopes. He who enjoys the literary beauty of a sermon by Bossuet cannot be touched by it religiously, and he who weeps for the death of Ophelia has no aesthetic sense. These two parallel categories of writers and readers constitute the two great types of cultivated humanity. In spite of shadings and overlappings, no understanding is possible between them; and not understanding each other, they despise each other. Their animosity extends in two wide, sometimes subterranean, streams throughout literary history.

. . . .

Style is a specialization of the sensibility. For us to make use of a word, it must represent something. Apart from the case where it is the symbol of a real object, clearly determined, which is very rare (as in science), a word can correspond only to a sensation—in the first place, to a vision, or an emotion, or, ultimately, to an idea.

. . . .

Other senses—taste, smell, and touch—have their influence in literature. Some writers have translated through words the impressions those senses provide; but these do not amount to much, vision and emotion remaining the two great sources of style. According to what it symbolizes, a word will therefore be plastic or emotive, depending on the construction of the sentence even more than on its sonority or its racial purity (which constitutes the proper beauty of words, and perhaps all beauty). In the state of pure notion, a word would represent an idea; but what is an idea? If it is immaterial, how can it be *felt* by the nerve cells, which are of good, real material? An idea is not an immaterial thing—there are no immaterial things. It is an image, but worn and therefore without force; it is usable only when associated with a feeling, when it has "become feeling." The two categories are again reformed to join definitively with the two divisions of style: concrete style, incorporating the sensibility and permitting art; and abstract style, where the sensibility remains exterior, associated only by direct contact, not permitting art, or permitting only a very special kind of art, almost geometric, one of inference rather than of reality. . . . The quality of an imaged style corresponds to the quality of the eye, to the quality of the visual memory, and also to the quality of the verbal memory. One learns to draw, one does not learn to paint; the sense of color is innate but the sense of equilibrium is an acquisition. . . . To speak of style is to speak of visual memory and metaphorical faculty, combined in variable proportions with the emotive memory and all the obscure support of the other senses. To gauge the proportions is to analyze the styles; you will never find any that is free of heterogeneous elements. I have explained elsewhere that the style of the pure visual, a style composed of nothing but completely original images, would be absolutely incomprehensible. Something of the banal and vulgar is needed as common bond, as cement serves the shaped stones. The two categories, abstract and concrete, are only limits.

Renan has written: "The finished work is one which has no literary afterthought, where one does not suspect for a moment that the author wrote just to write; in other terms, where there is no trace of rhetoric. Port-Royal[5] is the only corner of the seventeenth century where rhetoric did not penetrate." Carried away by his rationalist hatred of art (which he calls rhetoric, by intentional confusion), he does not seek the real cause of Port-Royal's apparent immunity; but if he had searched, he probably would not have found it. Now it is easy to formulate. Those solitaries wrote with a totally exterior style, incorporating scarcely a particle of their sensibility, keeping it entirely for their lives, for their religious activities. This is not a title of glory; it is a fact of psychology, and nothing more. Their books had an edifying or demonstrative purpose. They wished to prove the worth of their cause or win over disciples to their particular faith or, quite simply, to work for the glory of God. Art is incompatible with a moral or religious preoccupation. Beauty does not lead to piety, or to contrition, and the glory of God blazes forth principally in the works of most humble mentality and most mediocre rhetoric. Exempt from art to an inconceivable degree, Port-Royal cultivated, whatever Renan might say, a special glacial rhetoric, in which the fervor of faith is congealed into immobile phrases, into paralyzed epithets. Take up the preliminary discourse of the "Lives of the Holy Fathers of the Deserts" by Arnaud d'Andilly, and you will see there all the artifices of pious rhetoric: "The holy and happy retreat to which it had pleased God to call me through his infinite mercy—the holy delights—the grand marvels—the most faithful servants—such pious souls—those beautiful lives —the most celebrated authors—fervent prayers—powerful exhortations"—and throughout long dreary pages each sickly substantive is attached to its prop with a blade of rotten willow! Wretched rhetorical flowers in a sorry garden. It is disloyal to confuse art with rhetoric, Bossuet with Arnaud. Bossuet, too, wrote to edify or convince, but his general sensibility was so rich, his vitality so profound, his energy so violent, that he was split into two, and remained a writer while wishing only to be an apostle. Rhetoric is the putting into practice of processes of the art of writing previously dissected by a clever man. . . . Art is the spontaneous and ingenuous exercise of a natural talent. Saint-Simon, an extraordinary stylistic artist, is pure of all rhetoric. When he wrote, all his sensibility passed into his long, tough writings, and with it all his rancor, all his rage at being so obscure a duke, all the secret disdain of a man who judges for people whose importance, by the very judgment to which they are subjected, is lessened and limited. Saint-Simon is a great writer because he was a mediocre man of action. Apart from his writing, he must have been gross, wicked, inflexible, and maladroit.

If necessary, one can bring all French literature to bear witness that style is a specialization of the sensibility and that the more a writer approximates the artist, the less he is apt to cut a figure in the diverse forms of human activity. From the moment he starts to

write, Jean-Jacques changes his character; his entire sensibility
passes into his style. He agitates and remains calm. In his books, he
shows himself impassioned and talkative; in his life, he is can-
tankerous and mute. He is a sensitive bear; a bear in reality, a
sentimentalist in fiction. They are not absurd, those old expressions:
"To write lovingly—to caress one's sentences amorously." Racine,
whose style is rarely plastic, saves almost all his sensibility for his
mistresses first, then for his God. The profound sentiment of love
which was in him was passed only into the *acts* of his characters;
whereas they *expressed* extreme passions in an abstract, icy, and
diplomatic style. With Musset, sentiment swelled up around his
verses and spread out like a voluptuous perfume. This association,
completely external, was fugitive. The perfume evaporated, and we
are left with transparent poems, odorless vials which reveal to us the
absense of intimate and personal art. However sentimental, no one
has ever incorporated less sensibility into a work; he *lived* too much
"with love" to be able to *write* "with love." However, in periods of
undoubtedly less intense real life, he did let a little of that vagabond
sensibility filter into the marrow of his style, and that is in his theater. Chateaubriand, a type completely opposite to Musset, possesses
a serenity of absolute feeling. It is into his phrases that he puts his
heart. . . . He is all sensations; his organs are in constant communication with the external word. He looks, he listens, he smells, he
touches, and that sensorial harvest he pours unreservedly into his
style. Baudelaire is of the same physiological family, with a predominance of sensations of hearing, taste, odor, and touch. Victor Hugo,
on the other hand, represents the almost purely visual type. He is so
little auditory that he cannot render a musical sensation except by
transforming it into vision:

> Comme sur la colonne un frêle chapiteau,
> La flûte épanouie a montée sur l'alto.[6]

Both Hugo and Baudelaire, but Hugo more completely, incorporate
into their styles all the general sensibility which they have at their
disposal. Hugo's is a simple mechanism, almost elementary, and
perfect. All the sensations which he experiences—and he profits
especially from his eyes—he inevitably translates into words by
means of visual images; and similarly, when he tries to express any

notion acquired by reading or speech, it becomes a vision. He will say, by way of characterizing his influence on language which was immense:

J'ai mis un bonnet rouge au vieux dictionnaire.[7]

With such a faculty, a writer can have a barbaric style, eccentric and incomprehensible, but he will never be banal. Confronting the spectacle evoked by his memory or imagination, the writer must become a painter, or else abstain. It would be more difficult for him to use clichés than to arrange combinations of necessarily new words. However, while a paradoxical type of visual who writes by clichés is a possibility, the examination of the style alone would not permit us to discover it. Every sensation, current or stored up in the nerve cells, is proper to art. If, instead of sensations, material memories, the brain retains only the imprint of an emotion, or if the perception of the senses has been rapidly transformed into an abstract notion, or into an emotional idea, then art is no longer possible, for there is no art but plastic art and the material has fled, leaving only its traces along the way. One can therefore generalize and divide writers again into two classes: the sensorials and the ideo-emotives; or in other words, the plastics and the sentimentals. Leaving aside the question of style as a bit confining and accidental, one could well apply these two fundamental colorations, taking shadings into account, to all civilized humanity. One would then know almost exactly what is meant by the words realism and idealism, or rather spiritualism.[8] Recently a political group called itself "the intellectuals." In reality, these intellectuals are (or were) ideo-emotives, sentimentalists, spiritualists. There is no intellectual type, as pure intelligence cannot enter directly into contact with life. All its labor, whatever its apparent complexity, is limited eternally to taking cognizance, over and over again, of the principle of identity. In life, this principle is valuable only when associated with the emotions which corrupt it. There is no certitude except in insubstantial numerals; the realities are not comparable and resist identification. That is why the witness of the senses is superior to the witness of the intellect, which is always vitiated by an emotion born apropos of the object and not stemming from the object itself. Even when misleading, a sensation is physiologically true and can have the same effect as reality. The ideo-emotion, always hallucinatory, gives nothing of the external world but a fantastic image, futile and unsuited to react freely upon the physiology. Returning to the question of style: the ideo-emotives blossom forth in declamations; the sensorials, in descriptions. The material of one is sometimes too abundant; of the other, it is lacking: there is dearth, and they cry out in famine.

. . . .

Nihil intellectu quod non prius fuerit in sensu: the senses are the unique doorway through which enters all that lives in the mind, the very notion of consciousness, and the very feeling of personality. An idea is only a faded sensation, an effaced image. To reason with ideas is to assemble and combine, into a labored mosaic, faded cubes that have become almost indistinguishable. . . . If feeling does not intervene in the manipulation of ideas, it is pure parroting. . . . Reasoning by means of sensorial images is much easier and much more certain than reasoning by ideas. Sensation is utilized in all its verdure, the image in all its vivacity. The logic of the eye and the logic of each of the other senses suffice to guide the mind. When useless sentiment is rejected as a source of trouble, one achieves those marvellous structures which seem pure intellectual works but which, in reality, are the material work of the senses and their organs like the combs of bees with their wax and honey. Philosophy, which passes in average minds for the domain of pure ideas (those chimeras!), is lucid only when conceived and written by sensorial writers. That is what makes the solidity of the works of a Schopenhauer, a Taine, a Nietzsche; and it is that also which condemns them to the disdain of the ideo-emotive philosophers. But the disdain is reciprocal, the two classes of minds being irreconcilable. One thinks of the invective of Schopenhauer against Hegel, of Taine against the spiritualists and the spiritualists against Taine. It is undoubtedly a question of doctrines, but what is a doctrine if not the verbal translation of a physiology?

. . . .

The artistic faculties, based on the exercise of sensation, cannot be anterior to sensations. The senses are developed by that natural education which life gives. A sensorial style, an imaged style, is never precocious. It asserts itself in proportion as sensations accumulate in the neural cells and make the archives of memory denser, richer, and more complex. . . . It is life, the habit of sensation, that will create the stylistic image; but the mind, even in its undeveloped early years, manifests invincible tendencies. Taine's mind from the time of his youth was that of a visual and a sensorial. . . . "I ask pardon for these metaphors," he wrote. "One gives the impression of arranging sentences whereas one only recounts his sensations. . . . One does not give himself his style; he receives it from the facts with which he is dealing." This analysis is incomplete. It should read: "One does not give himself his style; its form is determined by the structure of the brain, from which he receives the factual material with which he deals."

Sensation is the basis of everything, of the moral and intellectual life as well as the physical life. Two hundred and fifty years after Hobbes, two hundred years after Locke, such has been the destructive power of religious Kantism that one is reduced to insisting on such elementary aphorisms. It is true as it is curious: the mechanism of that vital circulus, starting from sensation, returns there eternally and necessarily! Sensation is transformed into word-images; these into word-ideas; these into word-feelings. It is a closed circle; but there would be a perpetual fall into the void, if feeling did not have an almost irresistible tendency to pass into action. It must either die or reenter into life, a simple alternative, like life itself which is only the tireless propagation of circulatory movements. Thus, successively, sensation draws from and throws back into the vital torrent the images necessary to the exercise of the intelligence. Attenuated by the cerebral mechanism and become vain abstract ideas, images are gathered and revitalized by the feelings, and it is then that they act, poisonously or curatively, that they determine human activity, as sources of our strongest and most active sensations. This very much resembles (perhaps too much) the circulation of the blood. Disturbances of the circulation of ideas produce all literature, all art, all play, all civilization.

· · · · · · ·

Like all writers before, during, and after his time, Flaubert underwent the initial influence of Chateaubriand; which is neither miraculous nor very important. Emerging from any other school, Flaubert would inevitably have become what he was, himself. Life is a process of sloughing-off. The proper end of man's activities is to scour his personality, to cleanse it of all the stains deposited by education, to free it of all the imprints left by adolescent admirations. A time comes when the scoured coin is clean and shining with its own metal. But, to use another image, I think of the sloughing-off of wine which, freed from its disturbed particles, its vain fumes, its false colors, one day becomes gay with all its grace, proud with all its strength, limpid and smiling like a new rose. Since Flaubert is one of the most profoundly personal writers that ever existed, one of those who may be read most clearly through the lace of style, it is easy to follow in his work the progressive sloughing-off of the man. To do that, one must read successively *Madame Bovary, L'Education sentimentale, Bouvard et Pécuchet.* Only in this last book is the work completed, only there does the man's genius appear in all its transparent beauty. . . . There are no books but those where a writer has told of himself by telling of the manners of his contemporaries, their dreams, their vanities, their loves and follies. What are the descriptions of *Salammbô* and their long cadenced phrases compared with the brief notations and abridgements of *Bouvard et Pécuchet,* that book which is only comparable with *Don Quixote,* which amuses us as the novel of Cervantes amused the seventeenth century, and which, when the present period is over, will remain the archives where posterity will clearly read the hopes and disappointments of a century? And the soul of a man too. This book is so personal, so woven as it were from nervous fibers that no one has ever been able to add to it a page which did not produce the effect of a piece of cloth on a tulle dress. The miracle is that this work of flesh seems wholly spiritual. At first it seems like a catalog of little experiments which any industrious man could easily achieve. But it cannot be touched; it is a living animal which squirms and cries as soon as the needle plunges into it to make the seam. All Flaubert seems impersonal. It has become proverbial. As if a great writer, as if a man of such a strong, excessive, dominating, extravagant sensibility could be—what? the contrary of the one word that could define him! An impersonal work of art, an impersonal work of science! If I have ever been guilty of such an abuse of words, may I be pardoned. It was from ignorance. But I know now that only mediocre works are impersonal, and that there is more personality in the *Lessons of Experimental Physiology* of Claude Bernard than in [Musset's] *Confession of a Child of the Century*. There is not this and that kind of art; there is not science on one side and literature on the other. There are brains which function well and brains which function badly.

Flaubert incorporated all his sensibility into his works; and by sensibility I mean, here as elsewhere, the general power of feeling such as it is unequally developed in every human being. Sensibility includes reason itself, which is only crystallized sensibility. Outside his books wherein he transfused himself drop by drop to the dregs, Flaubert was not very interesting. He was nothing but dregs: his intelligence was stirred up, exasperated into an incoherent fantasy. He, whose written irony is duped by no social parading, no mask, no dream, allowed himself to be taken in by false talents (Sand) and false loves (Colet). He wallowed in poetic sentimentality or roared stupid insults against the bourgeoisie. Far from being impersonal in his works, the roles are here reversed: it is the man who is vague and made up of incoherences; it is the work that lives, breathes, suffers, and smiles nobly.

. . . .

I do not disapprove of the imaginary notation of things "not seen." Art must not be limited to the immediate data of the senses. The imagination is richer than the memory, but it is rich only in the new combinations it imposes on the elements furnished by the memory. To imagine is to associate images and fragments of images; that is not creating. Man cannot create either an atom of matter or an atom of idea. Therefore all imaginative literature, like positive literature, and like science itself, rests on reality. But it is freed from all care for absolute exactitude, remaining subject only to that relative exactitude which is general logic; and the laws of general logic are sufficiently flexible for us to admit the *Divine Comedy* or *Gulliver's Travels*. The methods of illusion of Dante and Swift are very different from those of Homer; but these great poets have nonetheless conquered the approbation and admiration of human generations.

IV. LAST WORDS

It is only in the final chapter—in fact, in the appendix—that M. Albalat approaches what ought to be the important part of his

book: "Style without rhetoric." One should come to that, and show
that there is only one style: an involuntary style, whether rich or
poor, imaged or naked. But this is not at all what M. Albalat means
by style without rhetoric; for he is thinking of Voltaire. But who, to
the contrary, is more inflated with rhetoric than Voltaire? When he
really sets his mind to something, he becomes oratorical; when he is
not witty, he is flat; and when he no longer makes you smile, he
puts you to sleep. Look at his idea of the natural: in the very letter
given to us as an example, he praises the ingenuousness of Mme de
Sévigné—that charmingly precious lady who never expresses a sentiment without embroidering it with affectations. Preciosity is not
disagreeable when it is sustained. She adorns her feelings in the
morning, as she adorns herself. She wears them as courtly attire. For
her, who delights in going to court, these precautions are not
affectations, but they certainly do not represent the natural. It is not
ingenuousness: it is merely being at one's ease. The "natural" of
Voltaire is made up of grimaces—painful when they do not amuse.
Voltaire is not simple: that is not a vice peculiar to intellectual people. The banal and vulgar man is never simple. If he were, we
would never see his banality. We see it, and therefore he affects a
stilted manner. The imbecile who writes is necessarily stilted. What
Duclos said of their acts is true of their style: "Fools who often
know what they are not, and who imagine it is only a flaw which
they should do something about, seeing the success of singularity,
take steps to become singular. . . . Having noticed or rather heard
that recognized geniuses are not always exempt from a grain of
madness, they try to imagine acts of madness, and commit stupidities." To write with images, when one does not have a visual imagination, is to play the "singular fool." It is to imitate the chamber-
maid who makes herself grotesque in her lady's cast-off clothes,
whereas, properly dressed according to her place, she could be
piquant and find herself preferred, by a man of taste, to the false
lady. Platitude and pomp are the two extreme reefs, sandy or
jagged, where those founder who are not made to play with words.
But if one has a certain intelligence, he can extricate himself, even
without a rudder, even without talent. It suffices to avoid all rhetoric, to use no word when one is not sure of its meaning—that is,
its symbolic connection with reality—to speak only of what one has
seen, heard, felt. An ingenuous fool is no longer a fool. Moreover,

sincere and true foolishness has its utility. It is the oil poured on the gears and joints of the social machine; it is the padding and packing straw. One of the most mediocre of mentalities, Eckermann, has left an immortal book, because he was content to be merely the wood shavings in a packing case containing precious porcelains.

However, M. Albalat, who is never disarmed, believes one should try to assimilate, as completely as possible, the Voltairian style. "The writer About," [9] he says in all seriousness, "sometimes earned the title of the grandson of Voltaire." Actually, he brought out the monkey that lurked in Voltaire, and it was all quite pointless. Is it a eulogy to write: "Anatole France has often written pages that are pure Renan"? To M. Albalat's mind, this is high praise, for it is one of the arguments which he believes crucial for his theory. But he is wrong to take Renan for a skeptic. The attitude of the old man spoiled by popularity cannot give a true image of the man's nature. Renan was a believer, a fanatic: a devotee of science, and more of a devotee than a true scientist.

Near the next-to-last page, we finally come upon a phrase regarding substance as opposed to form: "The substance of things has much less importance than the form. It is the manner in which one says things that makes them striking and original. Five talented painters will paint the same countryside in different ways. The material will not have changed; it is the execution that makes the difference." Here we have some fine idealism—which would be better still if conceived in terms of the painters' personalities rather than their hands. But let us leave painters aside. Whatever is worth painting is rarely worth being spoken; and vice versa, since no one has ever been able to illustrate a novel. There is less disparity between painting and poetry—at least between a certain descriptive poetry and landscapes born of passion and dream. All the same, the picture gives a synthetic impression and the poem an analytic or successive impression. It is therefore impossible to base, on relationships between such different arts, a theory as grave as one which sacrifices the substance to the form in literature. Substance is of little value in painting. That is granted, although we are not obliged to go the extreme of juxtaposing Chardin's cucumbers with Leonardo's androgynes. In literature, substance has an absolute importance.

Of the many kinds of literature none can avoid the necessity of being based on solidly cemented foundations. We will sometimes concede to the poet the right to make something out of nothing; but there are nothings and nothings. The trifles of love are nothings— but of prodigious importance, as is everything that bears upon the transmission of life. Decidedly, and in everything, it is the substance that counts. A new fact, a new idea is worth more than a beautiful sentence. A beautiful sentence is beautiful, and a beautiful flower is beautiful, but their duration is nearly the same—a day, a century. Nothing dies more quickly than a style that is not supported by the solidity of strong thought.[10] It shrivels up like a slackened hide; it falls in a heap like a rotten vine deprived of the tree it entwines. And if someone says that the vine keeps a tree with withered roots from falling down, I would agree. Style is also a force, but its value is that much more quickly diminished when it exhausts itself in preserving from annihilation the fragility which it embraces and sustains.

It is perhaps a mistake to try to distinguish form from matter. This scholastic reasoning served St. Thomas Aquinas in his discoursing on the union of soul and body. He easily proved that the form is the function of the soul and that, before or after the arrival or the departure of the soul, the embryo and the cadaver can only have illusory forms. But these distinctions are no longer valuable. There is no such thing as formless matter. Every thought has a limit, therefore a form: it only partially represents life—as true or possible, real or imaginary. Substance engenders form as the tortoise and oyster engender their shells.

The very philosophers who brought us new ideas brought them in new forms as well: Plato, Aristotle, Hobbes, Descartes, Pascal, Schopenhauer, Nietzsche are all great writers, and some of them great poets. We should distrust a philosophy entangled in the mud of scholasticism: it is bogged down because it lagged behind to set traps for the reason. The moment one believes Kant to have clean and free hands, he is setting the trap to catch the birds that he takes to Luther.

As for great scientists, almost all, from the moment they took the trouble to write, were perfect writers. These are invariably men of great visual imagination. Since they describe what one sees or will see, their words produce images: even the mathematician, the geometer, and chess-player are visuals. Linnaeus, Galileo, Leibnitz, Lavoisier, Lamarck, Gauss, Claude Bernard, and Pasteur wrote with certainty, with force. Goethe put no less literary genius into his scientific works than into his poems.

Form without substance, style without thought—what misery! This misery is miraculously realized in the prose of Banville—not to cite three or four of our illustrious contemporaries. The contrast between the supple and iridescent beauty of the robe and the corporeal skeleton has something moving about it, like a cemetery in flowers. Whatever the thought is worth, the style is worth—that is the principle.

Errors in judgment on this subject stem from the belief that there is no style when there is no "poetic style." An exception is made of Pascal, but it is only in order to enumerate his antitheses and arrange them on glossy paper like precious stones. Here we have the shadow of Montaigne. The true Pascal gives off such a light that the antithesis is drowned, invisible: as when he poses, as a principle, the error of utility, giving to the false and the true the same moderating value of human anxiety.

If nothing, in literature, lives except by its style, it is because works well thought out are always works well written. But the reverse is not true. Style alone is nothing. It even happens—since in aesthetics, as in love, everything is possible—that style, which made certain works live for a time, made others perish prematurely. Cymodocée [11] died, suffocated under her too rich and too heavy robes.

The sign of the man in the intellectual work is the thought. The thought is the man himself. Style is the thought itself.

—From *Le Problème du style,* 1902

Women and Language

The role of women in the work of civilization is so great that it would scarcely be an exaggeration to say that the structure is built on the shoulders of these frail caryatids. Women know things that have never been written or taught, and without which nearly all the matter of our daily lives would be useless. In 1814 some Cossacks, who had discovered a supply of stockings, put them on directly over their boots: a general example of our commonest acts, had woman not been, for centuries of centuries, the patient educators of childhood. This role is so natural that it seems humble. We are struck only by the extraordinary. The powerful machinery of a woolen mill overwhelms us, but who has ever observed with any emotion the simple play of two knitting needles? But compared to these slender shafts of wood, the most impressive power loom becomes nothing at all. It merely represents a particular civilization, whereas these wooden or metal needles represent absolute civilization. We must in all things distinguish the essential from the auxiliary. In civilization, the role of women represents the essential.

This is easier to feel than to prove, for it is a matter of precisely those acts which throughout life pass unnoticed—of all sorts of things which we never speak of, because we do not see them or do not grasp their importance. Thus the study of physiology was neglected for a long time, while man's curiosity was concerned with monsters. The continuous phenomenon ceases to exist for our senses. It was a city-dweller, or a prisoner, or a blind person suddenly cured, who first took note of the beauty of nature. There is an external physiology which disappears in habit. When analyzed, it reveals the most important voluntary acts of our lives—voluntary in that they are contingent compared with the primordial movements of the life of a species; voluntary, if we regard the will as conscious-ness of an unconscious effort.

Whether sense or faculty, speech cannot be logically separated from hearing, but the education of the ear is much less perceptible than that of the vocal apparatus. We can therefore consider them separately, or at least without observing a precise order in acquisi-tions which are intertwined like all the activities of life. Moving, lis-tening, seeing, speaking—all these are interrelated. Imitation imposes itself on all functions at once, though an appreciable order of birth can be established for each. That order is of small impor-tance in a study where it is a question, not of the intelligence that receives, but of the intelligence that gives—a question of the external and not the internal psychological life.

Speech is feminine. Poets and orators are feminine. Woman, be-cause she speaks as the bird sings, is alone capable of teaching the language. When a child tries to imitate the sounds he hears, the woman is there to watch him, to smile at him and encourage him. A mute contract of effort is established between these two beings, and what patience is shown by the one who knows in guiding the one who tries! The first words that a child pronounces do not corre-spond in his mind to any object or sensation. The child, at this mo-ment of his life, is a parrot, and nothing more. He imitates; he speaks because he hears others speaking. If everyone remained silent around him, speech would remain congealed in his brain. Hence the importance of a woman's chatter, an importance considerably supe-rior to that of the most beautiful poem and most profound philoso-phy. The function which makes a man a man is the particular work of woman. A child raised by a very feminine and talkative woman is formed for speech and consequently for psychological conscious-ness. Left to the care of a taciturn man, the same child would de-velop very slowly, and so slowly perhaps that he would never attain the limits of his practical intelligence.

If it were possible to assign an origin to language, we would say that it was the creation of women. But the secret of all origins will escape us eternally. Birds sing, dogs bark, men talk. It is no easier to imagine a dumb man than a dumb dog or a dumb finch. And if these species formerly existed without voices, it is not very clear why they should have acquired an organ which other animals, including birds of the south polar regions, get along very well without. If language is learned, or achieved—if, in order to discover the first rudiments, the celebrated roots, it were enough to find the common mother of Latin and Sanskrit, of Greek and Anglo-Saxon—it is hard to see why the dog does not converse with his master otherwise than with his tail, eyes, and yelps. But the dog will never talk, because the genius of an animal species is as rigorously determined as the form of crystalline species.

The notion that the most ancient language was composed of five or six hundred monosyllables corresponding to so many general ideas is an opinion of no value today, but it had its effect. It gave support to several hypotheses whose extravagance was not at first apparent. Yet nothing has ever been observed in any real language resembling an even unconscious reservoir of roots. Words are born one from another by derivation, coming into the world sometimes longer, sometimes shorter, than the first word. This derivation is always dominated by a concrete sense, real and alive. No man whose mind has not been spoiled by special studies has a sense of roots. The ba, be, bi, bo, bu of alphabets are, according to theory, so many roots; but a series of related meanings for each of these sounds has not been established. They are capable, even in the same language, of expressing all of them, either by chance or according to a logic whose laws cannot be determined.

What is primitive about speech is not the word, but the phrase. The phrase spoken by man is instinctive, like the phrase sung by the bird, the phrase yelped by the dog. The word is a product of analysis.

In order to give priority to the word over the phrase, one began with the idea that the word was created after the thing had been perceived, man acting as a nomenclator, like a professor of botany who gives names to sprigs of moss. Reality is different. A child babbles words before knowing the objects which the words designate. It is possible that man spoke—jabbered—a very long time before a fixed relationship was established in his mind between things and the familiar sounds coming from his mouth.

Thousands of tongues can thus have been jabbered successively in thousands of territories—imprecise tongues, primarily musical, a succession of phrases in which only certain sounds corresponded to realities. But these sounds, in spite of their importance, in spite of their utilitarian and representational value, may be supposed to have been at first almost as fugitive as the rest of the speech. A nonwritten language never outlives the generation that created it. Among savages, each generation remakes its language, so much so that a grandfather is a stranger among his grandchildren.

If this primitive chattering is admitted, it will also be readily admitted that the woman must have taken a large part in it, while stimulating the vitality of the males by her laughter and her attention. Woman has little capacity for verbal innovation. No woman, even among those who were nevertheless good writers, ever created a language in the sense that one says that of Ronsard, Montaigne, Chateaubriand, or Victor Hugo; but she repeats well, and often better than the man, what was said before her. Born in order to preserve, she plays her role to perfection. Eternally, untiringly, she rekindles from the dying torch a new torch identical with the old. It is in the hands of women—dancers of the ballet of life or melancholy vestals in the depths of caves—that the *lampada vitae* shines. What woman has been historically, she will always be, and as she always was, since before history began.

Certain words became fixed in primitive chatterings. This was the work of woman. Fated to pay attention because of the monotony of domestic labor,[1] she rebelled against the useless renewing of terms. Her life became complicated in those territories where game was abundant, where nature was fertile.

Men's needs grew with their wealth, and likewise women's chores. Having to work more, she had less time to listen to conversations and songs. Innovations coming in too rapid succession confused her. She corrected the language of men who, in their turn, were disconcerted. Thus were born words of common use; thus were multiplied the number of fixed sounds corresponding to realities in man's spoken song.

From the earliest times woman, whose memory is excellent, had no doubt also retained the most musical and rhythmical elements of speech—combinations of phrases similar to those melopoeias so insatiably reiterated by Negroes. Man created; woman learned by heart. If a civilized country should arrive one day at that state of mind in which every novelty is immediately welcomed and enthroned in the place of traditional ideas and mechanisms—if the past were to yield constantly to the future—then, after a period of frenzied curiosity, we would see men falling to the apathy of the tourist who never looks twice at the same thing. In order to regain possession of themselves, they would have to seek refuge in a purely animal existence, and civilization would perish. A comparable end seems to have been reached by some ancient peoples—they were so anxious to renew their pleasures that their passage through history left only hypothetical traces. It was excessive activity, far more than torpor, that led to the disintegration of many Asiatic civilizations. Wherever women were unable to intervene and oppose the influence of their passivity to the arrogance of young males, the race exhausted itself in fugitive undertakings. Therefore, we can be sure that wherever a durable civilization has been organized, woman was the cornerstone.

Standing up, like a reciter, before the creator, woman founded a repertory, a library of archives. The first notebook of songs was a woman's memory, and similarly the first collection of stories, the first bundle of documents.

However, the invention of writing came, as did all subsequent progress, to diminish the importance of woman as archivist. Everything that seemed worth remembering now being fixed by signs on durable matter, woman took on the responsibility and pleasure of keeping alive whatever men condemned to oblivion. She acquitted herself of her duty with a fidelity that matter has almost always betrayed; and thus it is that certain stories which were never written down, and which surely date from the most distant times, have come down to us. Women who had been amused by them as children, amused their own children with them in turn. In spite of the efforts of rationalist pedagogy to replace *Tom Thumb* with the history of the Revolution or the founding of the German empire, mothers still lull their good children to sleep with a tale, red or blue, of love or blood. Now it has been discovered that this oral literature, whose themes surpass in number those of written literature, was of the greatest beauty and consequently of supreme importance. We owe the almost complete salvaging of this treasure to the conservative genius of woman.

She also preserved songs, the music (and the dances that go with them) which man abandons at the moment he leaves his youth. For him they become pointless and he thinks no more about them; but for the woman they are the means of pleasing and she remembers them always; and when hope is gone, she falls back on them and relives past joys. Thus old women keep alive the youth of their hearts.

It does not appear that women played much of a part in the invention of stories and songs. They have preserved them, which is a manner of creating; but one finds, nevertheless, the mark of their minds on certain variants. Their tendency was to soften the ending of a story, to calm the exuberance of a too rollicking song. This intervention saved the lives of many small things by making them available to children, whose memories are most secure coffers.

Along with literature, women saved a whole array of notions difficult to determine. It is not a question of a long string of superstitions, but of what those superstitions, beliefs, and traditions contained in the way of practical science. In order to judge the importance of this chapter of human knowledge, one should make a sort of examination of his own consciousness; then, after long reflection, he will be able to distinguish between things learned from books and things that were never written but that everyone knows. Whatever is truly indispensable for our conduct in life has been taught us by women: little rules of politeness, those acts which invite the cordiality or deference of others, those words which assure our welcome, those attitudes which vary according to character and situation—the entire social strategy. It is by listening to women that we learn to talk to men, to insinuate ourselves into their good graces. For those alone who know how to please can teach others to please.

Even before he can talk, a child knows the value of a smile. It is his first language, and nothing proves that it is absolutely instinctive. An animal has no attitudes but those which signify a need. Some are beautiful, some are pretty, but none are voluntary. The smile of the smallest child often veils an intention. Woman has taught him the mastery of these exchanges—that, for an amiable gesture, one can acquire food and other things necessary to life. The little girl, better disposed than the boy to appreciate this teaching, knows the value of a curve of the lips and a wave of a rosy hand, and she knows it well before she knows the vocal signs which grant elementary reasoning to her tender brain. It is pure imitation on her part, but the act is favored by the memory of ends already achieved by the first attempts. And here we have a very curious and obscure example of an effect determining its cause in the physiological subconscious.

As women scarcely have anything in life except emotional relations, these primitive games remain the basis of their social tactic. Men, to the extent that they are alive, feel the need to complicate this elementary science, but it always remains their ultimate resource: to mellow one's conqueror, to please him—such is the last argument of the vanquished.

The art of the mime is the art of women. Even when silent, a woman still speaks, and often with a sincerity that her words lack. Even when motionless, she still speaks and often with greater eloquence than with words or gestures. The very conformation of her body makes a language of her breathing. The rhythm of her breast bespeaks the state of her soul and the degree of her emotion. To no other form of discourse is man more responsive. But women's eyes, though less effective, have at their disposal the broadest keyboard. With her eyes, with the various curves of her silent mouth, a woman can express the extremes of her thought. Her eyes grow dull or light up, her gaze rises or lowers, and we have desire or disdain, spite or promise—so many pages that a man understands from the moment he is interested in reading them. To these glimmers and movements, the play of eyelids adds its value—affirmative, negative, interrogative. It proffers a short and decisive yes, or a languorous and abandoned yes. It questions the tone of anger or complaint. It refuses by an abrupt closing of the pupil, which veils the eyes without closing them. But there are so many other nuances! And how rich in words is the smile as well! The whole woman speaks. She is language itself.

Her children will first of all be mimes. Like their mother, they will first learn to speak with everything that is silent—a precious acquisition. Darwin found the initial outlines of emotional expression among animals. There is an important element of instinct in human mimicry. Woman has cultivated these primitive movements; she has changed the nuances and has multiplied them. Signs of false emotions have come to join the true, and only then has language been created. An animal's expression of emotion is not a language, for they do not know how to feign. True language begins with the lie. There is a sense of reality in the famous saying:

language has been given to man that he may disguise his thought. The lie, which is the sole external proof of psychological consciousness, is also the sole proof that gestures are a language and not an unconscious mimicry. The lie is the very basis of language and the absolute condition of its being. Analysis of linguistic facts demonstrates this well enough, since every word contains a metaphor and every metaphor is a displacement of reality, when it is not an intentional and premeditated lie. But taking language such as it appears to be, and supposing that each word corresponds to an object, it may be said that if there existed a man who had never lied, then that man had never spoken. It is not speaking, in fact, to say "I am afraid" or "I am cold," when one is afraid or cold. It is expressing an emotion or a sensation by means of verbal signs, and is analogous to the trembling of an animal paralyzed with fear or hunger. But if, on the contrary, a man denies his emotion or sensation and says "I am warm" when he is cold and "I am not hungry" when he is hungry, then he is speaking. Whether he employ words, gestures, or written signs, it is by this, the lie—that is, by consciousness—that man is recognized. The word lie—in order that there be no misunderstanding—takes here the meaning: expression of an imaginary sensation. It is a matter of psychology and not of morality—two separate domains.

If woman is language, then she must be lie, and also consciousness. All three hang together and are of a piece. The first of these points has not been studied, but popular opinion is favorable to it. Not only do women speak more readily than men, but they use a better syntax and a less haphazard vocabulary. They pronounce well: one feels that language is their element. The second point, the lie, is not disputed; but it is considered a crime on women's part although it is the result of another gift and, moreover, an affirmation of their wit. Women lie more than men—it is then that they have a greater feeling of independence, a livelier consciousness. And so we arrive at the third point without, it seems, need of a detailed demonstration.

The hysterical lie has been spoken of. Here we probably have an abuse, not of the terms used, but of the intention that brings them together. If one means an unconscious lie, that is an absurdity. The lie is, to the contrary, the very sign of consciousness, and there can be a lie only where there is full and active consciousness. We must not confuse a deranged sensation expressed just as it has been felt with an intentional misrepresentation of a true sensation—or confuse the first term with the last. An animal never lies. How could it? It is obliged to express its sensation just as it experiences it. If it wants to bite, the dog curves his lips, shows his teeth. If you see it restrain itself, play the hypocrite, lie, it is because, through contact with man, it has probably acquired the rudiments of consciousness; it is because the training he has received finds itself, at that moment, in conflict with his instinct. Moreover, the ruse, especially when applied to self-defense or the search for food, is quite a different thing from the lie. It is an intensified form of prudence. The true lie has no purpose, no utility, except to assert a superior detachment. It seems like a denial of the ties that bind man to reality, and it is the means by which he approaches poetry and art, of which it is one of the elements.

Art is born, like the lie, of a lively awareness of sensations and emotions. It asserts a state of extreme sensibility, accompanied by a tendency to deny that reality which wounds man's senses. Art, whatever its form, implies a profound knowledge of signs and the will to transpose them without reference to their usual concordances. An artist is one who lies in a superior fashion, better than other men. If he lies with words, he is a poet; if with nonarticulated sound, he is a musician; if with forms whose attitudes he shapes, he is a sculptor, and his art is nothing but the extreme development of the language of gestures (which the dancer embodies in a very fugitive state); if with lines and colors, he is a painter, and what does he do but restore to the hieroglyphs of primitive writing their true aspect and all their natural scope? Art is a language, and it is only that.

But if woman is language, how does it happen that women are so poorly represented in the supreme activity of language? Critics, to flatter them, have alleged some sort of lateral heredity whereby it is demonstrated that, as they are daughters of mothers who are less and less cultivated, going back through the centuries, it is not surprising that their aptitudes are inferior to those of the male. This is not to be taken seriously, for if it is true that genius and talent are often directly related to early cultures, there are also sudden aptitudes developed by the immediate environment. Why should a girl not find that aptitude in her flesh as well as her brother? Moreover, consider the thousands of years that we have learned music from women, and yet it is in that realm that they have perhaps created the least. The cause lies deeper still. Woman is language—but useful language. Her role is not to create, but to conserve, and there she has performed admirably. She creates neither poems or statues, but she creates the creators of poems and statues. She teaches them the language which is the condition of their science, the lie which is the condition of their art, the consciousness which bestows genius. When the child, around the age of six or seven, leaves the hands of the woman, the man is made. He speaks, and that is man in his entirety.

The great intellectual work of woman is the teaching of language. Grammarians and their surrogates, schoolteachers and professors, imagine themselves to be the masters of language and that, without their intervention, the language of men would perish in confusion and incoherence. They have been supported for centuries in this illusion, yet there is none more ridiculous. Women are the elementary workers and poets the advanced workers of language, both of them unconscious of their role. The intervention of the grammarian is almost always harmful, unless it confines itself to a statement of facts—unless it has the courage to restore to the hands of women and poets an influence which science could exert only with injustice. Consider children who can talk: they go off to school to have a lesson in grammar. They speak and use all the forms of the verb and all shadings of syntax easily and correctly. They speak; but here is the school, and the master triumphantly teaches them what the imperfect of the subjunctive is. For a function, the pedagogue has substituted a notion. He has replaced the gesture with consciousness of the gesture, the word with its definition. He teaches grammar; he does not teach language.

Language is a function. Grammar is the analysis of that function. A knowledge of grammar is as useless for speaking one's native tongue as a knowledge of physiology is for breathing with one's lungs or walking with one's legs. Compared to the role of the ignorant mother who plucks like a flower the first word blossoming on her child's lips, the role of the teacher is almost nil. The mother herself has sown the newly blossomed word, for, if language is a function, it must be given the material on which to work. A woman's idle chatter, differing so slightly from that of a little girl talking to

her doll, is the child's first lesson, and one whose importance surpasses all others. So many words, so many seeds that are going to
germinate, sprout, and bear fruit in the young mind. Without this
ceaseless, random sowing, the child's linguistic functioning would
remain inert, and only vague and perhaps inarticulate sounds would
emerge from his lips. It has sometimes been wondered what language would be spoken by children raised together outside the
range of the human voice. They would probably not speak any. It is
a question no one can answer. In any event, they would speak only a
rudimentary language—that is to say, too rich, variable, and entirely
unknown—for there are no innate roots any more than there are
innate ideas. The child does not create his language, and still less
does he secrete it. He learns it. He speaks according to how people
speak around his cradle. He is a phonograph and is, at first, as mechanical as the instrument itself. Before he is able to situate vocal
signs with reference to objects, he possesses them in great number,
but in confusion, "helter-skelter." Later he will learn to use this
richness. Since he knows the words on the one hand, and the objects
on the other, the operation which will bring them together in his
memory will be most easy and natural for him. The woman happily
directs this apportionment, and she admires herself in admiring the
progress of her child. She believes that this double acquisition of
word and object is made exclusively at her command, and she takes
pride in it. Thus, ignorance of the psychological mechanism of the
child assures the success of the teacher.

   Later, as poet, storyteller, philosopher, theologian, or moralist
—as a creator of values, to use Nietzsche's powerful expression—the
child will gladly use, in her honor, the language that he learned almost entirely from woman. The greater part of literature is the indirect work of woman, made for her, to please or provoke her, to exalt
or denigrate her, to touch her heart, to idealize or curse her beauty
and her love. It was essential that the two sexes be so profoundly
dissimilar, so foreign, so opposite, in order that one might become
the idolizer of the other. With equality of tastes, needs, and desires,
the bodily differences might not have sufficed nor the injunction of
the species. Humanity could perpetuate itself without love [2] but love
might have been impossible without the radical divergences which
render man and woman two mutually incomprehensible worlds.
We can only adore the unknown. There is no religion where there

is no mystery. In all societies, woman, so long as she is young and beautiful, is, even as slave, the mistress of the civilization. Poets, whom her grace has inspired, enhance that supremacy by making her the object of their songs; and poetry, which wished primarily to speak only of the joys of possession or the pangs of desire, achieves its own evolution in creating love. For love, with all that the word contains of sentiment, passion, dreams, happiness, and tears, is essentially a verbal creation and the very work of the imagination of the artists of language.

It is through poems, stories, traditional narratives, that the ordinary man, inclined only to his own enjoyment, has learned to love, to enhance infinitely his mediocre joys and futile sufferings. To repeat Nietzsche's words: the poet was the creator of emotional values. But almost as soon as they were created, they escaped him. Taking possession of these new values, woman transformed them into instruments of sovereignty. She has, in all simplicity, culled the fruits of language, her own work.

How love evolved under this domination, along with all the benefits which have accrued from it, would be a long chapter in the history of civilization.

Note.—Philosophical deductions are valuable only if they are in exact agreement with science; by then they do have a value. I will therefore take advantage of an opportunity to complete a previous note regarding the lie considered as a vital reaction. Here is the scientific statement of the question:

M. R. Quinton has been led, in the course of his investigations, to recognize that all living creatures are divided into two great physiological groups, which correspond exactly to the two anatomical groups: *Invertebrates* and *Vertebrates*. Members of the first and lower group (Invertebrates) are always in equilibrium with the environment, submitting to all external conditions, however unfavorable they might be. The second and higher (Vertebrates), not accepting these conditions, reacting against them, are always in disequilibrium with the environment, maintaining internally the saline concentration of their origins, in opposition to the seas which become increasingly concentrated or to fresh water which loses its salt, and so maintaining the temperature of their origins in opposition to the terrestrial environment which grows colder, *lying to the environment,* in short, in order to maintain the most favorable conditions for living. The lie of which we speak is only the psychological form of that reaction of the *Vertebrate* to the hostility of the environment.

The obscure terms of this note (saline concentration, temperature of the origins) are explained in M. Quinton's book, *L'Eau de mer, milieu organique.*

—From Le Chemin de velours, 1901

Subconscious Creation[1]

Certain men possess a special gift which distinguishes them in a striking fashion from their fellows. Whether they be discus-throwers or generals, poets or clowns, sculptors or financiers, the moment they rise above the common level they demand the observer's particular attention. The predominance of one of their faculties singles them out for analysis, and for that analytical method which consists in successive differentiation. Thus we come to discern in mankind a class whose distinguishing trait is difference, just as, for common humanity, this trait is resemblance. We never know what some men are going to say when they begin to speak. There are few of these. We know what the others are going to say the moment they open their mouths. It is alleged that there are also noticeable disparities among members of this class, for it is undeniable that, even among those who most resemble each other at first sight, there are not two creatures which, at bottom, are not contradictory. It is the ultimate glory of man, and one which science has not been able to deprive him of, that there exists no true science of man.

If there is no science of the common man, still less is there a science of the different man, since the manifestation of his difference renders him solitary and unique, that is to say, incomparable. Yet, just as there is a general physiology, so there is a general psychology also. All beasts of the earth, whatever their nature, breathe the same air, and the brain of the man of genius, like that of the ordinary specimen, derives its primordial form from sensation. We have only a rough idea by what mechanism sensation is transformed into action. We only know that, for that transformation to take place, the intervention of the consciousness is not necessary. We also know that this intervention can be harmful—that it can, through its power to modify the deterministic logic, break the series of associations in order to create in the mind, and of its own volition, the first link of a new chain.

Consciousness, which is the principle of liberty, is not the principle of art. It is possible to express quite clearly what has been conceived in the unconscious shadows. Far from being tied to the functioning of the consciousness, intellectual activity is most often disturbed by it. We listen badly to a symphony when we know we are listening to it. We think badly when we know we are thinking: consciousness of thinking is not thought.

The subconscious state is the state of automatic cerebration in complete freedom, while intellectual activity operates at the extreme limits of consciousness, a little below it and beyond its reach. Subconscious thought may remain forever unknown, or it may, either at the precise moment when automatism ceases, or later, even after several years, rise suddenly into the light. These facts of cogitation do not belong, then, to the realm of the subconscious properly speaking, since they can become conscious. Besides, it will doubtless be preferable to reserve for this rather vast term the meaning given it by a particular philosophy. The subconscious state differs also from the state of dreams, though dreams may be one of its manifestations. A dream is almost always absurd, with a special kind of absurdity, and is incoherent or orderly according to its associations which are entirely passive,[2] and whose procession differs even from that of ordinary passive associations, conscious or unconscious.[3]

Imaginative intellectual creation is inseparable from the frequency of the subconscious state; and in this category of creations must be included the discovery of the scientist and the ideological construction of the philosopher. All who have invented or discovered something new, in any field whatsoever, have imaginative as well as observant minds. The most thoughtful, most deliberate, most painstaking of writers is at every moment, in spite of himself, enriched by the work of his subconscious. No work is so completely a product of the will that it does not owe some beauty or novelty to the subconscious. Perhaps no phrase, not even the most labored, was ever written or spoken in absolute accord with the will. The search for the right word in the vast and deep reservoir of the verbal memory is itself an act which escapes so completely from the control of the will that very often the word on its way flees at the very moment when consciousness is about to perceive and grasp it. We know how hard it is to find, at will, the very word we need, and we also know with what ease and speed certain writers evoke, in the heat of composition, the most unexpected or appropriate words.

It is, however, imprudent to say: "Memory is always unconscious." [4] Memory is a secret pool where, unknown to us, the subconscious casts its net. But consciousness fishes there just as readily. This pond, full of fish captured at random by sensation, is especially well known by the subconscious. Consciousness is less skillful at provisioning itself from this source, even though it has at its service several useful methods, such as the logical association of ideas and the localization of images. According to whether the brain works in the darkness or by the lamplight of consciousness, man develops a different personality; but, except for pathological cases, the second state is not so precise and well defined that the first cannot intervene without disturbing the operation. It is under these circumstances, and in accordance with this concerted effort, that most works, whether first conceived by the will or by the dream faculty, are accomplished.

In Newton's case (as a result of constant attention) the work of the subconscious is continuous, but connects itself periodically with voluntary activity. Now conscious, now unconscious, his thought explores all possibilities. In the case of Goethe, the subconscious is nearly always active and ready to deliver to the will the multiple works which it elaborates without its aid and at a distance from it. Goethe himself has explained this process in a miraculously lucid and instructive passage: [5]

> Every faculty of action, and consequently every talent, implies an instinctive force at work unconsciously and in ignorance of the rules whose principle is, however, implicit. The sooner a man becomes educated, the sooner he learns that there is a technique, an art, which will furnish him the means of achieving the regular development of his natural faculties. What he acquires would never be able to damage, in any way, his original individuality. The supreme genius is he who assimilates and appropriates everything without prejudice to his innate character. Here we are confronted

with the diverse relations between consciousness and unconsciousness. Through an effort of exercise, of apprenticeship, of persistent and continuous reflection, through results obtained, whether good or bad, through the movements of attraction and resistance, these organs amalgamate, combine unconsciously what is instinctive and what is acquired; and from this amalgam, from this chemistry that is at once unconscious and conscious, there finally emerges a harmonious whole which dazzles the world. It is nearly sixty years since the conception of Faust came to me, in the full flush of my youth, perfectly clear and distinct, all the scenes unrolling before my eyes in their proper order of succession. From that day the plan never left me, and living with it in mind, I took it up in detail and composed, one after the other, those segments which, at the moment, interested me most, with the result that, when this interest failed me, there appeared some gaps, as in the second part. The difficulty, at such times, was to obtain by force of will what could not be obtained, to tell the truth, except by a spontaneous act of nature.

It also happens the other way around—a work which is conceived in advance and whose composition is deferred, may end by imposing itself upon the will. The subconscious then seems to overflow and submerge the consciousness, dictating things written only with repugnance. This is the obsession which nothing can discourage and which triumphs over even the most lackadaisical indolence, the most violent aversion. Later, once the work is completed, one frequently experiences a sort of satisfaction, analogous to moral satisfaction. The idea of duty which, poorly understood, wreaks so much havoc in timorous consciences, is no doubt an elaboration of the subconscious. Obsession is perhaps the force which impels to sacrifice, as it is the one that impels to suicide.

Schopenhauer used to compare the obscure and continuous toil of the subconscious, in the midst of impressions imprisoned in the memory, to rumination. This rumination, which is purely physiological, may suffice to modify convictions or beliefs. Hartmann found that a hostile idea, at first pushed aside, succeeded, after a certain time, in supplanting in his mind the idea which he customarily entertained of a man or a fact.

If, after days, weeks, or months have passed, you have the desire or occasion to express your opinion on the same subject, you will discover, to your great astonishment, that you have undergone a veritable mental revolution—that your former opinions, which you had previously accepted as convincing, have been completely abandoned, and that new ideas have been implanted in their place. I have often observed this unconscious process of mental digestion and assimilation in my own experience; and instinctively I have always refrained from disturbing its course with a premature reflection, whenever it involved important questions bearing on my conceptions of the world and the mind.[6]

This observation might be extended to the exceedingly interesting problem of religious conversion. There is no doubt that people have suddenly felt themselves brought, or brought back, to religious ideas, when they had neither the desire, nor the fear, nor the hope for this sudden development. In conversion the will can act only after a long effort on the part of the subconscious and when all the elements of the new conviction have been secretly assembled and combined. This new force, which supports the convert, and whose origin is unknown to him, is what theology calls grace. Grace is the result of a subconscious effort. Grace is subconscious.

Alfred de Vigny—only instinctively and not, in his case, by philosophic preconception—entrusted the maturing of his ideas to his subconscious. When they were fully ripe, he recovered them. They came back to him of their own accord, rich with the results of their incubation. We can suppose that, like Goethe, he was essentially a subconscious person whose bills were payable only in long terms, for Vigny allowed exceedingly long intervals between his produced works. It is very probable that, if there are individuals in whom the subconscious is inactive, there are others in whom, after an active period, it suddenly ceases to work, either because of premature exhaustion, or because of a modification of relations in the brain cells. Racine offers the singular example of a twenty years' silence broken just halfway by two works which have only a formal resemblance to those of his earlier period. Can it be supposed that it was through religious scruple that he so long refused to listen to the suggestions of his subconscious? Can it be supposed that religion, which had modified the nature of his perception, had, at the same time, diminished the physiological power of his brain? Such a supposition would run counter to all other observations, which demonstrate, on the contrary, that a new belief is a new stimulant. It seems probable, then, that Racine fell silent because he had almost nothing more to say. It is a common experience, and he found in religion the common consolation.

A distinction should be made, then, between two kinds of subconscious: one whose energy is short-lived and strong, and one whose force is less ardent but more sustained. The two extremes are exemplified in the man who produces a remarkable work in his youth, then ceases; and by the man who offers for sixty years the spectacle of a mediocre, useless, and continuous labor. I am referring, naturally, to those works in which the imaginative intelligence plays the major part—works in which the subconscious is always the master collaborator.

More practically, and from a totally different point of view, M. Chabaneix, having studied the continuous subconscious, divided it into nocturnal and waking subconscious. If the former is a question of sleep or of the moments that precede sleep, it is oneiric or preoneiric.[7] Maury, who was particularly afflicted by the hallucinations which are formed the moment the eyes are closed in sleep, has given them careful consideration. It is not apparent that these hallucinations, called hypnagogic, and almost always visual, can have any special effect on the ideas working in one's brain. They are the embryos of dreams which can influence the course of thought only in the manner of dreams. It happens, at times, that the conscious effort of the brain is prolonged during the dream, even reaching a conclusion there, and that, on awakening, the dreamer finds himself, without reflection or struggle, master of a problem, or a poem, or a combination, which had escaped him the evening before. Burdach, a Koenigsberg professor, made, in his dreams, several physiological discoveries which he was afterwards able to verify. A dream was sometimes the point of departure of an undertaking; sometimes a work was entirely conceived and executed during sleep. It is highly probable, however, that it is the conscious reason which, at the moment of waking, judges and rectifies the dream spontaneously, gives it its true value, and divests it of that incoherence peculiar to even the most rational dreams.

During the waking state, inspiration seems the clearest manifestation of the subconscious in the domain of intellectual creation. In its most extreme form, it seems very close to somnambulism. Certain attitudes of Socrates (according to Aulus Gellius), of Diderot, Blake, Shelley, and Balzac, give force to this opinion. Dr. Régis [8] says that almost all men of genius have been "waking sleepers"; but the waking sleeper is rather frequently an "absent-minded" person —one whose mind becomes concentrated upon a single problem. Thus, both excess and absence of psychological consciousness would manifest themselves, in certain cases, by identical phenomena. What did Socrates think about during his days of inactivity? Did he think? Was he conscious of his thought? Do fakirs think? And did Beethoven, when, hatless and coatless, he let himself be arrested as a vagrant? Was he in a state of voluntary obsession or quasi-somnambulism? Did he know what he was pondering so deeply, or was his cerebral activity indeed unconscious? John Stuart Mill composed his work on logic in the streets of London, as he made his daily trip from his house to the offices of the India Company. Is it possible to believe that this work was not planned in a state of perfect consciousness? What was subconscious in Mill, says M. Chabaneix, was the effort of finding his way along the crowded street. "It was a case of automatism of the inferior centers." This reversal of terms—more frequent than certain psychologists have believed—can give rise to doubts about the true nature of inspiration. One ought at least to try to discover whether, from the moment when the realization—even when purely cerebral—of a work begins, it is possible for the effort to remain entirely subconscious. Mozart's letter explains only Mozart:

> When I feel well and am in a good humor, whether riding in a carriage or taking a walk after a good dinner, or during the night when I cannot sleep, thoughts come to me very easily and in vast numbers. Where do they come from, and by what means? I know nothing about it, and I have nothing to do with it. Those which please me, I keep in my head and hum—at least, so others have told me. Once I have my tune, another soon comes to join it. The work grows, I hear it continually, more and more distinctly, until finally the composition is entirely completed in my head, however long it may be. . . . All this takes place in me as

in a beautiful and very distinct dream. . . . If I then begin
to write, I have only to draw from the sack of my brain
what has previously accumulated there, as I have indicated.
Thus, in almost no time at all the whole thing is put on
paper. Everything is already perfectly arranged, and it is
rare that my score differs very much from what I had in
my head beforehand. It does not bother me if I am disturbed while writing. . . .[9]

With Mozart, then, the whole process is subconscious, and the
material labor of execution is hardly more than a job of copying. I
have seen a writer reluctant to correct his spontaneous production,
for fear of marring the tone. He was aware that the state in which
he corrected would be quite different from the one in which he had
written, and in which he had, at the same time, conceived his work.
A word overheard, an attitude glimpsed, an unusual person passed
in the street, was often the sole source for his stories, which he im-
provised in three or four hours. If he tried to follow a preconceived
plan, he almost always abandoned it after the first page, and finished his story according to a new logic, arriving at a conclusion entirely different from the one which had initially seemed best to him.
Some of these plans had been drafted under so strong a subconscious influence that later he no longer understood them; he recognized them only by the writing, and was able to determine where
they belonged in his past only by the kind of paper used, and by the
color of the ink. Other projects, on the other hand, associated with
longer works, recurred frequently. He was conscious of thinking of
them several times a day, and was convinced that it was these
reveries, even when vague and inconsistent, that made the work of
execution relatively easy. In fact, I never saw him seriously preoccu-
pied with works which were, nevertheless, supposed to have resulted
from rather laborious effort. He never spoke of them, and I really
believe that he never thought of them consciously except at the moment of writing the terrible first lines; but, once the work was
under way, almost all his intellectual life was concentrated on it,
with periods of subconscious rumination joining perpetually with
periods of voluntary meditation.

Villiers de l'Isle-Adam, as far as I am able to gather, used this
method of work. Once an idea had entered his mind—and it some-

times entered suddenly, usually in the course of a conversation, for he was a great talker and profited from everything—this idea, which had come in timidly, making no noise, through the side door, soon made itself quite at home, and invaded all the reserve spaces of the subconscious. Then, from time to time, it rose to the conscious level and actually obliged Villiers to obey it, obsessively. At such time, no matter who shared his conversation, he talked. He talked even when he was alone. Indeed, when he talked of his idea, he talked as if he were alone. Thus I heard, in fragments, several of his last stories, and one day when we were seated in the terrace of a boulevard café, I had the impression that I was listening to some truly incoherent maunderings in which this assertion cropped up periodically: "There was a cock! There was one!" I did not understand until much later, after several months, when *Le Chant du coq* appeared. He spoke in a low tone, without addressing me. Yet his conscious aim, in turning over his ideas aloud, was to try to guess the effect those ideas would have on a listener. But this aim became gradually obscured: it was the subconscious that was speaking for him. He worked slowly. There are five or six superimposed manuscripts of *L'Eve future,* and the first is so different from the last that only the name of Edison can serve to link them all together. It is rather often observed that, if a man has written little, he has done little work; but I am persuaded that Villiers de l'Isle Adam never ceased working for an instant, not even when asleep. In spite of the often absolute blockade that his ideas established around his attention, no mind ever worked more rapidly or was more talented at the sharp retort. He knew nothing of that twilight time of awakening, for, after the briefest night's sleep, he found himself, at a bound, in full possession of all his lucidity and verve. Though he was undoubtedly the man of his books, one could find in him the outlines of a double personality, in which the conscious and unconscious so overlapped that it would be difficult to disentangle them. It would be easy, on the other hand, to write two lives of Mozart—one on the social man, the other on the man in his second state, both perfectly legitimate.

Baudelaire used to say, "Inspiration means working every day." But this aphorism does not appear to sum up his personal experience. Work that is daily and regular is, so to speak, inspiration that is regularized, domesticated, enslaved. These terms are not contradictory, for it is certain that the second state, by becoming periodic, can only become more profound. Habit, so powerful, joins with nature to reinforce a psychological state which then becomes a veritable necessity. Anyone who departs from a daily labor to which he is accustomed and especially when he remains in the same locale, experiences, during and after the regular working hours, a certain uneasiness, sometimes a real suffering. Remorse, perhaps, has no other origin, whether it is a question of some habitual act which has not been performed, or of some unaccustomed act which has violently upset the customary march of days.

Inspiration, if it is a second state, can therefore be a second state provoked by the will. There is no doubt that artists, writers, and scientists can work whenever it is necessary, without preparation, prodded only by necessity, and that, on the other hand, works thus produced are quite as good as those whose execution has been determined only by a desire for realization. This does not mean that the subconscious has remained inactive during the effort initiated by the will, but that its activity has been provoked. There is, then, a subconscious state which is not spontaneous, which comes to mingle with the consciousness when the will has need of it, but which, little by little, in the course of some active effort, takes the place of the will. Often, one has only to set about his task, in order to feel all the difficulties that paralyze effort vanish one by one, but perhaps this reasoning is paralogical, and the work has become possible precisely and only because of the preliminary dwindling away of the obstacles which had confronted the mind in the first place. In either case, however, there is evident intervention of the subconscious forces.

How does a sensation become an image, the image an idea? How does the idea develop? How does it take the form which seems to us the best? How, in the process of writing, are contributions raised from the verbal memory? These are all questions which seem to me insoluble but whose solutions would be nevertheless necessary to whoever would wish to give a precise definition of inspiration. "For original creation," writes M. Ribot,[10] "neither reflection nor will-power can take the place of inspiration." No doubt, but reflection and will can yet play their role in the evolution of that mysterious phenomenon, and, on the other hand, cases of pure intellectual automatism are rather rare. It must doubtless be supposed that men capable of experiencing the happy influence of inspiration are also the men who, more than others, are capable of feeling forcefully and frequently the impact of the exterior world. Imaginative men are also the sensitive ones. The resources of their brains must be rich in elements. This supposes a constant supply of sensations, along with a very lively sensibility and an incessantly renewed capacity for feeling. This sensibility still belongs in large part to the domain of the subconscious. There are, as Leibnitz expresses it, "thoughts which our soul does not perceive." There are also sensations which our senses do not perceive, and it is perhaps these sensations which leave our brain as they entered it—subconsciously. The most fruitful observations are those which we have made without knowing it. To live without thinking about life is often the best way to learn to know life. After a half-century and more a man sees the surroundings, the landscape, the deeds of his indifferent childhood rise up before him. As a child, he had dwelt in the external as in an extension of himself, with a purely physiological concern. He had seen without seeing, and nevertheless, while the intermediate distance remains wrapped in mist, it is the period of his most fugitive sensations that returns and lives vividly before his eyes. It is quite evident that the sensation which reaches us without our being aware of it cannot, at any given moment, be voluntarily evoked; but conscious sensation can, on the contrary, return to us unexpectedly, with no assistance from the will. The subconscious, then, holds sway over two orders of sensation, whereas the consciousness has only one at its disposition. This can explain why reflection and will play such a restricted part in the creation of literature and art.

But what is their role in the rest of life?

In principle, man is an automaton, and it appears that in man consciousness is an acquisition, an added faculty. Let us not be deceived: the man who walks, who acts, who speaks is not necessarily conscious nor ever entirely conscious. Consciousness is, without a doubt—if we take the word in its absolute and precise sense—the prerogative of the very few. Gathered in a crowd, men become especially automatic. In the first place, their instinct to gather together, to do the same thing at a given moment, attests to the nature of their intelligence. How can we suppose consciousness and will to exist in the members of those mobs which, on days of festivals or troubles, all rush to the same point, with the same gestures and same cries? They are ants which come out from under blades of grass after a heavy rainfall, and nothing more. The conscious man who mingles naively in the crowd, who moves along in the direction of the crowd, loses his personality. He is nothing more than one of the suckers on the great artificial octopus, and nearly all sensations die away in the collective brain of the hypothetical animal. From this contact he will bring back practically nothing. The man who emerges from the mob, like a man saved from drowning, has only one recollection—that of having fallen into the water.

It is among the small number of the conscious elite that must be sought the truly superior examples of a humanity of which they are, not the leaders—that would be unfortunate and too contradictory to instinct—but the judges. However—and this is a grave subject for meditation—these elevated individuals do not achieve their entire value except at moments when consciousness, becoming subconscious, opens the locks of the brain and lets the renewed floods of sensation, derived from the world, flow back into that world. They are magnificent instruments on which the subconscious alone plays with genius. The genius, too, is subconscious. Goethe is an example of this dual man and the supreme hero of intellectual humanity.

There are men, no less rare, but less complete, in whom the will plays only a very ordinary role and who are nothing the moment that they are no longer under the influence of the subconscious. Their genius is often only the purer and more energetic because of this. They are more docile instruments under the breath of the unknown God. But, like Mozart, they do not know what they do—they obey an irresistible force. That is why Gluck had his piano moved out into the middle of a meadow, in full sunlight. That is why Haydn gazed at a ring, why Crébillon lived amidst a pack of dogs, why Schiller frequently inhaled the odor of rotten apples with which he had filled the drawer of his worktable. Such are the most innocuous fantasies of the subconscious. It can make worse demands.

—From *La Culture des idées,* 1900

The Roots of Idealism

Since writing, in *Physique de l'amour,* the chapter on "The Tyranny of the Nervous System," with its criticism of Lamarck's saying, "the environment creates the organ," I have come to have some doubts about the legitimacy of my ideas. I am going to state them without definitely taking sides either against myself or against subjective idealism, to which in the last analysis I remain in large part faithful.

Idealism is today the reigning doctrine in philosophy. It was bound to be sooner or later, after experiencing a period of ridicule, for reasoning leads invincibly to it.

We know that there are two idealisms. It is advisable, whenever using the word in any context which, then, is not purely philosophical, to define it. There are two idealisms, both qualified by words which appear identical, but which differ in meaning, for one derives from *ideal,* and the other from *idea.* One is the expression of a moral or religious state of mind. It is almost synonymous with spiritualism, and it is this term that M. Brunetière uses when that hardhearted man sentimentalizes on the subject of "the renaissance of idealism." There exists a certain *Revue Idéaliste,* marked by a serene religiosity, which belongs to the same clan, and in which it would be futile to seek enlightenment on Berkeley's doctrine.

The other idealism, which it would have been better to call "ideaism," and which Nietzsche has carried to the point of phenomenalism, is a philosophical conception of the world. Schopenhauer, who did not invent it, has given it the best formulation: the world is my representation—that is, the world is such as it appears to me. If it has a real existence in itself, it is inaccessible to me. It is what I see it, or feel it, to be.

Schopenhauer's formula stands up under every criticism. It is irrefutable. The doctrine which derives from it, if attacked directly, appears as an impregnable fortress: every reasoning blunts itself, impotently, against it. It is marvellous in that it is valid for the sensation, for the sentiment, as well as for the idea. It would be possible, if one so inclined, to found on it a theory of intelligence, like Taine's, as well as a theory of sensibility—something which has not yet been done. The commonplace statement to the effect that the same painful event does not affect with the same intensity two persons which it strikes with the same external force—that is idealism. The chapter on the subject of tastes and color (in which Nietzsche found so much amusement)—that, too, is idealism. Whenever we study life—facts, mentalities, physiologies, sensibilities—in order to discover, not resemblances, but differences, we are indulging in idealism. From the moment there is life, there is idealism. That is, there are, according to species or even to individuals, different ways of reacting to either internal or external sensation. Everything is only representation, for a bird as for a man, for a crab as for a cuttlefish. Reality is relative. A woman, even a nervous man, can suffer intensely, perhaps lose consciousness, by imagining the amputation of a leg, the scraping of the bones—but hardened soldiers have undergone such amputations without flinching. We must not suppose that civilizations which permitted torture, or those in which it is still countenanced, have any special tastes for cruelty. The refinements which the Chinese brought to physical torments were nothing more than clear evidence of insensibility. What makes a European suffer makes a yellow man smile. But there are, among men of the same social group, many degrees of sensibility. Pain, like pleasure, is a representation. The formula has been extended to groups: a group of people is what it believes itself to be, very much more than what it actually is. Most social ailments are merely collective representations.

But it is difficult to explain idealism by examining the facts of sensibility. They are too well known, too generally admitted to support a philosophical construction. It requires a more extraordinary and less easily understood point of departure. The phenomenon of vision generally serves here—it seems simple, but when analyzed, it is highly mysterious.

Seeing is the most natural thing in the world. Yet, what do we see when we see a tree? A tree, to be sure, but not the tree itself. What comes to us, as an object perceived, is not the tree in the state of a tree, but the tree in the state of an image. What is the image worth? Is it exact?

It may be supposed so, since it is obviously the same for the various persons who perceive it and since divergences of appreciation appear only when judgments of sentiment or interest come into play. This supposed exactitude is, in any case, strongly relative. An image is an image, a photograph, and it differs from the reality-tree (pure hypothesis) as much as a round, long, branching, leafy object differs from a graphic representation, without thickness. It is true that tactile sensation, or the memory of it, comes to our aid, adding to the tenuousness of the visual image the idea of consistency, or resistance, without which we would find it most difficult to conceive of matter. We can then—and thanks also to our observation of the opposing play of light and shade—give this vain image its true position in space.

But however complete and concordant the actions of our senses might be when it comes to knowing an object—and even when, as in sexual love, the six senses, including the genital sense, come into play simultaneously—it is nonetheless true that the object known remains exterior to ourselves. Moreover, the qualification "known" is not very appropriate to the object perceived, since it has an interior face, inaccessible at first contact with our senses. If we are dealing with a living being—and especially if this being is intelligent and complex—we must exercise all sorts of faculties and devote ourselves to minute analyses in order to arrive at nothing more than a near-illusory familiarity.

Knowledge ends, then, in a certain bankruptcy. From this stage to that of proclaiming the uselessness of the external world as a means of explaining the nature of knowledge itself, is not very far. It is only a step from uselessness to unreality. Idealist philosophers who carry their theories to extremes can say without paradox that everything occurs in vision, for example, as if the object did not exist—as if intelligence, while believing that it receives aid from the eye, actually creates the object to the extent that it wishes to know it. The phenomenon of hallucinations gives an appearance of reason to these exasperated idealists. Did not Taine, who was not exasperated, call sensation a true hallucination? But why true? Here we have a word which, under the circumstances, it is difficult to justify. It would be more just to say that hereditary habit inclines us to regard certain sensations as true, certain others as false. Perhaps utility serves us also as guide, and we imagine, in order to reassure ourselves, an external and fallacious world whose operations correspond to the movements of our physiology.

II

There is another way of knowing, at once more elementary, more intimate, more uncertain. This is absorption. The elements of our nourishment, in proportion as we "know" them, disintegrate, yield their solid parts to our organism, the rest being rejected in a form equally unknowable. If we deny, as we should, the primitive distinction between soul and body, if we admit only the body and believe everything to be physical, then this way of knowing should be studied parallel with those ways which spring from each of our various senses or from their collaboration. It is certain that absorption has taught men in all ages. It is by this, and not by virtue of some unknown instinct, that man has been able to separate vegetables and animals into good and bad, into useful, harmful, or indifferent. Our analytical methods are still unable, except perhaps in particularly expert hands, to distinguish between mushrooms as harmful or agreeable forms of nourishment. For this delicate operation, the expert himself must still be guided by a direct and real experiment of absorption. Man, when devoid of science, took himself as laboratory. None was surer: he acquired, by this means, some information which has been most useful for mankind and domesticated animals. Every now and then somebody rediscovers some medication which figured in very ancient pharmacopoeias: thus formate of lime or soda, recently prescribed as a muscular stimulant, contains scarcely a principle that did not figure in the old "water of magnanimity," obtained by the maceration and distillation of a certain quantity of ants. How did our ancestors, who were no doubt shepherds and laborers, come to distinguish the virtue of ants? Evidently by eating them. The foul Arabs and other base forms of humanity who eat their vermin find in them, perhaps, an analogous tonic. This practice, like all those that resolve themselves into absorption, is assuredly dictated by experience. Neither a man nor an animal can, in principle, lend himself to an act that might be harmful to him:

Between acts that are harmful and those that are salutary, there is a series of games, but it is difficult to admit that a daily game might be a harmful act.

Why is it that peasants will not eat certain abundant rodents? It is easy to answer by suggesting the pretexts of taste and disgust. But that would reverse the logical order of the terms of the argument.

A food does not disgust by its odor. The odor of a food disgusts because that food is harmful or useless. To understand this, without the necessity of insisting upon it, it is enough to think of all the foods with nauseating odors which we appreciate more than those which could be called pleasant. Such is the fruit of experience, that is to say, of knowledge. I believe that absorption should be considered one of the best ways that we have for appreciating the practical value of certain parts of the external world. Agriculture, kitchen-gardening, cooking, pharmacy almost entirely, are born of it. Assuredly men, even the most exceptional chemists and physiologists, could suck a kola nut for years without suspecting those virtues that savages found quite simply by cracking the fruit with their teeth.

They are amusing, those people who, ignoring not only the importance but the existence of that sixth or seventh or tenth sense, attribute to taste or to smell a mysterious power of divining the harmfulness of a plant or its fruit. How do they fail to see immediately that this preservative instinct, if it is hereditary, has had a beginning, and that, at this beginning, there was a fact of knowledge? The traditional notion of instinct must be left in the old repertories of theology and spiritualism. It serves simple people as an easy means of distinguishing man from the animals: animals have instinct, men have intelligence. There are proofs: man poisons himself with mushrooms, the frugivorous animals never. What man? Not the traditional peasant, surely. Only the *déraciné* or the city-dweller, who has naturally lost an instinct which had become useless to him. This proves only that it is dangerous for man, as for the other animals, or for plants themselves, to change their habitat. There is an uncertain, painful transitory phase. It is during this phase that we go into the woods, on picnic parties, and gather toad-stools. But rabbits in cages, when given wet grass or vegetables unknown to their instinct, allow themselves to be thoroughly poisoned. In a state of freedom, it would never have occurred to them to crop grass at dewfall, because their ancestors, dwelling in very thick woods, were ignorant of the very existence of the dew, and transmitted distrust of wet grass to their progeny.

Even in the state of semi-civilization, man is burdened with too much knowledge for it all to be transmitted by heredity; but there is no doubt that the oldest and most useful learning comes down to us in this manner. When we stroll through a forest, there are berries that tempt us—huckleberries, for example, but never alderberries. Who has taught us (I am supposing real ignorance) that the latter are purgative and even dangerous? Instinct? What is instinct? The hereditary transmission of knowledge.

This transmission can no doubt occur in the case of abstract ideas as well as practical ideas, that is, those useful for the preservation of life. Some of them, moreover, are really useful and even primordial. It is as reasonable to believe that they are inherited as to suppose them to be acquired personally. It might be possible to rehabilitate the theory of innate ideas, by revising it carefully and eliminating from its catalog all sorts of Platonic or Christian inventions, much too recent to have entered into our blood.

As to the direct knowledge of ideas, this is gained in a form apparently analogous to the knowledge of matter by absorption. Once they have entered us, ideas either remain inert, unknown, or else they disintegrate. In the first case, it is not long before they are expelled from the mind, somewhat like an indigestible fragment from the intestines. Their sojourn can produce a certain irritation, even lesions—that is to say, they can provoke absurd acts, manifestly without logical relation to the normal physiology of the patient. This effect is very apparent in different nations, but especially in France, at the time of great political or moral crises. We see people tormented by the presence of a parasitic idea in their brains, like sheep by the lodging of a trumpet fly's larva in their frontal sinuses. Man, like the sheep, has an "inflammation." It ends badly for the sheep—for the man also, very often.

In the second case, the external ideas that have entered the mind are disintegrated there and unite their atoms with the other atoms of knowledge already within us. An idea is digested, assimilated. Assimilated, it then becomes something very different from what it was when it first entered our intelligence. Like intestinal absorption, mental absorption is, therefore, an excellent though indirect means of acquiring knowledge. This is to say that, in both cases, ideas, like ailments, will be known, not immediately, but by their effects. Thus men know hereditarily that certain ideas are individual or social poisons, and that others are equally conducive to the welfare of the individual or the development of peoples. But, in this order, notions of utility and of harmfulness are much less precise. We have seen a certain idea, reputed to be very dangerous, conduce to the health of a man, a family, a society, even to civilization itself. Ideas are extremely malleable, plastic. They take the shape of the brain. There are perhaps no ideas that are bad for a healthy brain whose form is normal. There are perhaps no good ones for a brain that is sick and warped.

III

But let us return to our tree or our ox. This ox can enter us in one of two ways. First, partially, but really, in the form of food. What we absorb of it in that way obviously cannot be known as ox. It comes to our knowledge only by its effects: strength, health, gaiety, activity, depression. Even if this absorption were total in the case of a small animal, digestible in all its parts, the result, from the point of view of immediate knowledge, would be the same, since the object becomes resolved into elements which render its form unknowable.

The other manner—one which brings the external senses into play—will make us know the ox, in appearance as an ox, in reality as the image of an ox. What is the true value of this knowledge? We must return to this question here, in order to enter more easily upon the second part of this essay.

Truth has been very seriously defined as conformity of the representation of an object with the object itself. But that solves nothing. What is the object itself, since we cannot know it except in the state of representation? It is useless to push this discussion further. We would turn indefinitely around the fortress of idealism, without ever finding an opening, or any weak point. We shall never enter it, no argument serving as an effective bomb against its solid walls.

Nevertheless, we must consider carefully. Having thoroughly reflected, we will ask if this fortress is real, or if to the contrary it is not a representation without object, a pure phantom, like those sunken cities whose bells still ring for great festivals, but are heard only by those who believe in their mysterious life. This doubt will bring us to reconsider the reasoning of Berkeley and Kant and to determine whether it is soundly constituted. Does it start from the senses in order to reach the mind? Or may it not be, by chance, one of those mental conceptions which fall back upon the senses like an avalanche, freezing and smothering them?

How were the senses formed? This is the question. Has there always been opposition between the self and the nonself? There is nothing in the intelligence that has not first been in the senses. In this philosophical dictum, deriving from Locke, we must understand by the term "intelligence" the psychological consciousness. Let us leave aside the consciousness, which can only serve to complicate the problem. Consciousness is a phenomenon of a secondary order and, when restricted to man, is of an entirely sentimental utility. When extended to all sensible matter, it is commonplace and a matter of pure reflex. Let us consider this matter in what is perhaps its humblest manifestations, taking into account only actions and reactions, exactly as we might observe the influence of heat, light, or cold on milk, wine, or water. In living matter there will be, however, something more—decomposition will be compensated by assimilation, and if the assimilation is abundant, there will be generation. Other forms, resembling the first, will detach themselves from the matrix form. This represents life essentially, a living being, limited in duration by the very fact of its growth, which constitutes a labor and a loss. Let us consider a being whose senses are not differentiated, and let us see how it behaves toward the rest of the world, how it knows it.

The amoeba has no exterior sense. It is an almost homogeneous mass, and yet it is sensitive to almost the same sensorial impressions as the highest mammals. It feeds (smell and taste); it moves (sense of space, touch); it is sensitive to light, at least to certain rays (sight); its environment being in perpetual movement, ceaselessly traversed by sonorous waves, it doubtless reacts to these vibrations (hearing). Perhaps it even possesses, without special organs, senses which we lack and can recover only by study and analysis, such as the chemical sense, the one that judges the composition of a body, declares it assimilable or counsels its rejection. The exercise of all these senses demonstrates, first of all, a very long heredity. No doubt they have only been acquired successively, unless, the absence of one of them being capable of causing death, their presence is the strict consequence of the life of this humble beast. But it is useless to construct any hypothesis on this subject. It is enough to keep to the fact, and this fact is the existence of a living being without differentiated organs, that is, all of whose parts are equally qualified to react to every external excitation.

Why these reactions? They are one of the conditions of life. But could not life be conceived without them? It is possible. It is a question of environment. If the amoeba's environment were homogeneous and calm, if it were of a constant temperature and luminosity, if it furnished a suitable food in abundance, if the animal, in a word, lived in an alimentary bath, no reactions whatever would be necessary, and its only movements would be to open its pores for food, to reject any excess of this food, to divide itself, when swollen, into two amoebas. Why, then, does it possess all these senses which, though unorganized, are perfectly real? Because the environment obliges it to have them, by its instability. The senses, whether differentiated or spread over the entire surface of a living form, are the creation of the environment, and of an environment which—light, sound, material externality, odors, etc.—acts in accordance with different discontinuous manifestations. Constant or continuous, they would be without effect. Discontinuous, they make themselves felt. Discontinuous light created the eye, as the drop of water creates a hole in the granite.

A being, whatever it might be, whether vague and quasi-amorphous, or clearly defined, is not isolated in the vital universal milieu. It is the molecule of a diapason. It vibrates, not of its own accord, but in obedience to a general movement. The living cell, itself in internal movement and subject to all the reactions of external movement, no doubt perceives that movement in the form of a single impression. But when several cells come together and live in permanent contact, the impressions of external movement begin to be perceived in differentiated form. Is this, then, necessary? Do there then already exist luminous vibrations, different from sonorous vibrations? Assuredly, otherwise sensorial differentiation, being useless, would be inexplicable. The union of several cells permits the animal to divide its work of perception and to present an organ for each perceptible manifestation, or at least an incipient organ appropriate to receive it.

It is true that, from the idealist point of view, one could suppose that the senses are the creation of the individual, the outgrowth of his own life, and that he differentiates his cinematic impressions on his own initiative. That would be a phenomenon of spontaneous analytic creation, the analyzing instrument existing prior to the matter analyzed, or even, for the exasperated idealists, creating that matter according to needs determined once and for all by one's own physiology. It would be, then, a property of organized, living matter to fabricate its own senses and to diversify its own life in this way. This point of view is not easy to accept for several reasons, all purely physical.

First of all, if this sensorial differentiation were a faculty of living matter, we would not see it, as it is, limited in its powers. Even admitting certain senses unknown to man, such as the chemical sense, the electric sense, the sense of direction (highly doubtful), it is still apparent that the number of senses is extremely limited. But, even more important, the fundamental senses are found to be identical among most of the superior species, vertebrates and insects, with very few exceptions. The moment the animal achieves sensorial differentiation, that differentiation is made in response to the manifestations of matter.

The senses must, therefore, correspond to external realities. They have been created, not by the perceiving being, but by the perceptible environment. It is light which has created the eye, just as, in our houses, it has created windows. In environments without light, fish become blind. This is perhaps the direct proof, for if light is the creation of the eye, this creation can occur at the bottom of the sea quite as well as on the surface of the earth. Another proof: these same fish, having become blind, but nevertheless needing a luminous environment, create for themselves in their abysmal night, not eyes, but some apparatus that is directly productive of light—and this artificial light creates anew the atrophied eye. The senses are therefore indeed the product of the environment. Moreover, they cannot be otherwise, their utility being nil if the environment is not perceptible. One could still object that it is the nervous system which, having an intuition of an environment to perceive, created organs suitable for that perception. But this is merely begging the question, for either the nervous system has knowledge of the external environment, which means that it already has senses, or else it has no senses and thus can have no knowledge. A more serious objection would be that, the sensorial aptitude being a property of the nervous system, it would then create organs in order to perceive more distinctly and in more differentiated form the various natural phenomena. This manner of seeing would explain, up to a certain point, the creation of sensorial organs, but not the existence of the senses themselves as sensitive capability. It explains the vertebrate's eye, but not the amoeba's sensitivity to luminous rays. It is certain, moreover, that the nervous system acts more to tyrannize the organs at its disposal than to seek to modify those organs or to create them anew. That is a power which is obviously beyond it, and which, to the contrary, has devolved on external phenomena which, in acting mechanically on the living matter, has there produced local modifications. The organs of sense seem to be nothing more than surfaces sensitized by the very agents which, once the work is accomplished, will reflect in them their particular physiognomy. The eye—let us take up and repeat this example—is a creation of light.

Since they are themselves the work of principal general phenomena, the senses ought then to agree exactly—allowing for approximation—with the very nature of the environment which has evoked them. The luminous milieu, therefore, is not a dream, but a reality existing prior to the eye that perceives it; and the objects situated in that luminous milieu must be perceived by the eye in the form of an exact image, since the eye is the very work of that light, just as the drill which creates a hole, creates it strictly to its own size and form, in its own image. Bacon said that the senses are holes. Here this is only a metaphor.

IV

There remains the question of the coordination of the impressions received materially by the senses. This coordination, for elementary sensations, is evidently identical among all creatures. Both the snail whose horn is menaced and the man who fears for his eye make the same recoiling movement. Identical acts can only have, as cause, identical realities—or ones perceived as such. It is nonetheless true that a perception is a judgment. With judgment, we enter into the mystery. If light is constant, the judgment which allows its existence is variable according to the species, and, in the highest species, according to individuals. It is clear that all eyes are affected by light, but no one knows to what degree or according to what mode of spectral fragmentation. It is the same for all the senses. Even if we grant the reality of the palpable world, we must hesitate regarding the quality of that reality as a reality perceived and judged. We arrive, then, back at idealism, even though we had a very different end in view. We must retrace our steps and reconsider the ironic fortress and resign ourselves to never knowing anything but appearances.

Another fact remains, however, another fortress perhaps, erected opposite the other—which is that matter has existed prior to life. The gain seems slight, but it is equivalent to saying that phenomena perceived by the senses are anterior to the senses now perceiving them; and this perhaps means that, if life becomes extinct, matter will survive life. The proposition of the idealists, that the world would end if there were no longer any sensibilities capable of perceiving it, seems therefore untenable. And yet, what would a world be, which was neither thought nor felt? It must be recognized that when we think of a world that is void of all thought, it still contains our thought, or it is our thought that contains and animates it. Another phenomenon analogous to this has, perhaps, contributed much to the belief in the immortality of the soul, namely, that we cannot conceive of ourselves as dead except by thinking of this death, by feeling it and seeing it. The idea of our nonexistence still supposes the life of our thought. That we might have here an illusion due to the very functioning of the mechanism of thought, is probable enough, but it is difficult not to take it into account. It would be excessive to make of it a mere abstraction.

We can attempt it, however, and try a new path which would lead "beyond thought." It could be achieved by considering the general movement of things in which our very thought is closely implicated and by which it is rigorously conditioned. Far from thought thinking life, perhaps, it is life that animates thought. What is anterior is a vast rhythmic undulation of which thought is merely one of the moments, one of the ripples.

The position outside the world taken by man in order to judge the world is a factitious attitude. It is perhaps only a game, and too easy. Man's dividing himself into two parts, thought and physical being, one considering the other and pretending to contain it, is merely a philosophical amusement which becomes impossible the moment one considers it objectively. There is, in fact, a physics of thought. We know that it is a product, since we can curtail it by injuring the producing organ. Thought is not only a product, but a material product, measurable, ponderable. Unformulated externally, it nevertheless manifests its physical existence by the weight which it imposes upon the nervous system. In order to show itself externally, it needs the help of speech, writing, or some kind of sign. Telepathy, the penetration of thoughts, presentiment—if there are any facts in this category which have been verified—would in such a case be so many proofs of the materiality of thought. But it is useless to multiply arguments in favor of a fact which is no longer contested except by theology.

This fact of materiality gives thought a secondary place. It is produced, but it might not be. It is not primordial. It is a result, a consequence, no doubt a property of the nervous system or even of living matter. It is, then, through a singular error that we have become accustomed to considering it isolated from the ensemble of causes that produce it.

But if thought is a product, it is no less productive in its turn. It does not create the world—it judges it. It does not destroy the world—it modifies it and reduces it to its own measure. To know is to bring judgment; but every judgment is arbitrary, since it is an accommodation, an average, and since two different physiologies give different averages, just as they give different extremes. The path, once again, after many detours, leads back to idealism.

Idealism is definitely founded on the very materiality of thought, considered as a physiological product. The conception of an external world that is exactly knowable is compatible only with the belief in reason, that is, in the soul, that is, moreover, in the existence of an immutable, incorruptible, immortal principle, whose judgments are infallible. If, on the contrary, knowledge of the world is the work of a humble physiological product, thought, a product which varies in quality, in modality, from man to man, from species to species, then the world can be considered as unknowable, since each brain or each nervous system draws from its vision and its contact a different image, or one which, if it was at first the same for all, is profoundly modified in its final representation by the intervention of individual judgment.

If an object gives the same image on both an ox's retina and a man's, it will doubtless not be concluded that this image is known and judged identically by the ox and the man.

There are no two leaves, there are no two beings, alike in nature. Such is the basis of idealism and the cause of incompatibility with the amiable doctrines with which we still like to amuse ourselves.

The reasons for idealism plunge deeply into matter. Idealism means materialism, and conversely, materialism means idealism.

—From *Promenades philosophiques,* 1904

Art and Science

Art and science are equally useful in civilization. M. Edmond Perrier (Preface to *Nouveau dictionnaire des sciences*) summarily establishes the superiority of science. Only science, he says, can provide true high culture. "However decorative artists, men of letters, and poets may be to a strong nation, they are its amusement and charm, but not its energy and life." And, he adds, a too-exclusive esteem of literature and art is a sign that the sensibility is exalted at the expense of the intelligence. It is a mark of decadence.

If all this were true, seeing that science was outlined only a few centuries ago and established, provisionally, only a few years ago, there would be no civilizations prior to our own or different from it. The relativity of knowledge does not permit such an assertion: to-day's scientific culture may, in the future, appear puerile and vain. If it is a matter of good intentions and the desire to know, all centuries have shown an almost equal ardor. Science has always existed. What changes is its object.

But it is not historically that I view, and wish to pose anew, the question of the opposition of art and science. The contrasts which are easily made today could be reconstituted for certain European or Asiatic periods. The conflict is permanent, because it has its source in the very structure of the human being. Man wishes to live and man wishes to know. These two tendencies, far from being complementary and mutually strengthening, actually deny each other. Schopenhauer made this eternal conflict the basis of his metaphysics. Recently, M. Jules de Gaultier has made this point of view even more precise by showing the antagonism between the vital instinct and the instinct for knowledge.

Granting this, and it is essential to grant it, to what does art respond, and what science?

In art we will naturally include all aesthetic manifestations, including games in all their many forms, literature in its widest sense, and a good part of science—that which deals with notions and not facts, and which is clouded with sentimentality (such as popular sociology). To science we will relegate all the rest, that is, the ponderable and measurable immensity.

Of these two domains, one corresponds closely with the sensibility, the other with the intelligence—one the vital instinct, the other the instinct for knowledge. Art includes everything that stimulates the desire to live; science, everything that sharpens the desire to know. Art, even the most disinterested, the most disembodied, is the auxiliary of life. Born of the sensibility, it sows and creates it in its turn. It is the flower of life and, as seed, it gives back life. Science, or to use a broader term, knowledge, has its end in itself, apart from any idea of life and propagation of the species. Intelligence, that sublimation of the sensibility, that organ of the need to know, is sterilized sensibility. To know, and to know still more—the instinct for knowledge is insatiable, because the subject of knowledge is limitless.

Art and literature, which seem to be the luxury of the genius of the species, are, to the contrary, its daily bread. Their quality is a matter of indifference when they are considered as games, as stimulants. They are magic charms which have, for example, gradually brought that polygamous animal, the human male, to comply with regular marriage. And it is precisely when art declines, when the dreams of happiness it evokes are no longer strong enough to dupe the sensibility, that natural polygamy regains the upper hand over whatever weighs down the flight of life. Religions, those primitive and invariably superior forms of art, are powerful, vital aphrodisiacs. And those which exalt chastity are perhaps the ones which work most directly for the maintenance of life; for to speak against love or in favor of love is exactly the same thing. Nations without religion, without art, without literature, would escape to a considerable extent the tyranny of the vital instinct. They would still reproduce themselves, but with diminishing vigor. We see this clearly in France where the regions that have become sterile are those which modern forms of civilization have deprived of religion, art, and literature at the same time; while yet fertile regions, like Brittany, still live in an ideality of religion and poetry.

But it is not only the absence of art that dries people up. Almost all animals do without it, and their fecundity is often extreme, in singular rapport with the fecundity of the soil, that is to say, the abundance of food. Among certain very positive races, a state of well-being can replace music, dance, songs, parades, fairs, indulgences, hymns, legends, and tales. Yet there remains a void. If it is filled by the instinct for knowledge, if too large a part of the sensibility is transformed into intelligence, life is definitely vanquished.

I do not mean to say that this result would be bad, any more than I consider it, at the moment, to be good. It is a matter of indifference. The question is simply to know whether it is art or science that keeps alight the lamp of life.

To appreciate fully the role of science, we must distinguish pure science from applied science. Practical science has always existed. Its development does not follow that of theoretical science, but that of wealth. It also takes on more importance in proportion as wealth is mobilized and as men perfect methods of utilization which can increase its power a hundred-fold. The great practical discoveries are almost never scientific—they are empirical. The greatest useful invention of the nineteenth century—steam—was made long before the theory of steam was created. Science perfected; it did not discover. There was one other invention which was more important than steam; and that was printing, the work of the Middle Ages. There was never a less scientific invention. No doubt Pasteur's theory seems to have worked for life and not against it, although perhaps its beauty surpasses its utility, but would anyone dare to assert that chemistry would have been created by the vital genius, if such geniuses existed and if they were conscious?

Science could not work for life except by ceasing to be pure, by associating parasitical sentiments with its wholly intellectual preoccupations. A scientist who falsifies an experiment because he thinks the result would be harmful for mankind may be a very moral man, but he would not be a true scientist. Science wants to know and to make known. To know, and to know still more. Intelligence is the luxury of life, a dangerous luxury for the life which it contemplates with the eyes of Medusa and the Basilisk. Science is the food of the intelligence.

If anything really represents the dream, it is science. It manipulates life, kills it or fortifies it, impartially, according to the fortunes of its researches. And what does it seek? A chimera—the Truth. It seeks it while knowing well that it will not find it. Its disinterestness, repellent to life, is admirable and absurd. To know, and what for? To know, and to know still more! To go, not higher, for the world has neither high nor low, but farther, while knowing that the very farthest represents the diameter of a grain of sand compared to that of the visible universe. What is there beyond the molecule?— nothing or a world, an abstraction or a new beginning? Is matter something or a conception of the mind? In either case, it is divisible to infinity. Science says no, and it dreams. When it says yes, its dream will change its subject like that of the sleeper who turns on his back. And so it will go on from dream to dream until it has exhausted not the inexhaustible material of knowledge, but the material for knowing, the human brain.

Science is the only truth and it is the great lie. It knows nothing, and people think it knows everything. It is misrepresented. People think that science is electricity, automobilism, and dirigible balloons. It is something very different. It is life devouring itself. It is the sensibility transformed into intelligence. It is the need to know stifling the need to live. It is the genius of knowledge vivisecting the vital genius.

—From *Promenades philosophiques,* 1902

Selections from
The Young Lady of Today

Παρθένος, puella, virgo, pulcella, virgin, damsel, girl, young lady, and all the names of this state of being in all languages old and new—a common and exclusive idea permits of their being translated one by another; but whereas the translation is true for the basis of the idea, it would be false for the aspect which this idea takes on according to civilizations and their times. At present a woman of middling condition spends, in the state of a young "lady," a third of her sexual life and some of the years best fitted for love, sometimes almost all of them. A girl who marries at twenty-eight has spent fourteen years in not living, for outside of love there is no life for woman. This delay between the end of education and marriage was greatly shortened in the ancien régime. Sometimes there was none. The little girl became a woman without having ever been a young "lady." She was spared a painful transition; for it is certain that for most young "ladies" their state becomes a torment as soon as it is prolonged.

Yet there were young ladies in the past, and even in the eighteenth century. Not all were married on the morrow of their nubility, snatched from the convent for this new communion by which the first is confirmed. We see some of them in comedies, novels, and memoirs; but their character is not readily distinguishable from that of young married women. They never had any prudery and sometimes very little reserve. The moment they were admitted into society, they lived its life. There was no concern to hide from them either intrigue, escapades, or pleasures. They were guests waiting to be served, without impatience, since they were sure of being served. Those who were forgotten served themselves, and hardly anybody was surprised. On the eve of the Revolution, in those years of para-

dise whose pleasantness made the first dark days appear the more
cruel, virginity was not highly valued. There was a universal desire
to yield to nature. Today a Casanova would only conquer women or
courtesans; the young "lady" would escape him. He harmed a great
number of them, and that alone—an exact coincidence with the
morals of the times—would affirm the veracity of his admirable and
delicious memoirs. A witness of a lower level, Restif de la Bretonne,
confirms this facility of girls of the eighteenth century. They gave
themselves through sentiment and very quickly acquired the valuable taste for sensuality; for everything surrounding them—
manners, art, literature—urged them to a pagan life, enhanced only
by a bit of romantic dreaming. The young lady of Laclos belongs to
a society close to the Court; she scarcely differs from that of Casanova and Restif.

It is very apparent that, at that time, education possessed no
serious means of restraining the young lady. Hence, those very early
marriages. The parents were glad to be freed from their responsibility, and the husbands, without any illusions about the future, married young girls in order to be at least assured of one or two
legitimate children. This practice, in safeguarding the essential part
of the man's rights, respected the woman's liberty as much as it
could. She was not left free, or very rarely, to choose her husband;
but she chose her lover, and at an age when it is a pure pleasure to
love even more than a sexual necessity. At twenty-two or twenty-
three the woman of the eighteenth century had exhausted her
natural duties. She had children, often four or five. What more
could be demanded of her? Her husband, tired of her, left her tired
of him, with the hope of fifteen or twenty years of amorous life. At
the age when the young lady of today is exhausting herself over
sterile and—what is worse, stupefying—studies, the woman of the
past was in the full flower of maternity. In the provinces and other
restrictive environments, this flowering would be continued a long
time, leaving no room for outside pleasures for the woman, nor perhaps for the husband. Thus were produced those patriarchal families, the idea of which terrifies us, and very rightly, for social conditions no longer allow such developments. Some provinces retained
the tradition of early marriages down to the first years of this century. In my childhood I knew Mme de L. . . . married at fourteen,
and Mme de M. . . . married at fifteen. One had many children;

the other had only two. Neither could remember having been a young "lady," and they gazed with tender pity at their granddaughters who, at twenty years of age or more, blushed at the gallant stories the grandmothers related without scruple. For the elders there had been no interregnum between the lives of the saints and fashionable novels. They had passed, at one leap, from the doll to the husband, from puerility to maternity. They had the modesty of young women. The modesty of young "ladies" was a complete mystery to them.

In sum, there were young ladies before and during the eighteenth century, and always. There was no young "lady." The young "lady" was a creation of the last century. She was very naturally the product of late marriages, just as late marriages are the product of the suppression of hereditary situations.

. . . .

Women toiled for this new creature, for the virgin who had to spend five or six years in society at an age when she would naturally think of nothing but love. It was essential to thwart that tendency, to sidetrack it toward studies, toward pious sentimentality, toward ethereal reveries. Everything was good that would turn the young lady away from love, that would teach her resignation, modesty, obedience, the sentiment of duty, and an innumerable array of virtues of which the majority are nothing but paralogisms or an assemblage of syllables totally lacking in any appreciable meaning.

We know how literature for young "ladies" has proliferated. The book written for the young "lady" is the object of an important commerce, encouraged annually by the Academy and several other benevolent societies. It is for the young "lady" that the sad novels of Comming and Wood have been translated; for her that the old anthologies have been transformed into manuals of morality; for her that the journals and reviews which prefer to be "forgotten on the drawing-room table" offer repugnant and puerile travesties of life; for her that *Madame Bovary* was prosecuted, and for her that silence has been imposed on those French writers who fail to show a proper reserve in some matter of morals; for her that women's dresses have been stripped of their pockets (this is regarded as a great victory by pious ladies who have read in secret the *Memoirs of Count Grammont*); for her that subsidized theaters emasculate

Shakespeare; for her that the century of Louis XIV has been made out to be a period of virtue and moral dignity; for her that all the flavor has been taken out of art and literature and that man has been wounded in the first of liberties, liberty of manners and customs.

If the young "lady" has not caused us more harm—all the harm she has caused in Protestant countries—it is because France, being in the pagan tradition, like Italy, has developed a schism in her literature. With Gautier and Flaubert in the novel, with Baudelaire in poetry, a new literature was created—one which no longer took the young "lady" into account, nor the family of which she had become the soul and the center. This literature could have developed easily enough if it had been expected only to be considerate of the modesty of women; but it was also required to respect the modesty of virgins. Here we have the origin of the revolt, and the reason for the preface to *Mademoiselle de Maupin,* one of the finest pieces of free French literature. Sometimes, for thirty years now, "literary" literature has bordered on licentious literature. This is because authors, believing they were writing for an exclusively male public, have felt that they have had the right to say everything. Those writers whom the young "lady" has excluded from the "drawing-room table" (where I never see, myself, anything but flowers, cards, and knick-knacks) are no longer concerned about falling into the hands of young women. Some burned themselves in the inferno; others found it refreshing. There are some extremely honest young women in sensual literature's public; there are even some young ladies. Both prefer a good literature that shocks the heart a bit to a bad one which, in satisfying their sensibility, stains their intelligence. The mind also has its modesty.

—From *Le Chemin de velours,* 1901

PART III

Symbolism
and
the Symbolist Poets

Preface
to
Le Livre des masques

It is difficult to characterize a literary movement at a time when its fruits are still uncertain, when its flowering is not yet completed throughout the orchard. Some precocious trees, some backward trees, some doubtful trees which one hesitates to call sterile: the grove is very diversified, very rich, too rich—the density of leaves creates shadows and the shadows discolor the flowers and pale the fruit. Let us stroll through this opulent and shady grove and sit for a moment at the foot of the strongest, most attractive, and agreeable trees.

Literary movements, when they merit it by virtue of their importance, necessity, and appropriateness, are given a name. This name very often lacks precise meaning, but it is useful: it serves as a rallying-point for those who receive it, and as a point of focus for those who bestow it. Thus the battle is joined around a purely verbal standard. What does Romanticism mean? It is easier to feel than to explain. What does Symbolism mean? If taken in its strict, etymological sense, almost nothing. Going further, it can mean individualism in literature, freedom in art, abandonment of learned formulas, a tendency toward what is new, strange, even bizarre. It can also mean idealism, disdain for social anecdote, antinaturalism, the tendency to take from life only the characteristic detail, to pay attention only to the act by which a man distinguishes himself from other men, to wish to realize only results—essences. Finally, for poets Symbolism seems linked to free verse—that is, unfettered verse, whose young body can gambol at its ease, freed of the encumbrance of swaddling clothes and bonds.

All this has but slight relationship to the syllables of the word —for we must not allow the insinuation that Symbolism is only a new form of an old allegorism or of the art of personifying an idea in a human being, a landscape, or a narrative. Such an art is a total art, the primordial and eternal art, and a literature delivered from these concerns would be unthinkable. It would be nil, and of an aesthetic significance suitable to the cluckings of the guinea hen or the brayings of the wild ass.

Literature, in fact, is nothing more than the artistic development of an idea, the symbolization of the idea by means of imaginary heroes. Heroes, or men (for each man is a hero in his own sphere), are merely outlined by life. It is art which completes them by giving them, in exchange for their poor sick souls, the treasure of an immortal idea, and the humblest man may be called to participate, if he is chosen by a great poet. How humble is that Aeneas whom Virgil burdened with the idea of Roman might, and how humble that Don Quixote on whom Cervantes imposed the appalling weight of being, at the same time, Roland and the four sons Aymon, Amadis, Palmerin, Tristram, and all the knights of the Round Table! A history of Symbolism would be the history of man himself, since man can assimilate ideas only in symbolized forms. We must not insist here, for it is possible to believe that the young disciples of Symbolism are ignorant of even the *Vita Nuova* and the person of Beatrice, whose frail and pure shoulders manage to remain straight under the complex weight of symbols with which the poet has burdened her.

Then whence comes the illusion that the symbolization of the idea is a novelty? From this: We have had, in recent years, a very serious attempt to establish a literature based on a contempt for the idea and a disdain for the symbol. The theory is well known, and appears culinary: take one slice of life, etc. M. Zola, having invented this recipe, forgot to make use of it. His "slices of life" are weighty poems made up of a muddy and tumultuous lyricism, a popular romanticism, a democratic symbolism, but always pregnant with an idea, always big with allegorical significance—*Germinal,* the Mine, the Mob, the Strike. The idealist revolt did not rise up against the works (unless against base works) of naturalism, but against its theory or rather its pretensions. Reverting to anterior and eternal necessities of art, the rebels, in professing their desire to reintegrate the idea into literature, thought they were affirming new and even surprising truths. They only relit the torch. But they also lit, all around them, many small candles.

A new truth—and there is one which has recently appeared in literature and art—is entirely metaphysical, a priori (in appearance), and quite young, since it is only a century old and truly new, and since it has not yet done service in an aesthetic order. This truth—evangelical and marvelous, liberating and rejuvenating—is the principle of the ideality of the world. In relation to man (the thinking subject), the world (all that is exterior to the self) exists only as the idea formed of it. We know only phenomena; we can reason only about appearances. All truth, in itself, escapes us. The essence is unattainable. This is what Schopenhauer has popularized in that clear and simple formula: the world is my representation. I do not see what is; what is, is what I see. So many thinking men— so many diverse and perhaps different worlds. This doctrine, which Kant left by the wayside to throw himself to the aid of a ship-wrecked morality, is so beautiful and so flexible that one can trans-pose it, without bruising its liberal logic, from theory to even the most demanding practice. It is the universal principle of emancipa-tion for all men capable of comprehending. It has revolutionized only the world of aesthetics, but here we are concerned only with aesthetics.

Handbooks still give us definitions of the Beautiful. They go even further: they give us formulas by which an artist arrives at the expression of the Beautiful. There are institutes where one learns these formulas, which are only the consensus and summary of earlier ideas or appreciations. Aesthetic theories, being as a rule ob-scure, are supplemented by the example, the paradigm, the model to be followed. In these institutions (and the civilized world is but a vast Institution) every novelty is considered as blasphemous, and every personal affirmation becomes an act of madness. M. Nordau, who, with a bizarre patience, has read all contemporary literature, has propagated the notion, so villainously destructive of all intellec-tual individualism, that "nonconformism" is a capital crime for a writer. We are of a violently different opinion. The capital crime for a writer is conformism, imitativeness, submission to rules and teach-ings. The work of a writer must be not only the reflection, but the enlarged reflection, of his personality. The only excuse a man has for writing is to write himself—to reveal to others the kind of world reflected in his individual mirror. His only excuse is to be original. He must say things never said before and say them in a form not yet formulated. He must create his own aesthetic—and we must admit as many aesthetics as there are original minds, and judge them according to what they are rather than what they are not.

We acknowledge, then, that Symbolism, even if extreme, untimely, and pretentious, is the expression of individualism in art.

This definition—too simple, but clear—will serve provisionally. In the course of the following portraits, or later, we will no doubt have occasion to complete this definition, but its principle will still serve to guide us by prompting us to seek out, not what these writers ought to have done, according to tyrannical rules and traditions, but what they have tried to do. Aesthetics has become itself a personal talent. No one has the right to impose it, ready-made, on others. One can compare an artist only to himself, but there is profit and justice in noting dissimilarities. We will not try to indicate wherein the "newcomers" resemble one another, but wherein they differ—that is, in what way they exist, for to exist is to be different.

This is not to pretend that, among most of these writers, there are not obvious similarities of idea and technique—that is inevitable, but so inevitable as to be without interest. We do not pretend, moreover, that this flowering is spontaneous. Before the flower there is the seed, itself fallen from a flower. These young persons have their forefathers and masters: Baudelaire, Villiers de l'Isle-Adam, Verlaine, Mallarmé, and others. They love them dead or living; they read them, they listen to them. What foolishness to believe that they disdain those of yesterday! Who, after all, has a more admiring and more affectionate court than Stéphane Mallarmé? And is Villiers forgotten? Or Verlaine forsaken?

To join yesterday to today, I have interpolated known faces among the new; and then, instead of recasting a physiognomy familiar to many, I have sought to illuminate, not the whole, but some rather obscure point.

—1896

Stéphane Mallarmé

Every twenty years the world of men renews itself, as does the world of nature. When we look around us, in a contemplative moment, we rediscover almost nothing of what charmed and gave direction to our youth. Where are those whom we called our masters and to whom we fervently listened for the enchanted word? I have seen Henri de Régnier blush at a discreet compliment from Stéphane Mallarmé, and now it is he who arouses such emotions in the hearts and on the cheeks of young poets. Where is the small room in the rue de Rome, where the cry of locomotives came to mingle with our aesthetic effusions?

Stéphane Mallarmé was a contemporary of Villiers de l'Isle-Adam, Coppée, Verlaine, Mendés—of that Parnassian generation whose last representative and last prince today is M. Léon Dierx. Around 1885, I believe, Mallarmé's literary gatherings began to attract some young writers of rather diverse tendencies, who admired in him the most perfect of poets and most sage of men. He so enriched my mind that no other person has given me, as he did, the illusion of listening to a new Socrates. His speech was measured, fine, gently ironic, but for his listeners skilfully benevolent, without banality, for he knew how to restrain true praise and distribute it with care and tact. He had none of the sarcastic tone which Leconte de Lisle, considerably older, kept until the end and which earned him many enemies. Mallarmé, but only much later, also had his enemies. Critics reproached him, as for a crime, for the obscurity of some of his verses, without considering all the lucid parts of his work and with no attempt to understand why the very logic of his symbolist aesthetic had led him to express only the second term of a comparison. Classic poetry was so clear—but so monotonous—

because it expressed both. Victor Hugo and Flaubert united them in a single complex metaphor. Mallarmé *disunited* them and let only the second image be seen, which served to illuminate and "poetize" the first. The result is a new language, imprecise as the very dream that it evokes and whose contours it does not feel obliged to encircle. Words, in this second manner of the poet, are chosen for their complementary qualities, somewhat like colors by the painter. Also, we must not analyze the sentence according to grammatical methods, just as we must not examine at close range the paintings of Impressionists, not even those of Claude Monet. The education of the eye is more advanced in France than the education of the poetic sense. One might make the style of Mallarmé somewhat better understood by remarking that he is the Claude Monet of poetry. Neither his verses, nor the luminous daubs of the painter, lend themselves to the teaching of grammar or of design, and nevertheless whoever has experienced these two expressions of art will feel that they serve a purpose nonetheless—to please certain observers and certain sensibilities:

> Surgi de la croupe et du bond
> D'une verrerie ephémère
> Sans fleurir la veillée amère,
> Le col ignoré s'interrompt.

Is this really obscure, really enigmatic? If the poet described for us in direct words the vase whose tormented belly and sharp-pointed neck, flowerless through neglect, seems, lacking a rose, to be brusquely broken, would we see it better and with more melancholy pleasure? It appears that, all the things of life having been said a thousand times over, it only remains for the poet to point them out while murmuring some words to accompany his gesture; and that is what Mallarmé has done. Even more, he has the air sometimes of talking to himself with words linked by simple juxtaposition, in appearance illogical and unconnected; and surely, at such moments, the ellipsis has intoxicated him. Then, to be sure, we are no longer able, without the aid of his commentary, to retie the ends of the thread broken by the gestures of his vision, and we understand him either not at all, or too little and with too much difficulty. Champollion rediscovered the language of hieroglyphics, thanks to a bilingual inscription. It is with that second language that we decipher the poets, when they have the art of letting it show through the first. Mallarmé has effaced all traces of it, and that renders more difficult the task of the decipherers. The second language, which flows beneath the first, is composed of known and commonplace locutions, of immediately clear clichés whose clarity, dull but indispensable, illuminates the new parts of the discourse. Mallarmé wanted to write without clichés. We might say that he used only words coined to measure. His obscurity seems to involve no other mystery. He was led to it by an excess of art. His example, after having been followed during the first years of Symbolism, soon became a severe lesson, and poets learned again to mix, in their verses, the known and the unknown in carefully proportioned quantities. It is good, perhaps, to have passed through that school, to have experienced the pride of spontaneous obscurity of style, in order to enjoy fully the joys of a tempered clarity. A style must not be too illuminated. The ready-made phrase, the expedient locution, must hold only a strictly limited place. Perhaps the genius of writing is to know the proper proportion and not to know that one knows it.

Stéphane Mallarmé did not immediately reach the limits of his art, which he exceeded to find the abyss afterwards. His beginning verses, with already some quite mallarméan affectation and preciosity, were clearly Parnassian, but with none of the impassivity advocated by that school. To the contrary, a lively sensibility was always allowed to show through, although he was careful, later on, that it not be too obvious. Moreover, as a disciple of Baudelaire, more so than of Banville, and living quite isolated in the provinces, he was not a man who lent himself to a discipline, and it is in this regard only that he distantly resembles Verlaine. Like Verlaine, however, but even more fervently, he remained faithful to romantic verse and accepted only in conversation the new techniques brought by the Symbolists. To him, and to his rather rigid and hieratic manner, nothing could have been more repugnant than free verse.

These first poems, which have something most reassuring and timeless about them, and which offer a better harmony of thought and expression, must most assuredly be ranked among the most beautiful in French poetry. Baudelaire, who at that time was the very expression of poetic tradition, was able to read a few of them before dying to the intelligence, and he was disturbed, it is said, by this poet rising from his ruins all at once so beautiful and so strong. I do not know if they were *les Fenêtres, les Fleurs, Azur* or *Brise marine,* pieces which appeared in *l'Artiste,* in the first *Parnasse,* in the rare collections of the time, but Baudelaire could believe himself the inspirer, at least indirectly, and claim at the same time that he had a successor toward whom the admiration of the young would soon veer. Victor Hugo, perhaps without feeling it very much, had understood what Baudelaire had brought and, in one of those words employed only by poets, he had warned men of the "new thrill" so ill-restrained in *Les Fleurs du mal.* Baudelaire, less generous, and unmoved by the efforts of the contemporaries of Mallarmé, had recognized and acknowledged him by his very anxiety. Thus, from generation to generation, thought and sensibility are knitted together in French tradition, and the very ones who believe themselves outside it are in reality only links in the eternal chain.

It is indeed useless today to gather up against Baudelaire the growing mound of reasonable criticisms. He is encased in admirations which have been piled around him to a mountain's height, and the excavations of the most ingenious and fertile of our critics will never reach a comparable level. It is the same with Mallarmé, whose destiny has been strikingly parallel to Baudelaire's. Like him, he is a poet who is respectful of the old forms and who pursues them with an as yet unrecognized rigor; like him, he is a prose writer of the first rank, more meditative, more retiring, but equally sufficient master of expression to make, with simple prose and in the manner of prose, some memorable poems; like him, nourished on Poe and marvelously aware of his rare poetic English; like him, living and dead, scoffed at by the reasonable mob to which he is exhibited like an extravagant rag; like him, finally and in spite of everything, one of the gods of youth and, soon, of all lovers of life and beauty. But if Baudelaire is still contested, is it not honorable that Mallarmé should also be. I do not propose the complete works of either one, although they are already "selected" works: that is the prerogative of those for whom art is half of life; but—and here I refer to Mallarmé—I wish that one might meditate sometimes, having in hand the anthology in which he himself has collected his finest pages: *Vers et prose.* I include here, chosen for its brevity, a selection entitled *Soupir,* one which is scarcely esoteric:

Mon âme vers ton front, où rêve, ô calme soeur,
Un automne jonché de taches de rousseur,
Et vers le ciel errant de ton oeil angelique,
Monte comme dans un jardin mélancolique,
Fidèle, un blanc jet d'eau soupire vers l'azur!
Vers l'azur attendri d'octobre pâle et pur,
Qui mire aux grands bassins sa langueur infinie,
Et laisse, sur l'eau morte où la fauve agonie
Des feuilles erre au vent et creuse un froid sillon,
Se traîner le soleil jaune d'un long rayon.

Why this limpid poetry, and so much exquisite prose, have not preserved Mallarmé from the reproach of obscurity—if not of mystification—which has darkened his reputation, is easy to explain. Men are primarily simplifiers. For us to remember a writer's name, he must have but one quality; and when it was known that Mallarmé had written his sonnets, which in appearance are only verbal music, denuded of precise sense and deprived of that diplomatic clarity which it is proper to attribute to French masterpieces, his poetry was all relegated to the category of enigmas. He himself later seemed to prefer his pieces of most difficult orchestration, and the young readers who looked for novelty looked for it there and thought they had found it. There is no doubt that it is less for his poetic genius than for the mysterious character of that abstruse genius that he was chosen to be the master of a segment of the new school. It was found that the other consul, Paul Verlaine, used on the contrary a sometimes soft and negligent language. So contrary tendencies and wills found themselves satisfied, and the government of Symbolism was instituted, even before it had found its definitive name.

This movement, which the press discovered in 1885,[1] actually dated back nearly twenty years. Arrested by the war, it acquired all its force the day when some young poets, guided by a famous chapter in Huysmans' *A Rebours* and discovering Mallarmé and Verlaine at the same time, found themselves enthusiastic and, so to speak, fecundated on the spot. They recognized in the two men the contradictory realization of their confused aspirations: they suddenly took confidence in themselves. Also it required, in order that the movement might burst into broad daylight, the arrival in France of a bold young foreigner, somewhat churlish, not in touch with our literary prejudices or else disdaining them—Jean Moréas. He published *Les Syrtes* in 1884, and thus released the small spring which must be touched to put into motion the greatest of machines. At that moment, Verlaine and Mallarmé had made or were putting the finishing touches to the work which they had pursued in silence for nearly a quarter of a century. As early as 1867, in Villiers de l'Isle-Adam's review, *La Revue des lettres et des arts,* Mallarmé had published, under the title of *Pages oubliées,* some prose poems which appeared later, in 1886, under the same title at the head of the first number of *La Vogue,* as a sort of manifesto. They seemed so new, those old pages, that they brought about that blossoming of prose poems that soon filled the little reviews. *Le Phenomène futur* was not a part of those which, nearly twenty years earlier, the *Revue des lettres* had discovered. Where then had it appeared, that piece which is one of the most exquisite pages in all the literature of the nineteenth century? Complete knowledge of the reviews is difficult, and I only possess it in part. It is nevertheless the sole authentic source for the literary history of our century. I write surrounded by all their yellowed papers, from which escape all sorts of poems whose beauty is revived on seeing the light again.

While these forgotten pages are well representative of the verbal genius of Stéphane Mallarmé, they also give a rather good idea of the state of mind of the Symbolists and of their intellectual attitude toward the Naturalists, who were so heavy and grossly optimistic. The Symbolists really wanted anything except descriptions satisfied with present conditions and the stable-litter,

Où le bétail heureux des hommes est couché.[2]

It is thus in all revolutions, whether political or literary, and it is not so much the desire for the better that determines them as the need for the new. This need Mallarmé had the gift of satisfying, at least for a time and in part. I admit that his poetry is not for the masses, but what poetry is, outside of some *vase brisé,* some song of sadness or facile smile? It remains that his *Après-Midi d'un faune* is, all the same, a *date,* as well as a sort of touchstone. One likes it or one does not like it, and that makes two realms and two bands of promenaders in the garden of French poetry. The faune, hallucinated by the play of the sun, dreams of the nymphs which he believed he saw among the reeds, and he constructs a poem of love:

> Moi, de ma rumeur fier, je vais parler longtemps
> Des déesses; et par d'idolâtres peintures,
> A leur ombre enlever encore des ceintures:
> Ainsi, quand des raisins j'ai sucé la clarté,
> Pour bannir un regret par ma feinte écarté,
> Rieur, j'élève au ciel d'été la grappe vide,
> Et soufflant dans ses peaux lumieuses, avide
> D'ivresse, jusqu'au soir je regarde au travers. . . .

I say that we have never before known such verses of sensual passion, freshness, and light, and that we must not let this treasure be lost. All those who could quench their thirst there have not yet drunk there; and perhaps more than one dreaming woman, once knowing the mirror of Hérodiade, will gaze at herself in none other:

>   O miroir,
> Eau froide par l'ennui dans ton cadre gelée,
> Que de fois, et pendant des heures, désolée,
> Des songes, et cherchant mes souvenirs qui sont
> Comme des feuilles sous ta glace au trou profond,
> Je m'apparus en toi comme une ombre lointaine.
> Mais, horreur! des soirs, dans ta sévère fontaine,
> J'ai de mon rêve épars connu la nudité!

What, alas, can remain of a poet, when once the color of his sensibility is no longer fashionable? Some fragments of verse, occasionally and no more, are retained because their meaning or their music end with the same verse and one thinks he has always known them—belated witnesses to the glory and superior business of the craftsman. We already knew this one, echo of lassitudes in the midst of life:

> La chair est triste, helas! et j'ai lu tous les livres.

Even when one is ignorant and jovial, this can be said and can disquiet. Such verses, full and perfect, composed of words seemingly soldered together (one of his doctrines), abound in his brief work and ask that, for having been read, they might be learned by heart. This might serve:

Et le vomissement impur de la bétise.

And these, though a bit esoteric:

Les noirs vols du blasphème épars dans le futur.

Or

J'aime l'horreur d'être vierge et je veux
Vivre parmi l'effroi que me font mes cheveux.

Or this supreme charm of the ear:

Je t'apporte l'enfant d'une nuit d'Idumée.

It is astonishing, the divine music that a dozen French syllables can make!

All this (and the quotations could be continued indefinitely) is as solid as Malherbe and Baudelaire. He had, himself, like those two poets and like Victor Hugo, the tendencies of the grammarian, and never, to the contrary of the unequal Verlaine, did he write haphazardly.

There are no anecdotes about Mallarmé. He was a professor of English, for which some writers have had the stupidity to reproach him, and a good teacher, who knew his business, received a retirement pension for a very short time, and retired near the Seine and the forest of Fontainebleau. He had been a long while at Tournon, whence some very precious letters are dated. I have wished to begin these notes with him—notes which are not intended to be well-balanced criticism—because he had the most distinct and most intellectual influence on Symbolism. Verlaine yields little apart from sentiment and never learned to write in prose. Mallarmé was master on the double-flute, admirable performer and most sagacious theoretician. Whistler's lithographs, at the head of *Vers et prose,* give his very attitude, the manner and aspect that he had at his chats in the Rue de Rome—intelligent and gentle. His head, to be a portrait of the time of the Pléiade, lacks only the inscription:

Et le divin laurier des âmes exilées.

—From *Promenades littéraires,* 4me série, 1912

Paul Verlaine

Paul Verlaine was the other consul of Symbolism. I am not establishing priority, for both were loved to distraction—Mallarmé with more respect, Verlaine with more familiarity. The first time I saw him was at the Bibliothèque Nationale in Paris, a good place to hunt out great writers, for nearly all pass through there some day, mingling with the laborious herd. Even if his name-card had not called him to my attention, his face would have struck me. It was one, I imagined, of a Suabian or Hun—one of those formidable barbarians who so frightened Sidonius Apollinaris that he could not describe them without shuddering. This impression was not far off the mark. Had he not just ravaged poetic art as they had ravaged Roman majesty? I did not see him again except in the cafés and on the sidewalks of Boulevard Saint-Michel. He no longer left the quarter, after so singular a life, except when his capricious health sent him off to the distant and benevolent refuge of hospitals. His destiny was fulfilled, after the apotheosis of 1891, in Vaudeville, in a sort of quivering calm, amidst his too familiar friends, his too curious admirers. They came to breathe in his present the odor of his past.

The cafés were never so fashionable. A photographer, publishing *Nos écrivains chez eux,* established Verlaine at the Café de la Source, next to an absinthe. What a contrast with the sumptuous library, in the same series of pictures, where M. Ohnet, in bearskins and in the shadows of candelabras, renders himself visible to the masses! The corner of a table, and, as the sum total of his equipment, a tall narrow glass, a battered carafe, an inkwell, a pen and blotter: such was the work study of the last great French poet. If he did not make his best verses there, it is perhaps because absinthe was

more tempting than sheets of letter paper. I have a photograph of
the tomb of Edgar Poe where there stands out, in enormous letters
on the wall of a building near the cemetery, the word LIQUOR.
The fateful word *alcohol* hovers over the life of the poor Lélian.[1]
His life—why not tell of even its bad episodes? They readily tell of
Villon's, who was a highwayman, a fugitive from the noose; and it
proves only one thing—that there is no connection between morality
and genius. "Better he should be an assassin and have some talent!"
said Huysmans amiably, when confronted by some bad verses and
the dedicated conduct of a young poet. The excessiveness of the paradox contains a truth. One may find it immoral, but it is a fact
which existence teaches us perseveringly—and one which we had
better receive graciously—that lives can be base and works exalted.
The method of Sainte-Beuve and Taine is at fault here, and I have
never known with what to replace it. Unless we must believe that
the judgments of men about morality are highly uncertain, unless
we must read nature by placing ourselves, like Nietzsche, above
good and evil. And then—and this, at least, is not uncertain—there
is a physiological fatality. This is what one should say to himself
when contemplating, in the Luxembourg Gardens, the mystery beneath the gentleness of that uncouth face, of that great child in
whom are joined the brutality of male instincts and the frailty of a
woman with languid nerves. Verlaine was all that. He was the little
child who piously recites his prayer and the faun who prowls about
like an ogre. He was Saint Teresa, drunk with divine love, and also
Sappho, who loved only her own kind. He was the dreamer touched
by the autumn nightfall, who quivers at a whirling leaf as he would
at a fluttering scarf; and he was also the bad *gallant* who slept in
taverns. Verlaine was intimate with all feelings and all sensations.

I do not know how those people read who see in *Poèmes
saturniens* nothing but poetic exercises or impersonal notations. It is
possible that he might have intended to obey Leconte de Lisle's rule
of impassivity, but his nature refused. His sensibility was already
overflowing. His muse is a statue, no doubt, but one which speaks:

> Son regard est pareil au regard des statues,
> Et pour sa voix lointaine, et calme, et grave, elle a
> L'inflexion des voix chères qui sont tues.

All of Verlaine's poems are in bud and the leaves already visible
in the *Poèmes saturniens*. Certain prosodic liberties, concealed here

and there, make me doubt that he had ever been a true Parnassian [2] in the bottom of his heart, in the bottom of his nerves. Whoever swoons on hearing

> Les sanglots longs
> Des violons,

was not Parnassian, nor was anyone who wove new metaphors of love:

> Baiser! rose trémière au jardin des caresses!

or who wrote as a prelude to his future poetic art:

> De la douceur, de la douceur, de la douceur.

This volume, published at the same time as Francois Coppée's *Le Reliquaire,* naturally had no success. It was seen lying hopelessly, for a long time, in the window of Lemerre's, passage Choiseul, among the euchologies of the successor of Percepied, seller of rosaries. One day, following *Le Passant,*[3] *Le Reliquaire* (which sometimes sold because of its title),[4] was taken away. *Les Poèmes saturniens* remained, awaiting their sisters, *Les Fêtes galantes,* who came to join them three years later, in 1869, and who did not enjoy a better fate. Verlaine, in spite of his friends' having put him in the first rank of new poets, was obliged to remain unknown to the public until 1884 or 1885, the year of *Jadis et Naguère.*

Poor *Fêtes galantes*—they would arrive unseasonably, at that time of political debates and riots, on the eve of the war and the Commune! In 1871, a new mentality had emerged. Was it the time to dream

> Au calme clair de lune triste et beau,
> Qui fait rêver les oiseaux dans les arbres
> Et sangloter d'extase les jets d'eau,
> Les grands jets d'eau sveltes parmi les marbres?

Was it the time to repeat to oneself, under horizons still bloody and inflamed:

> Le soir tombait, un soir équivoque, d'automne:
> Les belles, se pendant rêveuses à nos bras,
> Dirent alors des mots si spécieux tout bas
> Que notre âme depuis ce temps tremble et s'etonne?

At the very most, one would have murmured, while still shiver-
ing from the ancient fear:

Dans le vieux parc solitaire et glacé
Deux formes ont tout à l'heure passé. . . .

But no one was murmuring anything of the kind, and in order
that Verlaine's words, congealed by a terrible political winter, might
retain their sound and accent, it was necessary that the children of
around 1860 reach adulthood and that there appear, hungry at last
for something that had the smell of art, a generation tired beforehand of oppressive political and social strife.

Meanwhile, Verlaine had lived. Two years before the *Poèmes
saturniens,* he had entered the Hôtel de Ville [City Hall], where he
found in the various offices the poets Lafenestre, Velade, and Mérat,
and many afternoons were spent at the Café du Gaz in feverish dis-
cussions of art. He then admired Leconte de Lisle and seemed quite
taken by the precious poems the young Stéphane Mallarmé was
publishing in the *Parnasse contemporain.* Like Albert Samain, who
later succeeded him at the Hôtel de Ville, he did not deign to advance past the rank of clerk, although he had a good education, and
it is in that status that he remained until the fire.[5] Not having dared
to present himself again at the reconstituted offices in the Luxembourg, he passed for a communard, and that was the first of the
legends that weighed on his life, and the most grave, the one which,
casting him into a kind of vagrancy and misery, predisposed him to
bad adventures.

Verlaine's office years were the only good years of his life. Supported by a mediocre security, but all the same a security, he married for love. He believed he had found, in Mathilde Mauté de
Fleurville, the half-sister of the musician Charles de Sivry, the very
realization of all that was divine in his youthful poetry:

En robe grise et verte avec des ruches,
Un jour de juin que j'étais soucieux
Elle apparut. . . .

The thunderclap was reciprocal. Ecstatic, Verlaine lived in a
fairy land, awaiting the hour—that is the expression of his attentive
friend and biographer, M. Pelletier. Verlaine had not yet known
love, or an affair, or a caprice. His youth, as wild as a young god's,
but less chaste, had drunk only at the springs of chance, sudden

gushings forth at the kick of desire. The young girl intoxicated him with a new inebriation sufficient unto itself. He forgot alcohol, he became himself again—a naturally gentle being, a dreamer, rather timorous, with the heart of a child—so timid that he paid court by letters, by letters that were verses, which became *La Bonne Chanson!* Like a Sully Prudhomme, he sang the poetry of duty:

> Ce sera le devoir heureux aux gais combats. . . .

He was married to the noise of the first cannon shots, still distant, and the terrible year was for him the happy year.

However, favored by the enforced idleness of the seige and the barrack-room life of the guard-corps, the demon of alcohol retook possession of Verlaine, at the same time that another demon, perhaps more terrible still, came into his life: Arthur Rimbaud. That was the separation: Verlaine parted from the wife whom he had loved so much and was obliged never to see again. In 1872 he led Rimbaud off. What was this Rimbaud? Alas, Rimbaud, if not also a great poet, was one of the most conspicuous of the poets then in evidence. This urchin of genius who wrote only between the ages of sixteen and twenty, and then disappeared so completely that he was believed dead, was a freak of nature, a *lusus naturae,* as they used to call outlandish stones or crazy petrifications. After leaving the Charleville high school, he disembarked fraudulently at Paris, in February 1871, and improperly gained entrance to the atelier of André Gill; whence, uncouth, ill-bred, impertinent, brutal and wild, he introduced himself into the literary world where he provoked a sort of stupor. One could hate him, but not despise him, for the vicious child recited an incredibly high-strung poetry of a miraculous boldness and intense coloring—*Les Premières communions, Les Assis, Le Bateau ivre.* These pieces and others were published too late to have a real literary influence, but they attested to a singular and mature precocity. One of these verses has been long repeated in an ironic manner:

> Avec l'assentiment des grandes héliotropes.

The following are truer words that reveal the profound melancholy of the bad boy of genius:

> Mais vrai, j'ai trop pleuré. Les aubes sont navrantes,
> Tout lune est atroce, et tout soleil amer. . . .

His famous sonnet of the *Voyelles,* which was cited at that time as the very type of decadent poetry, revealed, to practitioners of physiological psychology, the not very rare phenomenon of color audition. A mountain of writing has been raised, for twenty years, on that question.

Was it Verlaine who carried off Rimbaud, or Rimbaud who carried off Verlaine, the Verlaine with a woman's nerves? I have my own ideas on that, but we will pass on. They stayed together in London for nearly a year. Verlaine tired first and fled to Brussels, where Rimbaud, recalled by Verlaine, joined him. Here we have some facts and a psychology, both equally obscure, especially seeing that to this intimacy was added, in some of Verlaine's letters dated from that period, the constant memory of the wife he would have liked to regain. Finally, to a request for money by Rimbaud, Verlaine responded with a revolver. That resolved a situation without explaining it. Had Verlaine been the victim of Rimbaud's frightful vanity, who was then parading all his vices? Perhaps, but Verlaine concealed, beneath his superficial naiveté of a child, a complicated nature, triple and quadruple, so that one could not make head nor tail of it. He spent two years in prison at Mons. It has been recently proposed that a commemorative plaque be placed on the jail. I believe silence would be more appropriate, if silence were possible. Still we cannot forget that it was there that he wrote the book that made him one of France's greatest Catholic poets: *Sagesse. Romances sans paroles* had appeared, during the very time of his imprisonment, through the good offices of M. Edmond Lepelletier; and it is there that is found the famous arietta, so loved and so often repeated:

> Il pleure dans mon coeur
> Comme il pleut sur la ville.
> Quelle est cette langueur
> Qui pénètre mon coeur?

If his conversion, which was very sincere and was to be reflected in the last fine books, *Amour* and *Bonheur,* sometimes modified the nature of his poetic inspiration, it had no influence whatever on his life and habits. Hence some people have concluded that his conversion was primarily literary. I do not believe it. Verlaine was scarcely capable of dissociating reason from feeling, but he was always the slave of sensation and could never resist a physical desire. His drunkenness, his wraths, his loves were equally terrible. Dominated by his senses, he was a frightful man. When he escaped from their tyranny, he became the pure and gentle poet once again, the finely ironic conversationalist, the good comrade, the promenader of dreams and smiles. Unfortunately, as the days passed, he lost the little mastery he had over himself, and his last years slipped away in a kind of vulgar spree in which he was encouraged, to his misfortune and their shame, by young persons, today much wiser, whose sole glory will be to have drunk with Verlaine. At least, he who seemed destined for the hospital, had the happiness of escaping from it in his last days, and of dying in the small lodging of a steady worker, cared for by his last mistress.

Verlaine was a great poet and he has had a great influence on French poetry. One can say that whatever the material form our poetry has affected—free verse, liberated verse,[6] romantic verse—it has been entirely and still is under the domination of Verlaine. The most recently celebrated poets, like Mme de Noailles, are still Verlainians by a certain manner of breaking the rhythm while preserving the flow, of avoiding any display of eloquence, of voluntarily neglecting the rhyme. It was not until rather belatedly, in *Jadis et Naguère* (1885) and in terms at once picturesque and somewhat prophetic, that he addressed to M. Charles Morice, who was destined to best penetrate Verlaine's genius, the *Art poétique* wherein generations of poets have found their justification: Music above all. —Do not be too precise: fear excessive clarity.— Not the color but the shading.— Avoid epigram, wit, laughter.— No eloquence: strangle it.— Rhyme? It is a cheap bauble that rings hollow and false under the file.

> Que ton vers soit la bonne aventure
> Eparse au vent crispé du matin,
> Qui va fleurant la menthe et le thym. . . .
> Et tout le reste est littérature.

Despite certain licenses, as Théodore de Banville used to say, it is rather in the language itself than in the prosody that Verlaine is an innovator. His phrases rise and fall in tone, suddenly split up, are forgotten as in a suspension of distracted thought, set out again, arrive at the goal of which caprice never loses sight. Verlaine's verses never suggest effort, erasures, or repeated starts. The short poem, often a sonnet, unrolls with a perfect certainty, in conformity to a free unity of rhythm, a music that sings from within. Verlaine's poetry, form and thought, is entirely spontaneous; it is a "lost wax casting",[7] it is or it is not. Nothing suggests a retouching. The style does not change: whether the inspiration be religious or libertine, it is the same pure fluidity; whether the stream flows over grass or gravel, the voice sings always the same amorous song; whether his love laughs at women or angels, it is nearly the same sensuality. He himself has blended, in his *Parallèlement,* these two nuances of his dream: eroticism and mysticism.

Verlaine, renovator of poetic feeling, creator of his diction and verse, sincerely believed himself the very type of decadent poet. He has expressed it magnificently:

Je suis l'empire à la fin de la décadence. . . .

The idea and the word came from Huysmans, who portrayed in des Esseintes, the famous puppet,[8] the very type of lover of all decadences. It had consequences. A good part of the younger generation willed itself decadent. It is an amusing chapter of the literary history of our time, but it needs the details which will be said another time, now that the portraits of the masters are being finished, those who must stand in the frontispiece of those memories, like patrons and protectors.

—From *Promenades littéraires,* 4me série, 1912

The Sensibility
of
Jules Laforgue

Jules Laforgue, author of the *Moralités légendaires* and *Fleurs de bonne volonté,* was an exquisite person and a charming genius. He died at the age of twenty-seven, too young for us to judge him—we can only love him.

He is one writer whose complete works it is not ridiculous to collect. True, they amount to three volumes. As he loved to write, these three volumes, if he had lived, would have greatly multiplied; and his contemporaries, in this current year when he would have been forty-four years old, would already and for a long time have had to make difficult choices. We write too much. The exercise of thought has become too easy. Laforgue was inclined to follow his facility: the gods have, perhaps, shown him clemency.

His intelligence was very lively, but closely linked to his sensibility. All original intelligences are so composed—they are the expression, the flowering, of a physiology. But, in the process of living, one acquires the faculty of dissociating intelligence from sensibility. This happens, sooner or later, by the acquisition of a new faculty—skepticism. Laforgue died before reaching this stage.

Full of good will, like his verses, which often did not have other merits, he sought to free himself from his youthful sentimentalism. Irony was the instrument he used; but his sentimentalism resisted and he never succeeded in vanquishing it. At the moment when he first had an inkling of the advent of skepticism, a fortuitous encounter took place which cast it back into the realm of simple sentiment. He himself has told of the adventure. It is a delectable tale, to which truth adds a certain pleasure but which it can do without. We find it in one of the letters he sent to his sister from Berlin.[1] To many young men, this letter will seem childish. Few young ladies, on the

other hand, will read it without emotion; and men who have passed
the age when sentiment is expressed with such ingenuousness will
regret no longer being capable of such candor.

Have I told you this winter about a young English girl,
from whom I have taken some lessons in pronunciation?
Well, it was day before yesterday evening that I declared
myself and she said yes, and we became engaged. Since day
before yesterday my life no longer belongs to me alone, and
I feel all the grandeur of that idea. . . . I have not yet
kissed her. Yesterday I was seated near her in a carriage, in
the evening, and while looking at her the idea came to me
that I could caress her hair—*my head swam at the
thought* . . . [Gourmont's italics].

Love, at the first blow, vanquished irony. The mocking bird of
the *Moralités légendaires* became the touching little blue bird. The
tale ended with a marriage, the delicious nuptials of two consump-
tives who were soon to die and had to drink ardently at the fast
evaporating spring.

Before this most normal of emotional crises, experienced with
such joy, Laforgue had thought much about women and love,
which is of course completely natural. Did his early biased opinion
of women differ noticeably from that derived of Miss Leah Lee?
He said in his *Aphorismes et réflexions:*

At bottom women are commonplace creatures.

Women, those mediocre and magical beings.

A loved woman who has the consolation and distraction of a magnificent head of hair to look after is by that
token less of an encumbrance in our lives.

Women often affect me like babies, important babies,
monstrously developed.

No matter how realistic and routine life may be, the irresistible argument—absolutely irresistible in conquering a
woman—is the threat of suicide. Think about it—it's magnificent!

But he also wrote some small bits of tenderness entirely comparable to those which fill the letter announcing his engagement: "Part, caress that fine blonde hair . . . is it possible! Nature will not shudder at it? Could it happen?" Take away the irony which is so obvious, especially at the end of the paragraph, which I have not quoted, and it is the same attitude of adoration before the mystery of virginal purity. The young girl (he was interested above all in young girls) is for him an almost supernatural creature. He sees her, like Dante and his contemporaries, in a radiant, celestial atmosphere which isolates her from the vulgar world. But all the same, what dominates these first notes is irony. He mocks or pretends to mock. Perhaps, at bottom, he plays the dupe, but he does not want it to seem so—not even to himself. From the time of his engagement, his ideas change—that is, they dissolve into sentiment. The ironist becomes an amorist. The entire section of thoughts entitled *Impressions* belong to this period, although the editors have inserted it between two chapters, both from an earlier period. These *Impressions* are no longer thoughts "about woman," as the general title states. With the immodesty of writers who compose their works with everything that is most intimate in their lives, Laforgue converses with us about his own woman. And it is a hymn:

> How pure she is, absolute, exceptional!—I love her as
> life itself. I would forget life for her, her hands in mine.
> . . .

He is conquered, and he will not have time to reconquer himself.

Intelligence was of a fine quality in Laforgue. He would have reconquered himself, if a long life had been given him. His irony would have gone very far. There was genius in this young man, the stuff, perhaps, of a Jonathan Swift; but of a Swift tempered by sentiment and poetry. He might have spent his entire life, even if it had been a very long one, watching the perpetual struggle in himself between intelligence and sensibility, and that might have given us the most beautiful and lively of works.

He has left us the *Moralités légendaires,* some verses, some letters, some thoughts, and these are the bases of a palace scarcely risen above its foundations, but already sufficiently visible to attest to the genius of the architect. Laforgue is missed by our literature of today where he counts so many friends, where he would have had few equals, and where no one represents that extraordinary sentimental irony of which he is the sole master.

From *Promenades littéraires,* I, 1904

PART IV

Criticism and Critics

Sainte-Beuve,
Creator of Values

The importance of Sainte-Beuve, which is becoming increasingly apparent and unchallenged, affirms the importance of criticism.

Poets and artists create phantoms which sometimes become immortal in the traditions of mankind. The critic, like the philosopher, creates values. The work of art does not conclude. Wherever there is conclusion, there is criticism. Persons of small perspicacity used to ask of Sainte-Beuve: "But what is your conclusion?" "My conclusion," he would reply, "begins with the first line of my study." The critical mind seeks intentions and attributes them necessarily to the very works which are most lacking in them. Who has given Helen her value? The critics, and Goethe in particular, whose poetry itself is a collection of judgments. There are certain legends, certain popular stories, which have never acquired their full value, even though the world knows them by heart, because they have never found the critic to extract it. Who will say, for example, everything that is to be found in *Beauty and the Beast?*

It is due to the absence of sacerdotal criticism, much more than to transformations in the language, that old French poetry has fallen into disrepute during the last centuries. *Pantagruel* is almost as difficult to read as *Berthe aux grands pieds;* but criticism began, supported by the printing press, and Rabelais' popularity, attested to by innumerable editions, became his glory, thanks to the judgments of his contemporaries, rewritten year after year. In the middle of the seventeenth century, Boileau appeared and established for three centuries the catalog of good poets of his time. Boileau was a great creator of values. His authority, in spite of Romantic reputations, has been but slightly diminished down to our own time. Against a Théophile or a Saint-Amant, such a highly talented writer always had ready some verse of *Satires.* Later, with less good fortune and only momentary authority, Voltaire tries to assume the role; but minds were becoming less docile and the very notion of taste fading away, effacing forever the Temple of Taste.

Laharpe, for a time, fixed literary values. His authority was uprooted only by that of Sainte-Beuve. Only Sainte-Beuve's *Causeries du Lundi* could overcome the *Cours de Littérature.* Despite appearances, Sainte-Beuve was almost the only critic of the nineteenth century, the only creator of values. Although since the Consulate and until the last years of the century, works and pages of criticism have abounded, almost no other critic has had the power to establish durably the image of one of his contemporaries or to bring current opinion to revise old judgments. Théophile Gautier's *Grotesques* would have been one of the exceptions, if the author of that agreeable and just book had not first acquired the reputation of a poet and fantasist. All the others, and those who had for forty years the most brilliant authority—the Villemains, the Nisards, or, lower down the scale, the Pontmartins, and so many others of good minds and good will—of them there remains nothing but some worthless pages, unless one can smile at anecdotes or sneer at malice. The critic who is a creator of values is as rare as the great poet.

What we call a critic today is a former "good student" who has contracted, first from his secondary school and then usually from Ecole Normale, the taste for wearisome studies. After having been a professor for a time, he passes into journalism, and writes appreciations of new books. He gives his advice, prudently, cites the authorities, ends by insinuating that none of this has any importance. And it is true. Sainte-Beuve, even before he had any inkling of a vocation in criticism, and from the time of his very first essays, seriously interrogated his literary conscience. He had the sense of relationships and relativity. He knew how to dissociate men and works, although his method seemed, on the contrary, to unite them much more closely than anyone—except perhaps the ancients—had ever dared to do before. But he was not unaware that there are men superior to their works, and vice versa. The values that he creates from that moment on are not definitive: he feels and he speaks. But, actually, even if he often has to retouch, he rarely has to erase.[1]

With perhaps the exception of the *Méditations,* none of his first romantic works passed directly into the hands of the public. Each was announced, prepared by clever notes confided to the newspapers. Then, once the books appeared, the critic mounted the podium and explained the new gospel to the people. Sometimes Sainte-Beuve was this sermonizer; but, more often, he preferred to hold back, to wait until the impression of astonishment had died down a bit. For relaxation, he studied Racine or even Delille. He accustomed himself to the impartiality of portraiture, while in the very midst of the battles, which he was waging, along with his friends, against antiquated forms of style and thought.

The essential image which we have of Romanticism has been provided by Sainte-Beuve. Writers which he has discussed will always have at least a profile in literary history. We will always have to go to some trouble to make out the lineaments of those about whom he was silent. And this situation will persist, in spite of all efforts, until such a time as another creator of values comes and revises these paintings. But a parallel with Boileau could be drawn here: for a long time his authority will probably fare like that of the satirist. It will die down momentarily only to revive again. After all, a rule is necessary, that is, a limitation, even in literature—memory is limited, and limited are our capacities for admiration and even for taste. Supplements, pages added to the catalog, are scarcely ever consulted. Thus it is with judgments aimed at rehabilitation or dismissal. What is done is done.

During the period following Sainte-Beuve, his authority decreased remarkably, and that in proportion as the years passed. The phenomenon is not unusual and conforms to all that we know of human psychology. It stems from the fact that literary judgments are not purely intellectual—they involve a good deal of sentiment. Now sentiment diminishes with age; or at least, our sympathetic faculties not being infinitely extendible, there comes a time when the literary production of the latest arrivals, even if it still interests us, no longer arouses us. We feel clearly enough that there is a struggle going on, but it is to be settled among men of another season. Our part is done, or at least recorded, barring flukes. Those who are coming along may begrudge us our role, but they cannot seriously dispute it. The result of all this is that the judgments of one generation about the work of following generations often reveal a certain flabbiness. Sainte-Beuve was fond of Baudelaire, but he did not dare to say so. *Madame Bovary* interested him, but he did not know how to distinguish between it and Feydeau's *Fanny*. I think that instead of reproaching Sainte-Beuve for these weaknesses, we would do better to profit from them. Young people could also draw this conclusion: that instead of seeking our judgment, they would do better, as we did fifteen years ago, to judge themselves and each other. This attitude does not prevent cordial relations, nor mutual esteem or admiration; but it would avoid the errors from which the two parties suffer. It is more worthwhile to refrain than to write Sainte-Beuve's articles on *Salammbô*.

But Sainte-Beuve could no longer refrain. He was too involved and had moved too far toward the status of Oracle of Delphi. He regained his plenitude of judgment quickly enough when he again turned his attention toward the past, that is, toward his youth, toward the books he had seen born or those which, at the age of twenty-five, his curiosity had discovered.

For this category of works he was no less a creator of values than he was for those of the Romantic period. It is even possible to state that the most certain and definitive values that he created were those which found their place between Ronsard and Victor Hugo.

It is he who created Ronsard and the whole Pléiade, and all the excavations that have since been organized into sixteenth century soil.

Today it seems quite natural to love Ronsard and to reread, from time to time, some sonnet from his *Amours*. Before Sainte-Beuve, and outside of a rather narrow circle of inquisitives, Ronsard was esteemed almost to the same extent as Nostradamus. France did not move beyond the singularly erroneous evaluation of this great poet created by Boileau. It is the only judgment of Boileau's that posterity might have cleanly shattered, and it could not do it except with the aid of a Sainte-Beuve. His *Tableau de la poésie française au xvie siècle* seems a bit timorous today, but remember that it was written for the slaves of Boileau, the students of Laharpe, the admirers of Delille. Its judgments, however, are clear and sound, and one finds almost nothing but just appraisals. M. L. Séché, who knows the Pléiade and the cénacle[2] equally well, thought very highly of the *Tableau;* I owe this appreciation to him. It can serve to measure the creative power of the critic, which could support itself, in this work of thaumaturgy, only on its genius alone.

The second of Sainte-Beuve's creations in the past—we can all name it—is *Port-Royal*. But there he did more than indicate the places where he guessed treasures to be—he himself sank the pickaxe into the burial mound and brought up before astonished eyes a civilization which, while contemporary with *Phèdre* and *Tartuffe,* was also one of catacombs. The discovery of these wild Christians was not without influence on the evolution of religious minds, nor on that of Sainte-Beuve himself. Thus, he knew, in passing from Ronsard to Pascal, the extremes of man's tendencies: he needed no longer be surprised at anything.

To what extent did Sainte-Beuve create the value of Chateaubriand? Such an evaluation would be a delicate matter. There is general agreement in the belief that he intended to disparage Chateaubriand rather than praise him. He appreciated the immense importance of the author of the *Génie,* but he cared little for the man and still less for his tendencies, perhaps because he had submitted to them at the time of his crisis of religiosity. After having first appeared slightly satirical, Sainte-Beuve's portrait of Chateaubriand ended by achieving, in its turn, the perfect resemblance. Certain ecclesiasts today are alone in still affirming the profound religious sincerity of René.[3] Right up to the end Chateaubriand sustained nobly the role he had elected at the very first, through political views and sentiment; but he was the "great disenchanted" because of religion as well as all the rest. For his secret life was passionate. The hand of Sainte-Beuve was sacrilegious, perhaps, only because it stripped away the veil a few years too soon. It was, at the same time, creative: the Chateaubriand that it conjured up is indeed our own, such that his value was created from that moment in 1848, in Liége.

Sainte-Beuve fixed the characters of almost all the French writers and some men and women who played an intellectual role from the Renaissance until after the middle of the nineteenth century. The middle ages necessarily escaped him, except for a few figures more historical than literary, and similarly there escaped him, for the reasons that have been given, his contemporaries making the latest news. But everything in between received his mark—he stamped French literature with his own image, and that coinage is still in circulation.

The grandeur of that role is beyond compare, and it really matters little that, among so many heads, some might have been missed in the engraving or demolished by the impact. No work is definitive. Every century is obliged to recast even the finest and most venerated poems in order to be able to read them, to feel and understand them. And it is the same with art. One might say, though with the fear of not being understood, that Chateaubriand and Victor Hugo recreated Gothic architecture. It was dead, it had been scorned for two centuries. Nobody was in the least concerned with it until after the Revolution, when the Consulate suddenly provoked the flowering of a springtime in which everything appeared renewed and rejuvenated. Chateaubriand had portrayed Notre Dame from afar, like a dream-vision. Victor Hugo went inside, made himself at home, rang its bells, and all cathedrals began to resound and revive. Sainte-Beuve, at that very moment, undertaking exactly the work that his century was waiting for, set about remaking French literature. His method, or rather *the* method, for there is only one —was the renewal of motives. Bossuet has been constantly admired for three centuries: but for each century the motives for admiration have changed. The one who changes them is the creative critic. In renewing the premises of our judgment, he renews that judgment itself, although it may not vary in its substance, and the work, under this unexpected illumination, appears fresh and almost original. There is also creation through the alteration of environment. Thus a beautiful architectural monument lost among ramshackle hovels suddenly emerges in all its splendor, as when one destroys the matrix which encloses the diamond. There are ancient motives for admiration which lead more readily to contempt, because little by little they have become heaped up around the masterpiece until they have spoiled one's view of it. The critical genius of Sainte-Beuve lay in creating gardens and planting trees around chapels which superannuated motives for admiration used to conceal from our own admiration.

Of this very important function, Sainte-Beuve, from a certain moment on, at least, was fully aware. He wrote, about 1850, among some thoughts collected at the end of *Derniers Portraits:* "In criticism I have played the lawyer enough—let us now play the judge."

He played the judge and his judgments have created the literary values according to which we judge in our turn.

—From *Promenades philosophiques,* 1904

M. Brunetière

I have no great faith in the customary hierarchical distinction, in literature, between critics and creators. It is difficult for me to admit that Taine was any less creative than his contemporary in time, Octave Feuillet, or, if we move to the highest level, that Aristotle was less creative than Shakespeare, his contemporary in space. Whether one writes a novel or a history of French literature, the structuring of the work is a matter of establishing new, or seemingly new, relationships between known facts. It is a matter of providing the reader with new grounds for understanding or new grounds for feeling. In both cases, there is creation. But if the usual distinction still obtains, it must be based, not on the quality of the performer, but on the materials of his performance. Here, to make the issue clearer, let us change our terms and compare the novelist and the critic. The one aspires to touch our sensibility in a new way; the other aspires to interest, in a new way, our intelligence. The two workers ply different trades, but they have in common the fact that both are obliged either to be original, each in his own line, or to be nothing at all. They must both be creators of values, one in the order of the sensibility, the other in the order of the intelligence. In short, it takes as much genius to be a great critic as to be a great novelist.

I do not mean to say that Brunetière had genius; but it is still possible, with a well-managed talent, to cut a figure in the world. Brunetière cut a figure, and a good one. Very few of his literary contemporaries were his superiors, and I cannot see—to continue my initial line of reasoning—in what way, for example, he would have been inferior to Paul Bourget, his comrade in difficult times. He did not write novels, but what becomes of our novels? Is there indeed, today, a novelist who believes in himself and hopes to be presented, in full glory, to future generations? And were there any yesterday? Would it be Alphonse Daudet, towards whom Brunetière was indulgent, or Emile Zola, towards whom he was cruel? Some stories of Villiers de l'Isle-Adam and Maupassant are perhaps all that posterity will know of the French imagination of that period, which was the period of naturalism. We will have to seek out summaries and judgments, the remains of books which are currently out of favor and which will gradually acquire the value of Merovingian cemeteries or Egyptian tombs. Some of Brunetière's books will be among them. And are not the novelists already of this opinion, those who entreat us to talk about their works? They are ingenuously aware that, if no one talked about them, they would not exist. There, perhaps, is the triumph of the critic. He is the grave-digger, at least, and during the time he is performing his duty, he survives the deceased he is responsible for burying. Sometimes he is a marble-mason and sets up a small monument on the freshly turned earth. That is what survives: the bust survives the city, and, sometimes, the city of books.

The duty of the critic is one of coordination and, even more, of architecture. He does not shape the stones, but he gives them their proper place in the ensemble of the monument. Brunetière, at one time in his career, understood this rather well. He even designed completely new plans, according to which literary architecture would indeed have had to take on an entirely new face. It was his great conception—only he neglected to put it into effect. That was about 1890. The ideas of Darwin had finally entered into general circulation. Taine, on the other hand, had launched his famous trio of terms: race, milieu, and moment. Brunetière, boldly joining Darwinism with Tainism, traced a marvelous plan of the evolution of literary genres, based on—or rather the counterpart of—the evolution of animal species. He set about, first of all, teaching us about literary genres considered as kinds of living organisms subject to transformations. Then, he showed us how these singular animals submit to the actions of vital competition and natural selection. There was also the question of heredity and individuality, of the homogeneous and the heterogeneous, and several other mysteries. For a brief moment Brunetière, who was then concealing his secret ideas, passed for a fiery revolutionary. What kind of man was it who came along and overthrew the old critical considerations and coolly replaced Boileau with Darwin and Sainte-Beuve with Haeckel? He was a man who was deceiving himself and who, moreover, was not slow in perceiving it. The program of the evolution of genres was never put into effect. All that we knew of it was contained in an innocent study on *The Evolution of Lyric Poetry in the Nineteenth Century,* an honorable work and one which any conscientious professor might have successfully carried out; for nothing is really less mysterious than the transformations in French poetry from Népomucène Lemercier to Francis Vielé-Griffin. Darwin, for the purposes of this study, seems to offer only modest assistance.

Why, then, did Brunetière try to graft his method onto Darwinism? It is because Darwin—like all other historians of animal life, moreover—made abstractions of individuals. Natural history knows only species, and it assumes, in principle, that all normal individuals of the same species are identical, at any given moment, to one another. The scientific method pleased Brunetière because it enabled him to combat individualism, which always seemed to him dangerous both socially and intellectually. Nevertheless, when speaking of personal works, one ought to mention persons; but this will only be accorded a secondary place. Literary history will no longer be a sequence of portraits, of individual lives. It is the poetry and not the poets which will be the concern of history. It will be a matter of poetry and history, and not of poets or historians. We will study works, without giving too great an importance to the authors, and we will show how works engender one another by natural necessity; how the species poetry gives birth to the species sonnet and madrigal; how, under the influence of environment, the variety lyricism is transformed, without losing its essential characteristics, into eloquence, and many other such metamorphoses.

This was the first madness of Brunetière. It was short-lived, however, and was soon followed by a violent reaction of reason. Brunetière, by virtue of his dullness, seemed endowed with great levelheadedness; but he was, on the contrary, a man of strong feelings. Whenever he found himself obliged to reverse a judgment, he did so in a most immoderate fashion. Hard on others, he proved to be equally hard on himself: "Darwin's *The Descent of Man* or Professor Haeckel's *Natural History of Creation* are, to call them by their right names, merely scientific novels." He recognized, on the other hand, that it was impossible to make of criticism "a science analogous to natural history." This last declaration should suffice: Brunetière was not a scientist, but neither was Darwin a novelist. All the same, there should be in this experience a point to bear in mind. It should be clearly visible, and it should at least lend support to Taine and the influence of environment and time. Brunetière had succumbed to Darwin because Darwin was highly fashionable in the Sorbonne environment where Brunetière had spent his youth. And his was not the only fine mind to be unseasonably subjected to the Darwinian method and to try, with greater or lesser success, to transplant it to new soil. About the same time, Arsène Darmesteter was writing his *Life of Words,* a delightful and absurd book, in which the details are new and exact—but whose conception is so insane that it almost derailed the entire study of philology. It took the good sense of Michel Bréal to make us understand how senseless it is to try to study languages by making abstractions from human psychology and individual will. I believe that M. Bréal contributed to putting Brunetière back on the right track.

Of this painful contact with science, Brunetière retained a most disagreeable memory. Not having been able to bend science to his own use, to a predetermined use, he believed that it was not good for anything. As it had not responded when he interrogated it regarding the evolution of literary genres, he believed that it was incapable of making any useful response whatever, and so, with impetuous haste, he proclaimed its bankruptcy. This was Brunetière's second madness, and the one which established his reputation as the most reasonable of men. It was already greatly to his credit to have repudiated Darwin, and when he repudiated all of science, he became the master of those who feared science but did not dare to confess their fear. But did he repudiate all science? Here we find a singular misunderstanding. Brunetière, at one time, was without doubt one of those who believed that science was going to revive, not renovate, metaphysics, religion, morality—that it was going to take on, on its own account, the comforting role which Christianity still played for some good souls. At the very least, science, so they thought, was finally going to give them, in one sense or another, some certainties. But science, and this alone is certain, brought them nothing but negations, and these negations it set forth with a grand air of indifference. There followed a profound disillusionment, and those who suffered from their doubts resigned themselves to turning once again to the old traditional affirmations. The failure of science, which Brunetière proclaimed, was a failure of metaphysics.

When one needs metaphysics, one soon needs religion. Metaphysics is the first step on the stairway of mysticism. Brunetière climbed it to the very top and there he could rejoice at having accomplished in the spiritual order what he had always labored to accomplish in the literary order: he had tied together the strands of tradition. So he believed. He believed that he had contributed to a stabilizing enterprise. To restore the spirit of authority in all domains; to make men understand that there is a higher will to the orders of which they must subject their instincts, their sensibilities, and perhaps even their reason; to teach that all activities must be regulated and limited by rules, which exist in politics as in grammar, in morality as in art; to accept this universal authority for oneself and, having accepted it, to impose it on others—all this Brunetière found in Catholicism. He was Catholic, and, to tell the truth and in spite of his access of transformist madness, he always had been. Nobody is converted—a man reverts to what he was, at the beginning of his life, and what he has secretly remained, in spite of appearances. Brunetière's taste for the classical seventeenth century was one indication: nobody converses daily with Bossuet unless he has a certain taste, avowed or latent, for religious verities. Another indication could have been furnished by Brunetière's covert tendencies—the aversion he almost always showed for modern literature. Even when it is mediocre, contemporary literature has the very great interest of being alive, of reflecting the tendencies of the moment, that is to say, reflecting what is of immediate importance to us who have at our disposal only a moment of life. But Brunetière always liked to live in eternity, and for him all moments were equal, those of the past and those of today, in the sense that he understood only the life of the mind, that he was not interested in men, but only in works.

Among his publications, however, there are two volumes entitled *Essays* and *New Essays on Contemporary Literature,* but we should not expect to find in these works a picture, even fragmentary, of the literary movement as we feel it, as we live it. True contemporary literature, with its fevers, its naivetés, its audacity—its incoherence, if you wish, but inquisitive and even impassioned—of this Brunetière knew nothing. His tastes have always led him towards the reasonable, conventionable work, towards the wise imitations of wise works. If, by chance, he dares to pause before a book that seems to flout tradition, his moral preoccupations prevent him from finding any pleasure in it. Since he has, all the same, a certain sense of art, he admires; but morality takes over, and he condemns. Sainte-Beuve's timidity was often hypocritical; Brunetière's is fundamental and therefore logical, in perfect harmony with his principles. In one of his books, however, he comes to grips with contemporary literary reality, in the volume entitled *The Naturalistic Novel*. How I savored, in those times, its harsh injustice! I will always remember a chapter on Huysmans, where Brunetière demonstrates that *A Rebours* is constructed like a vaudeville. It is the only time that he ever made an amusing criticism. But how inappropriate it was! It mistreated a novel by a naturalist, without realizing that it was not a naturalistic novel. Wishing to strike one literary group, he wounded another. Believing that he was harrowing naturalism, he was railing at nascent symbolism, which was soon to produce several minds rather disposed to enjoy, something in which they were fortunate, classicism and French tradition. Such as it is, with its exaggerations, its scorn or bad humor, this book remains perhaps Brunetière's best effort—one, at least, which testifies that he did not live always and exclusively in the past, and that innovations did not always catch him napping.

Nevertheless, I admire his perseverance in working with those old subjects; for this, when one possesses a good method of investigation, is not at all a useless business. Brunetière's method is the historical method, and it is there alone that his notions on evolution find a logical application. He uses it, in fact, in his studies to establish the genealogy of ideas and literary forms. He confronts the texts and, while being careful not to confuse intentions with works, he is pleased to discover unexpected and even remote origins for conceptions which one would have thought to be most recent. Then, he addresses himself to the question of hierarchy, which for him has a capital importance. He declassifies and reclassifies with such solicitude that he cannot help evoking smiles: he would have been quite capable of presenting us with a prize list of French literature, from the first prize to the five-hundredth honorable mention. It might even be supposed that he read all of the works whose titles he cites, for more than half his life must have been spent in serious reading —required reading, those readings in which one takes notes and checks back in order to compare two ideas given in different passages. One of these hierarchical studies, only thirty pages long, contains the titles of fifty-five dramatic pieces—it is staggering. The erudition of Brunetière is not indulgent. Should I say that it is the erudition of pedantry? No, it is rather one of excessive precision, and also of conscientiousness—he likes to offer proofs at every step. If his judgments, supported by such apparatus, do not satisfy all who are subject to the law, they do satisfy the judge, for Brunetière exhausts the facts of the cases in question. In order to reconsider them after him, we should steer clear of all erudition. We will need a method that is completely different as well as more difficult to apply; but it would still be a method, and one preferable to my taste. Let us take a work, recent or old, and see if it recommends itself to our intelligence, if it provokes us to reflection, if it arouses our sensibility, if it evokes in us desires or dreams, if, in short, it flatters our ideal of beauty. But Brunetière shrugs his shoulders at such a program: he despises the critic "of tastes and colors." As if he would indeed demonstrate that if red is a beautiful color, violet is necessarily a detestable color!

This man was an inveterate rationalist. He believed in nothing but reason. He gathered everything under its principle, forgetting that the domain of reason is, in the final analysis, extremely limited and that the logic which guides us is almost always, as M. Ribot expresses it, only the logic of the feelings. He himself granted this sometimes, and especially toward the end of his career, when religion became his source of inspiration, when he bowed before dogmas from which reason, precisely, is absent, when he demanded of his beliefs grounds for aversion or preference. But we should recognize that, even at times when he returned to entirely literary subjects, Brunetière no longer compromised with his rationalist principles. His last book, his *Balzac,* is the proof. The militant catholic, the preacher of *Science and Religion,* does not show through—to the extent that one might well wonder if the conversion of M. Brunetière had not been a maneuver dictated by politics rather than a maneuver of conscience.

I consider his work to be a repertory of literary facts, ideas, and judgments, and a valuable one. But we should not look there for anything else. Brunetière has never had anything but objective ideas, those which are the product of the will or of a method, which can be acquired. These ideas are reasonable, they are just, they are not original. What Brunetière lacks is the ferment of idealism. I read in his *Balzac:* "Not only is it not true, as a matter of fact, that everything appears to each of us under a different aspect which would determine its 'idiosyncrasy'—and we have there only a prodigious and impertinent illustration of pride—but the same reality imposes itself on all intellects; and, for each thing, there is only one vision which is exact and 'conformable to the object,' just as, for each fact, there is only one formula which is scientific." This quotation, better than a lengthy discourse, shows the limitations and nature of Brunetière's mind. With his principles, one comes to deny the legitimacy of all individual activity. Art completely disappears. Originality becomes a breach of good taste. Every object, every deed allows of only one valid representation, which is therefore true; and ideas are necessarily divided into two classes—the true, and the non-true.

Brunetière lived his life bogged in this infantile philosophy. Who says, then, that he continued the work of Taine? Let us remain firmly attached to the principle—unassailable, moreover—of subjective idealism: "The world is my representation." It is the only fertile principle, the only one which permits, which demands, the free development of minds and sensibilities.

—From *Promenades littéraires,* 3me série, 1909

Jules Lemaître

"The imagination could not invent so many diverse contrarities as exist naturally in the heart of man." It is a very just maxim of La Rochefoucauld. To make it fully understood, we would have to put it into modern language, replace "contrarities" with "contrary tendencies," and "heart" with "sensibility." The language of the seventeenth century has become, for the common reader, almost as obscure as that of the thirteenth. We think we grasp its nuances at the first glance, but it requires study. M. Jules Lemaître, whose education was entirely classical, could translate this maxim much better than I. Moreover, he should know it intimately, for it contains the elements of his literary portrait and the secret of his psychology.

These "contrarities" or contrary tendencies, when they exist in very great number and pronounced form in a conscious sensibility, inevitably engender skepticism. We dare not condemn tastes which we are not far from sharing, though we might not have yet satisfied them, nor opinions which are quite acceptable to us at certain times, nor acts which make us secretly envious. Our good will does not vacillate. It is, like our sensibility, successive: there are few utterances that do not please it, each in turn, just as inimical pieces of music, if our ear is free from principles, can be pleasing one at a time.

This skepticism by excess of aptitudes for feeling is rather rare. There are other kinds, less estimable. There is the skepticism of the fool, who is not interested in anything; that of the coward, who does not dare to speak his thoughts for fear of responsibilities; the skepticism of the timid, who fears being judged; that of the weak, whose shiftiness sometimes has the appearance of diversity; that of the prudent, who does not dare to make decisions; that of the ambi-

tious, who prefers to sit on the fence and wait; that of the voluptuous, who lets himself, like the clever swimmer, drift from wave to
wave with the rhythm of life. The state of skepticism is so attractive
that it has always made the common run of men envious. They attribute to it their vices and failures: the hypocrisy of skepticism is
one of the most widespread and most difficult to unmask.

But life almost always succeeds in doing just that. The fool
ends by being interested at least in himself, in that self to which
time has given a certain importance, as it does to most stupid and
ugly, but very ancient, things. The weak man, some day, becomes
angry, and we know, by the source of his anger, his secret inclina-
tion. The coward has found shelter in a coterie, which allows him to
display a certain bravado. The prudent man betrays himself, in finally bringing his anxieties to bear on a single point. The voluptu-
ary soon becomes weary even of voluptuousness, and we see that his
skepticism was nothing but laziness. Satisfied, the ambitious man
can no longer conceal his goal, since he has reached it.

There remains the man of "diverse contrarities," who will be, in
this case, M. Jules Lemaître. Let us see by what mechanism he
moves from skepticism to partisanship. A man cannot exercise his
diverse aptitudes equally except by dividing among them the sum
total of activities he has at his disposal; but this division, which
seems easy during the time of youth, during the years of growing
energy, starts to become troublesome the day when energy ceases to
increase. It is frankly insupportable from the moment that, even to
an imperceptible degree, energy begins to diminish. Then we have
to choose. We become resigned, we unburden ourselves. Some persons suddenly unload all the burdens but one; others are content,
provisionally at least, to arrange them in greater equilibrium. A hierarchical order of activities is established. This lasts for some years,
then a new arrangement pushes to the fore an activity which up to
that time was only rarely exercised. It is not until after numerous
attempts at equilibrium that the excessively endowed man is finally
resolved to free himself of everything which hinders the full development of his major tendency.

M. Jules Lemaître had, himself, numerous contrary tendencies:
professorship, poetry, criticism, novel, theater, oratory, politics. Except for the last, he exercised almost all of them simultaneously, or
at least in groups of three or four at a time. He has been, as several

of his former students have testified and as a successful career proves, a very good professor, fulfilling the role of the master which is, even more than to teach, to pique intelligences, to astound them, and then to keep them on the alert. As poet, he was amusing, when, as M. Sansot-Orland [1] puts it "with an equal abandon of intimacy and prosody," he initiates us, in the manner of François Coppée, to his ephemeral love affairs as student and young professor. But poetry itself was for him one of these brief love affairs. He found a certain pleasure in it, no doubt, and a little of that special consideration—almost ironic but real—which is readily accorded, in France, any man of spirit who can turn out a sonnet and who does not overdo it. In the case of Jules Lemaître, it is all right; of Jean Aicard, it is too much.

The critic was already in evidence before the poet, who was soon silenced. Two pieces, equally agreeable, sufficiently perverse, moderately wicked, revealed M. Jules Lemaître to different literary publics at the same time, around 1884: his "Renan" in the *Revue bleue* and his "Huysmans" in the *Revue contemporaine*. Neither of these studies has any great critical value. They are curious because of his determination not to be fooled; but it is not a bad thing—it is, after all, a sign of superiority—to be credulous when confronted by genius, by talent, by loyal and disinterested effort. The snob is more useful to civilization than the antisnob, than the critic who, with cold water or lukewarm, dumps on our enthusiasms the shower of his anger or banter. I do not mean to say that M. Jules Lemaître would go so far as to banter; but he has come very close, and he has certainly escaped the temptation to let himself go only because of the strong classical education which had formed his tastes. The day he came the closest was when he amused himself, before a gallery delighted at such dexterity, by dismembering Georges Ohnet, then the great novelist of the bourgeoisie; but in this case the waggish, bantering tone was marvelously suited to the insignificance of the literary personage. The scalpel was a paper knife and the operating table was a conjurer's stand.

The literary criticism of M. Jules Lemaître has the merits of clarity, finesse, and good sense. We can regret that it does not also have—not principles, which it can get along very well without—but a direction. It marches along rather at random. It was denied to this witty author to have the experience, even for two or three years, of a literary faith. But it is the most fortunate of intellectual disciplines. A person learns to judge for other reasons than his personal taste; he feels the necessity of certain aesthetic sacrifices; he understands that works might have, even in a limited field, a social interest independent of their artistic interest. The literary coteries are highly useful: they initiate a person to a certain quality of injustice, which has a great edifying value, because it is one way of opposing a greater injustice. But the nerves always calm down rather quickly and the moment of certain concessions always comes too soon. Boileau, so cruel in his verse, is indulgent in his letters and his commentaries in prose. But, good or bad, his work was done. If the symbolists had not shown themselves so disdainfully unjust toward Victor Hugo, they would never have staked out their place in the sun. The great failing in the criticism of M. Jules Lemaître, then, is its not having any purpose. It lacks force, because its author lacks discipline. We can say as much for his works of imagination, novels, or theater. Except for certain initiatory works, nearly every literature derives its value from its conformity with a momentary aesthetic ideal. It is necessary that a contemporary of romanticism be romantic; otherwise, whether he is Béranger of Viennet, he is nil. Is it permissible, even for a Shakespeare, not to belong to some school? Shakespeare carried on theatrical practice, at first, just as he found it. It was the misfortune of some of our contemporaries, otherwise well endowed, to be neither Parnassians, nor naturalists, nor symbolists. This isolation made derelicts of them, floating at random, while the ship that they once skirted close to has long since arrived in port, where it reposes awaiting a new crew and a new passage.

If M. Jules Lemaître has misunderstood the necessity, in the literary realm, of clearly accepted disciplines, he did not do so in the political realm. That is perhaps because his true vocation lay there. Unburdened of all his secondary habits, the dilettante was finally shown to be what he really was: an excellent man of action, a social apostle. When a man has been a brilliant critic, an excellent novelist, a successful dramatist, is it so degrading to play the generally humble role of political journalist? A man never "falls" when he practices with talent and authority the occupation he has chosen, after having practiced several others. To the contrary, it seems that he has finally found himself and discovered, however belatedly, his own way. And besides, it is less politics that occupy M. Jules Lemaître as

it is social medicine. I think that the very persons who are least inclined to taste remedies he advocates are nevertheless admiring of
the mastery of the clinician.

Medicine, even social, is not incompatible with a certain skepticism: to the contrary. It will be interesting to follow M. Jules Lemaître in the exercise of his new trade, his new faith. For the five or
six years that he has been active, he has given almost as much anxiety to his friends as to his enemies. One could say at times that he
was beginning to dissociate himself again. Just as he was at one and
the same time an author and a drama critic, he might indeed reveal
himself one of these days as both an author and a political critic.
There is a book, which I know only by sight, which bears this title:
The Motives for Doubting and the Reasons for Believing. M. Jules
Lemaître is quite capable of putting, one of these days, the reasons
in place of the motives, and vice versa.

—From *Promenades littéraires,* 1903

Notes

The Dissociation of Ideas

1. *Les Travailleurs de la mer;* IIe partie, livre Ier, VII.
2. Technical term.
3. A character in *Les Travailleurs de la mer.*
4. About 1870—the time of the Franco-Prussian War.

Success and the Idea of Beauty

1. At the Hôtel de Bourgogne, while at Guénégaud Racine's rival, Pradon, was performed to great applause—the work of the duchess of Bouillon who bought up, and left empty, all the seats of Racine's theatre, in order to insure the success of her favorite, Pradon.
2. Bayle. And Racine, recognizing his adversary's craft, said: "The whole difference between Pradon and myself is that I know how to write."
3. Damiens (Robert François), having struck Louis XV with a cane, was tortured and quartered. Ravaillac (François) suffered a similar fate for having assassinated Henry IV. (G.B.)
4. Racine wrote *Phèdre,* Pradon wrote *Phèdre et Hippolyte.* (G.B.)
5. In another essay, *Women and Language,* I discuss the lie as a characteristic which distinguishes man from the animal. The superiority of a race, of a group of living beings, is in direct ratio to its power of prevarication, that is, of reaction against reality. The lie is merely the psychological form of the vertebrate's reaction against its environment. Nietzsche, anticipating science, says: "The lie is a condition of life."
6. There is an anticipation of this in Montesquieu's remark, recently published, that it is conformity that makes for beauty: "Esthetics—Father Buffier defined beauty: the assemblage of what is most common. When his definition is explained, it is excellent. . . . Father Buffier says that beautiful eyes are those of which there are a great number of the same kind; the same for the mouth, the nose, etc. This is not to say that there might not be a much larger number of ugly noses than beautiful noses, but that the ugly are of different kinds, and each kind of ugly nose exists in far smaller

225

number than the beautiful kind. It is as if, in a group of a hundred men, there are ten each dressed in a particular color: green would be the predominant color."

Glory and the Idea of Immortality

1. Intelligence can thus be conceived as an initial form of instinct, in which case the human intelligence would be destined to crystallize into instinct, as has occurred in the case of other animal species. Consciousness would disappear, leaving complete liberty to the unconscious act, necessarily perfect in the limits of its intention. The conscious man is a scholar who will reveal himself a master the moment he has become a delicate but unerring machine, like the bee and beaver.
2. *La Survivance de l'âme et l'idée de justice chez les peuples non civilisés.* Leroux: Paris, 1894.
3. Barth, *Religions de l'Inde,* in *l'Encyclopédie des sciences.*
4. *Des Réputations littéraires. Essai de morale et d'histoire.* Première série. Hachette: Paris, 1893.
5. Philoumeste Junior, *Livres perdus: Essai bibliographique sur les livres devenus introuvables.* Brussels, 1882.
6. These privately printed editions of three hundred copies or less have necessarily been worn out in proportion to their success.
7. *Opera et Fragmenta veterorum poetarum latinorum.* London, 1713.
8. This was written on the appearance of M. Louis Proal's work, *Le Crime et le suicide passionnels* (F. Alcan, 1910), in which, referring to sex dramas in the criminal courts, Racine is quoted, every ten pages, for reference and comparison. Everyone hesitates to say just what an age of passion and of carnal madness the *grand siècle* really was.
9. *L'Étang.* This poem forms part of the set of five odes in which Racine celebrated Port-Royal des Champs: *L'Étang, Les Prairies, Les Bois, Les Troupeaux, Les Jardins.*
10. *Le Promenoir des deux amans.*
11. Vapereau, *Dictionnaire des littératures.*
12. An excellent doctoral thesis on Tristan l'Hermite, by M. V. M. Demadin, bears precisely this title: *Un Précurseur de Racine.*
13. The first volume, and that alone, of Restif de la Bretonne's *Monsieur Nicolas* should be excepted.
14. *Recueil de quelques pièces nouvelles et galantes, tant en prose qu'en vers.* Cologne, 1667.
15. Paris, published by Jacques Dugast, aux Gants Couronnez, 1632.

Stéphane Mallarmé and the Idea of Decadence

1. It must be remembered that the Abbé Delille was not at all, as is commonly believed, a poet of the Empire. Almost all his poems and his glory date from the ancien régime.
2. P. Stapfer. *Des Réputations littéraires.* Paris, 1891.
3. Main character of J.-K. Huysmans' novel of decadence, *A Rebours.* (G.B.)

4. A genre which has degenerated into the "complaint." But the complaint has had its great period. The oldest poem in the French language is a complaint and inspired, precisely, by one of the poems of Prudentius.

The Value of Education

1. "A work," continues the translator, "which can profit the reader, and which brings marvellous contentment to those who frequent the courts of the *grands seigneurs,* and who wish to learn to discuss an infinite number of things contrary to the common opinion."
2. *L'Appel au soldat.*
3. Someone said in the course of a conversation: "The peasant is serious; he is a scientist, a physician." Every modern political effort tends to make of this physicist a metaphysician. This effort is well under way for the working man, who is beginning to scorn labor and to esteem phrases. His surprise is immense when he finds that words have no effect whatever on reality.
4. *De Kant à Nietzsche.*

On Style or Writing

1. On the importance and influence of Protestantism at this time, see the work of E. Hugues, pilfered by Protestant writers for the last twenty-five years: *Histoire de la restauration du Protestantisme en France au XVIIIe siècle* (1872).
2. A book so little known and so disfigured in its pious editions. Nothing could be less pious, however, or less edifying, beyond the first volume, than this curious and confused encyclopedia wherein one finds *René* and statistical tables, *Atala* and a catalog of Greek painters. It is a universal history of civilization and a plan for social reconstruction. Here is its complete title: *Génie du Christianisme ou beautés de la religion chrétienne.*
3. When we speak of the eighteenth century, we must always make an exception of the grandiose and solitary Buffon, in his tower at Montbard, who was, in the modern sense of the terms, a scientist, a philosopher, and a poet.
4. Some day an attempt will be made, in a study of the *World of Words,* to determine whether words really have a meaning—that is to say, a constant value.
5. *De l'Enseignement de notre langue.*
6. M. Albalat has italicized everything he deems "banal or useless."
7. See the chapter on the cliché in my book, *l'Esthétique de la langue française.*
8. Literal translations:

> Those monsters which from afar seem a vast reef.
> The animal covered with his thick crust,
> One whose shell is rounded into a vault [arch].

> The equivocal inhabitant of the earth and the waves.

And that speaking bird whose sad beauty
Does not compensate for its sterility.

And those living branches, those populous plants,
The miraculous rival races of two kingdoms. (G.B.)

9. *The Art of Writing,* p. 138.
10. "Un style désécrit." (G.B.)
11. Or, rather, had them copied by his secretaries. He afterwards reworked the clean copy. There is a whole volume on this subject: *Les Manuscrits de Buffon,* by P. Flourens, Paris, 1860.
12. On this point there is a nice passage from Quintilian, quoted by M. Albalat, p. 213.
13. I am assuming that we no longer believe that the Homeric poems were composed in a haphazard manner by a multitude of rhapsodists of genius, and that it only required stringing these improvisations together to get the *Iliad* and *Odyssey.*

The Problem of Style

1. In a work entitled *The Art of Writing Taught in Twenty Lessons.* This book enjoyed considerable vogue in its day and can still be seen in bookstores near the Sorbonne. (G.B.)
2. Paris, 1901.
3. A satirical work by Flaubert. (G.B.)
4. *M. de Pourceaugnac* is a "comedy-ballet" by Molière; *Le Lac* is a romantic poem by Lamartine. (G.B.)
5. Originally a convent, Port-Royal became in the seventeenth century a center of Jansenism and residence of a number of reclusive scholars.
6. Literally: "The blossoming flute has surmounted the alto as the fragile capital surmounts its column." (G.B.)
7. "I have put a red cap on the old dictionary." (G.B.)
8. In fact it is proper to reserve the word idealism for a philosophical state of mind that is much closer to a certain materialism than to a vulgar idealism: Nietzsche is an *idealist,* that is, a *phenomenalist;* M. Brunetière is an *idealist,* that is, a *spiritualist.*
9. Edmond About (1828–85), an anticlerical journalist and writer of witty tales. (G.B.)
10. Elsewhere Gourmont says that "subject" is of small importance in literature. He sees "subject" and "thought" as two different things. (G.B.)
11. Heroine of Chateaubriand's *Martyrs,* the very model of the chaste and timid woman, who died before any profane thought could penetrate her innocent soul. (G.B.)

Women and Language

1. The idea of thus introducing attention into the world through woman is M. Ribot's, in his *Psychology of Attention.*
2. Copulation might have sufficed for that. A shared life after fecundation is extremely rare, except among primates and birds.

Among carnivorous insects, the union is often fatal for the male whom the stronger female devours.

Subconscious Creation

1. Suggested by *Physiologie cérébrale: Le Subconscient chez les artistes, les savants, et les écrivains,* by Dr. Paul Chabaneix. This study was already written when M. Ribot's masterly work, *L'Imagination créatrice* (July 1900), appeared.

2. For example, in a dream related by Maury (*Le Sommeil et les rêves*) the word *jardin* causing the dreamer to visit Persia, then to read *L'Ane mort* (Jardin–Chardin–Janin); and in another dream, the syllable *lo* leading the mind from the word *kilomètre* to *loto,* via *Gilolo, lobélia, Lopez.* However, the poet (by reason of rhyme or alliteration) experiences similar associations, but he must be able to render them logical, a thing which very rarely happens in dreams pure and simple. Victor Hugo, a veritable incarnation of the subconscious, reveled in these associations, which were at first involuntary.

3. With regard to dreams, M. Chabaneix says (p. 17) that those who often think in visual images are subject to dreams in which the images are objectified in amplified form. A personal observation contradicts this, but in mentioning it I am only opposing a single observation to many observations. I refer to a writer who, although besieged, when awake, by internal visual images, sees images rarely in dreams and never has any characteristic hallucinations. Recently, having reread Maury's book during the day, he experienced that night, for the first time, two or three vague hypnotic hallucinations, caused doubtless by the desire or fear of knowing this state. . . . This case may serve to explain the contagion of hallucination by books. He saw kaleidoscopic flashes, then grinning heads, finally a figure clad in green, of life size, of whom the dreamer, looking out of the corner of his right eye, saw only one-half. At this moment, he was awaking. The figure evidently came from an illustrated history of Italian painting, which he had glanced at in the forenoon.

4. *Le Subconscient,* p. 11.

5. Letter to W. von Humboldt, March 17, 1832 (*Le Subconscient,* p. 16). Goethe was then eighty-three. He died five days later. The whole letter is quoted by Eckermann.

6. *Le Subconscient,* p. 24.

7. That is, having to do with dreams. (G.B.)

8. Preface to *Le Subconscient.*

9. Jahm, quoted in *Le Subconscient,* p. 93.

10. *Psychologie des sentiments.* W. von Humboldt said: "Reason combines, modifies, and directs; it cannot create, because the vital principle is not in it." (*Ideas on the New French Constitution*).

Stéphane Mallarmé

1. Report by Paul Bourde in *Le Temps* of August 6, 1885.

2. "Where the happy herd of men are bedded." (G.B.)

Verlaine

1. Paul Verlaine's anagram for his own name was "pauvre Lélian." (G.B.)
2. The "Parnassian" poets, a mid-nineteenth century French movement, advocated an impassive and objective verse. (G.B.)
3. A one-act verse comedy by Coppée (1869). (G.B.)
4. *The Shrine.* (G.B.)
5. A fire that destroyed part of Paris during the Communard insurrection in 1871. (G.B.)
6. "Le vers libéré": verse freed from pre-existing restrictions. (G.B.)
7. A process used in metal casting, in which a wax model melts and is replaced by molten metal. (G.B.)
8. In J.-K. Huysmans' novel of decadence, *A Rebours.* (G.B.)

The Sensibility of Jules Laforgue

1. *Mélanges posthumes.* Paris: Société du Mercure de France.

Sainte-Beuve, Creator of Values

1. Except when personal passions are brought into play. But this point of view has no place in a general outline.
2. And who had just published a most interesting *Sainte-Beuve* full of new and curious facts.
3. The title character in a book by Chateaubriand. (G.B.)

Jules Lemaître

1. *Les Célébrités d'aujourd'hui: Jules Lemaître.* Bibliothèque internationale: Paris, 1903.